From HEARING
to HEALING

WILEY SERIES
in
CHILD PROTECTION AND POLICY SERIES

Series Editor: Christopher Cloke, NSPCC,
42 Curtain Road,
London EC2A 3NX

The NSPCC/Wiley series explores current issues relating to the prevention of child abuse and the protection of children. The series aims to publish titles that focus on professional practice and policy, and the practical application of research. The books are leading edge and innovative and reflect a multi-disciplinary and inter-agency approach to the prevention of child abuse and the protection of children.

This series is essential reading for all professionals and researchers concerned with the prevention of child abuse and the protection of children. The accessible style will appeal to parents and carers. All books have a policy or practice orientation with referenced information from theory and research.

Published Titles

Bannister, Barrett & Shearer	Listening to Children	0-471-97282-7
Butler & Williamson	Children Speak	0-471-97219-3
Cloke & Davies	Participation and Empowerment in Child Protection	0-471-97218-5
Cloke & Nash	Key Issues in Child Protection	0-471-97217-7
Platt & Shemmings in association with NISW & PAIN)	Making Enquiries into Alleged Child Abuse and Neglect	0-471-97222-3
Wattam	Making a Case in Child Protection	0-471-97225-8
Wattam, Hughes & Blagg	Child Sexual Abuse: Listening, Hearing and Validating the Experiences of Children	0-471-97281-9

Forthcoming Titles

Cloke	Primary Prevention of Child Abuse	0-471-97775-6
Parton & Wattam	Child Sexual Abuse: Responding to the Experiences of Children	0-471-98334-9

From HEARING to HEALING

Working with the Aftermath of Child Sexual Abuse

Second Edition

EDITED BY

Anne Bannister

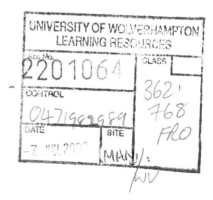
JOHN WILEY & SONS

Chichester · New York · Weinheim · Brisbane · Singapore · Toronto

Other Wiley Editorial Offices

John Wiley & Sons, Inc., 605 Third Avenue,
New York, NY 10158–0012, USA

WILEY-VCH Verlag GmbH, Pappelallee 3,
D-69469 Weinheim, Germany

Jacaranda Wiley Ltd, 33 Park Road, Milton,
Queensland 4064, Australia

John Wiley & Sons (Asia) Pte Ltd, 2 Clementi Loop #02-01,
Jin Xing Distripark, Singapore 129809

John Wiley & Sons (Canada) Ltd, 22 Worcester Road,
Rexdale, Ontario M9W 1L1, Canada

British Library Cataloguing in Publication Data

A catalogue record for this book is available from the British Library

ISBN 0-471-98298-9

Phototypeset in 10/12 pt Palatino by Intype London Ltd.
Printed and bound in Great Britain by Biddles Ltd, Guildford and King's Lynn.
This book is printed on acid-free paper responsibly manufactured from sustainable forestry, in which at least two trees are planted for each one used for paper production.

CONTENTS

About the Editor vii

About the Contributors ix

Foreword to First Edition—John Pickett OBE................................ xi

Preface xiii

Introduction... 1
Anne Bannister

1   Crimes Against Children... 5
    Anne Bannister

2   Confronting the Shame—the Interactive Approach in Action 22
    Anne Bannister

3   To all the Flickering Candles:
    Dramatherapy with Sexually Abused Children................................... 35
    Di Grimshaw

4   The Interface Between Assessment and Therapy 55
    Corinne Wattam

5   Empowering Mothers of Sexually Abused Children—
    a Positive Framework.. 72
    Bobbie Print and Carol Dey

6   Working with Adult Female Survivors of Childhood Sexual Abuse   96
    Helen Sheldon and Anne Bannister

7   Young Children who Exhibit Sexually Abusive Behaviour 118
    Carol Dey and Bobbie Print

8   Therapeutic Issues in Work with Young Sexually
    Aggressive Children 142
    Anne Bannister

9   Brother Nature? Therapeutic Intervention with Young Men
    who Sexually Abuse their Siblings 152
    Simon Hackett, Bobbie Print and Carol Dey

10 Secondary Abuse 180
    Jeff Hopkins

Index 197

ABOUT THE EDITOR

Anne Bannister, for 10 years the Manager of the NSPCC Child Sexual Abuse Consultancy, is now a freelance Psychodrama Trainer, Dramatherapist, Supervisor and Consultant, specialising in child sexual abuse issues. She has published widely on psychotherapy and child protection. Her latest book is *The Healing Drama: Psychodrama and Dramatherapy With Abused Children*. (Free Association Books, 1997.)

ABOUT THE CONTRIBUTORS

Carol Dey, CQSW, is employed by NSPCC and is a part-time G-MAP staff member. She has been qualified for 17 years and has previous experience of probation and family court welfare work. She was a member of the NSPCC's national Child Sexual Abuse Consultancy and, for the last five years, has been Team Manager of NSPCC in Merseyside.

Di Grimshaw is a dramatherapist and play therapist. She has worked with children and women who have experienced sexual abuse, and with children with challenging behaviour. She teaches on the Roehampton Dramatherapy and Play Therapy Diploma courses and is the present chairperson of the British Association for Dramatherapists. She has contributed to several books on the subject of therapy with children.

Simon Hackett, CQSW, MA, is employed by NSPCC as a Programme Director of G-MAP, an independent multi-agency organisation providing a comprehensive range of services to young people who have sexually abused, their families and the professional community. He has developed and co-ordinated a number of therapeutic work programmes with a range of agencies and is regularly involved in training a wide variety of practitioners in work with young people who have sexually abused. He has published journal articles in this field and is particularly interested in all aspects of work with young men, both as perpetrators and survivors of sexual abuse.

Jeff Hopkins is a Lecturer in Social Work at Keele University, Staffordshire. He has taken a particular interest in the effect of child protection work on workers and managers. He has wide experience as a consultant on staff care to a number of social work agencies and staff, and he is currently working on several related projects with UNISON and the British Association of Social Workers.

Bobbie Print, CQSW, is a Programme Director of G-MAP, an independent multi-agency organisation providing a comprehensive range of services to young people who have sexually abused, their families and the professional community. A founder member of NOTA (The National Association for the Development of Work with Sex Offenders), she remains a member of its national executive committee. She has authored a number of publications in this area and regularly trains staff from across all professional disciplines in the UK.

Dr Helen Sheldon is a feminist psychodynamic psychotherapist working as an adult psychotherapist in the Department of Clinical Psychology, Royal Bolton Hospital. She has previously worked in the voluntary sector in a feminist counselling and therapy service. In addition to many years' experience of working with survivors' groups in both voluntary and statutory agencies, she has organised and facilitated supervision and training for women working with survivors and has articles published in psychiatry and psychotherapy journals.

Corinne Wattam is NSPCC Research Fellow at Lancaster University and a member of the Pigot Code of Practice Policy Steering Group. She has published a number of papers and articles on the subject of child sexual abuse including, 'Teachers' Experiences of Children who may or may not have been Sexually Abused', and 'Truth and Belief in the Disclosure Process'. She is also co-editor of *Child Sexual Abuse: Listening, Hearing and Validating Experiences of Children* (Longman, 1989).

FOREWORD TO FIRST EDITION

Progress can only be measured in retrospect. In the over-heated climate of the latest child abuse scandal the many achievements of the past two decades are easily lost sight of. This book could not have been written 10 years ago. It is only in the past decade that the helping professions and the public have come to accept that the sexual abuse of children is a significant social problem. It is hardly surprising, therefore, that our understanding about causation, management of the problem and therapeutic methods is still at an early stage of development. There is still a great deal to learn and the authors of this book are making a valuable contribution towards increasing our understanding and knowledge.

The writers reflect on where they are at this time in their practice experience. This is not the dogma of 'experts' but the sharing of insights in the process of struggling towards a better understanding of the problems and ways to help children and adult survivors. It is a daunting task because we know that if we fail to effectively help today's victims many of them will suffer all their lives and some will become the perpetrators of tomorrow.

The NSPCC and Childline have led the way in promoting the rights of children to be listened to. The messages they give us are painful and disturbing and challenge our capacity to hear them and take them seriously. Our natural instinct is to recoil from what we hear and to deny the reality of what is said. The sexual abuse of a child involves the most fundamental betrayal of trust and abuse of power with devastating consequences for the child, undermining the basic needs of the child for a trusting, dependable and loving relationship. This is why the child not only needs to be heard, but also to be healed. The child's right to be respected as an individual person is unquestionable, but a long way from being generally accepted in our society.

The management of the effects of child abuse has vastly improved as the helping professions have learned to collaborate together in responding to the problem. We are now faced with the challenge of developing methods and resources to provide the child with remedial care. This book describes one approach, the interactive method, clearly child-centred and child-focused. The chapter of Corinne Wattam is of particular importance in explaining that child-centredness does not have to be sacrificed for evidential reasons and the needs of adults. The method is built on an eclectic approach to theories of causation and treatment and draws on a wide range of research and practice experience.

It is no easy task for busy social work practitioners to write about their practice. They need to be encouraged to do so. They need to be helped to believe in their ability to influence theory and practice. They, too, need to be empowered. Anne Bannister and her colleagues have produced a valuable book from which there is much to learn. I am proud to have been closely associated with Anne Bannister's work for many years; her skill and commitment to abused children, and that of her colleagues, is an example to all of us in our efforts to help such victims.

John Pickett OBE
Director of Inspection Services
NSPCC
October 1991

PREFACE

In the five years since the first edition of *From Hearing to Healing* was published, the debate about child sexual abuse has continued both in the media and in professional circles. The work of the NSPCC Child Sexual Abuse Consultancy, which is described in the book, has continued and moved on. There is now even more demand for therapeutic work with children who are seriously disturbed as a result of their early abuse. The extent of the emotional damage which accompanies sexual abuse when it is perpetrated within families, is now more fully realised. The Consultancy has, therefore, employed a dramatherapist, and more recently an art therapist and a group analyst to further its work.

We hope that the book will encourage childcare workers to increase their understanding of abused children so that the children can be facilitated to heal themselves. There are too few child psychotherapists in Britain and not enough creative psychotherapists are willing to specialise in the difficult but rewarding work with children. The use of the creative therapy of psychodrama, in particular, is described in the opening chapter and the new chapter by dramatherapist, Di Grimshaw, illustrates very clearly the effectiveness of such creative approaches.

The advent of the Children Act (1991) has, on the whole, been helpful to children although the emphasis is strongly on legal and evidential matters, rather than the therapeutic needs of the children. There has recently been a realisation that although much money and resources are expended on investigating child sexual abuse, too little is then done for the children subsequently. Children are then left 'wishing that they had never told'. Mothers of abused children feel bewildered that the intense interest which they received during an 'investigation' evaporates immediately afterwards. Sufficient resources are not available in the public sector and the NSPCC and other charities struggle to fill the gap.

As a consequence, more children are feeling hurt and angry and perhaps it is no coincidence that we are receiving even more reports of boys and girls who are sexually abusing other, younger children. The original chapter on this subject, by Carol Dey and Bobbie Print is still very relevant in assessing such children. A recent study, conducted by the Consultancy, and referred to in Anne Bannister's new chapter on treatment of sexually aggressive children, shows that workers, parents, and the children themselves, are often reluctant to acknowledge the numbers of children who are starting to abuse others. This area is often neglected and therefore, in addition to the new short chapter on young children who abuse, we have included a comprehensive chapter by Simon Hackett, Bobbie Print and Carol Dey which describes G-Map, their renowned treatment programme for young men who sexually abuse. The writers have concentrated particularly on another neglected area, those who abuse their siblings.

Knowledge of child sexual abuse, and the extent of it, has increased dramatically during the last two decades. As we move into the next century we hope that the work of hearing and healing abused children will help to prevent this crime against young people in the future.

Anne Bannister
Manchester, October 1997

INTRODUCTION

Anne Bannister

On 23 June 1987 the NSPCC and Greater Manchester Child Sexual Abuse Unit held a Press Conference as an official launch to the project, which had opened earlier in the year. The Unit was founded with cash made available from the dissolution of Greater Manchester County into its 10 constituent boroughs. The NSPCC provided premises and a management structure. Three social workers were appointed, one as manager. All were highly skilled in therapeutic practice with children and all had extensive child protection experience. Administrative and research staff were also appointed. The aims of the venture were: (i) to advance understanding about the phenomenon of child sexual abuse and effective methods of intervention; (ii) to increase the knowledge and skills of practitioners and managers dealing with cases of child sexual abuse; and (iii) to achieve these objectives by the provision of services through staff who are active practitioners.

The Press Conference was very well attended. One reporter began to ask questions about events in Cleveland. The Unit staff and the other Press members were puzzled as to the relevance. Cleveland was in the North East surely, not the North West? Enlightenment followed: 23 June 1987, the day of our launch, was also the day the 'Cleveland Crisis' hit the headlines. Public awareness of sexual abuse escalated from that date, although professional awareness had been steadily growing since the late 1970s.

The prevalence of child sexual abuse in the general population can only be estimated by retrospective studies since it is known that sexually abused children find it extremely difficult to disclose their abuse. In San Francisco in 1983 Diana Russell and her team of highly trained researchers found that up to 38 per cent of adult women said they had been sexually abused in childhood (Russell 1984).[1] In Britain a Mori Poll of over 2,000 men and women found that 10 per cent stated that they were sexually abused before the age of 18 (Baker & Duncan 1985).[2] Careful studies of the existing literature and the information from those running adult Helplines reveals that child sexual abuse has been known for decades. Statistics were not collected in Britain, however, until the 1980s. NSPCC Annual Statistics for

1986/87 showed that there were 2,300 referrals for child sexual abuse. This increased to 2,900 the following year, to 3,680 in 1988/89 and to 4,385 in 1989/90. The NSPCC is only able to deal with a small proportion of child abuse referrals since Social Service Departments are the statutorily responsible body in the major part of England and Wales, so it follows that the actual number of child sexual abuse referrals was very much higher.

Detailed local research was still very necessary in 1987 and one of our first projects was to institute research into the children who were being placed on the Child Protection Registers, for reasons of sexual abuse, in the whole of Greater Manchester. This necessitated great co-operation from all 10 boroughs and this co-operation by the Child Protection Co-ordinators was an added bonus from the research. The results of the research were published regularly during the next three years; the final report: *Child Sexual Abuse in Greater Manchester*, appeared in May 1991 (CSAC, 1991).[3] Mainly the report confirmed national and international studies.

The number of children placed on the child protection registers for sexual abuse rose by 57 per cent in the second year and by 21 per cent in the third year. Eighty-two per cent were girls but we agree with other surveys that this may represent under-reporting by boys. In the main, child protection registers are only concerned with intra-familial abuse and there is evidence to show that boys are more likely to be abused outside the family. The ages of the children ranged from five months to 17 years.

Ninety-seven per cent of the perpetrators were male, aged 35 on average, and natural fathers were by far the largest category, followed by step-fathers, male cohabitees and brothers. Many of the older children had been abused for years and had been presenting disturbed behaviour for some time.

Our report also confirmed that criminal prosecutions were brought in only about one-third of the cases, probably due to lack of corroborating evidence and to a natural reluctance to subject children to court proceedings. Most of those charged, however, were convicted and most went to prison. In the third year we noted the appearance of multiple perpetrators and of organised abuse. We also found that only a small minority of sexually abused children were offered treatment or therapy.

When the funding for the Unit expired in March 1990 the NSPCC took responsibility for the work and renamed us the Child Sexual Abuse Consultancy. About a third of the staff's time was already spent in training others and demand for this, throughout Britain and abroad continues to be high. Acting as professional consultant and 'expert witness' also takes nearly a third of resource time and the remaining time is spent on direct assessment and therapeutic work with children and adults.

In the five years of our existence we have seen the demand for our work increase, but also change. The level of knowledge about child sexual abuse is much higher amongst the child protection workers. Basic courses and awareness exercises are 'the norm'. We devised and packaged a basic course for multi-agency audiences in 1987 and a joint course for police and social workers in joint interviewing and assessment in 1988. Both these courses have been superseded as our knowledge and experience has grown.

In our work on joint interviewing of children who may have been sexually abused we realised that there can be no such thing as a 'neutral' interview in these circumstances. If we are indeed dealing with a sexually abused child the feelings of powerlessness, betrayal and so on will be already present. The child will be highly sensitive to any interaction which he or she does not understand and which is perceived as increasing the powerlessness, fear or stigma. Our experience has been confirmed by the work done by Corrine Wattam in Preston, and she has written Chapter 4 of this book.

In the past three years the demand has been for courses to teach therapeutic skills for those involved in child protection. From our therapeutic experience we devised a training course, 'Working with the Aftermath of Child Sexual Abuse'. The success of the course provided the impetus for this book.

Whilst running this course, often with multi-agency groups, throughout the country, we have been particularly concerned with the level of support needed for workers in this highly charged area. Jeff Hopkins' chapter at the end of this book explains the dilemmas and the need for action.

The author edited, with Kevin Barratt and Eileen Shearer, *Listening to Children* about the experiences of a number of different professionals who, in their work, interviewed children who may have been abused. 'Listening to Children' has been a theme of NSPCC publicity campaigns for some years. Listening, in an active, responsive way, is the first step in a process whereby an abused child may receive healing. *From Hearing to Healing* is our answer to all those children who have been brave enough to break their silence and who are demanding 'What now?'. If we are to serve the interests of sexually abused children in an ethical way we must move beyond an acknowledgement that abuse occurs. We must learn how to facilitate self-healing, to enable abused adults to parent their own children and to allow survivors of child sexual abuse to celebrate their survival.

REFERENCES

1. Russell, Diana (1984) *Sexual Exploitation* (Sage: Beverley Hills, California).
2. Baker, Anthony W. and Duncan, Sylvia P. (1985) 'Child Sexual Abuse: a study of prevalence in Great Britain', in *Child Abuse and Neglect*. Vol. 9 pp. 457–467.
3. NSPCC Child Sexual Abuse Consultancy (1991), *Child Sexual Abuse in Greater Manchester—a Regional Profile of child sexual abuse registrations*.
4. Bannister, Barrett and Shearer (1990), *Listening to Children* (Longman: Harlow).

1

CRIMES AGAINST CHILDREN

Anne Bannister

Crimes against children are the modern form of slavery.

Interpol spokesperson, national newsbroadcast, 3 April 1991

In her book, *For Your Own Good*, Alice Miller (Miller, 1987)[1] quotes the statement of a German woman about her anti-semitism. The woman had been brought up very strictly and had not been allowed to have a career because she was kept at home to help her parents after her brothers and another sister had left home. She read about the 'crimes' of the Jews and felt a sense of relief at being able to hate someone so unequivocally. Miller explains that the young woman (later a friend of Miller) felt anger and resentment against her parents and siblings, but because this was an inadmissible feeling for a 'good little girl', she found great relief in projecting this on to a whole race, the Jewish people. Her anti-semitism was acceptable in the society in which she lived (Germany in the 1930s and 1940s) so she felt no guilt at her murderous and vengeful feelings.

Society has always found an acceptable scapegoat on which to deposit its scorn, hatred and fear. Black people have been a prime target, hence the quote about 'slavery' at the head of this chapter. Women, too, have been feared and kept in submissive roles and, of course, people with disabilities have suffered similarly. Our language is expressive of this tendency. We talk about 'being the underdog', and 'kicking the cat', when things go wrong, reminding us that animals, too, do not escape our need to abuse power.

It seems that it is almost inevitable, that as anti-racist and anti-sexist laws are passed and small victories are won for campaigners, people simply find another group on which to vent their fury. Is there nothing that can be done to change this? Would not society be healthier if people could safely express resentments, as they occurred, directly to the people concerned, that is, those with the power? The powerful ones could then look at their actions, without being over-defensive, and either justify them or apologise. What an ideal world, especially when we realise the origins of this interaction. The 'powerful ones' are parents or carers of children and the 'people feeling resentful' are children. Children are the original underdogs.

Donald Winnicott (Winnicott, 1964)[2] disliked the use of the word 'training' to describe the way children are encouraged to use a potty or stay dry at night. 'Training is for dogs,' he says, 'not children'. In helping children to become socialised to live in families and communities we underestimate their abilities to think and feel and confuse children's needs for boundaries with our own needs to control. Children are simply lacking in knowledge and experience. Their intelligence, and their capacity to experience emotions, is often much sharper than that of adults. Our feelings and perceptions can become distorted or blunted with misuse.

If adults began to respect children, rather than treating them as an inferior species that may sometimes need protection, then children would not grow up with repressed resentments about past injustices. These resentments would not then have to be expressed inappropriately, against a race or class of people. Most important of all, those adults who themselves become parents or carers, would not then need to express their own anger against vulnerable and powerless children and so perpetrate the cycle of abuse.

This is the basis of the child-centred philosophy that informs the work that is carried out at the NSPCC Child Sexual Abuse Consultancy in Manchester. For five years we have researched and studied the problems of child sexual abuse (CSAC, 1991)[3] and worked with children and adults who are suffering because of it. We have struggled with the difficulties of investigating possible cases of abuse and with the inter-agency and political differences that become apparent when this is done. We have realised constantly the necessity to make careful assessments of all those involved in the abusive situation and we have recognised the largely unmet needs for treatment. The sub-title of this book *Working with the Aftermath of Child Sexual Abuse* is the title of a training course which we devised to meet the needs of social workers, psychologists, psychotherapists and others who were asked to provide therapy after child sexual abuse had been disclosed. We use the word 'Aftermath' deliberately since the devastation that is caused by child sexual abuse, to individuals, families and communities, cannot be underestimated. It is similar to that caused by major disasters. Indeed, a proportion of children (perhaps 30 per cent) who have suffered child sexual abuse can also be diagnosed as suffering from Post Traumatic

Stress Disorder (Finkelhor in Wyatt and Powell, 1988),[4] a cluster of symptoms common amongst survivors of hostage and torture, battles, prisoner-of-war camps, and the like.

We realised that we would need to share all our skills within the team if we were to provide anything approaching comprehensive help for abused children and their siblings, for non-abusing parents, for adult survivors of abuse and for the abused children who had started to abuse. We are also involved in providing treatment for young offenders, but have deliberately not extended this to adult perpetrators because of the need to conserve resources. Most of us, in our changing team, already had social work skills and, in addition, we each had some specialist skill and knowledge in psychology, family therapy, groupwork, dramatherapy, research, and psychodrama. Because of our team approach we have been able to share these skills and provide a response tailored to the needs of the client or clients. The Consultancy was not set up to show that one particular approach was 'the best' in cases of child sexual abuse but rather our methods evolved from the perceived and expressed needs of our clients, coupled, of course, with our own knowledge.

Often, when sharing particular ways of working that were especially successful, we would recognise the theoretical background that supported the work. We may have assimilated the theory some years ago and almost unconsciously brought it into play when a client seemed to need it. Thus the child development theories of Winnicott (Winnicott, 1964)[5] and Erikson (Erikson, 1977)[6] remembered from social work courses, seemed particularly apt. The person-centred approach of Carl Rogers and the psychology of C. G. Jung with its emphasis on symbolism, dreams and archetypal memories, proved helpful. All of us admired the childcentred philosophy of psychoanalyst Alice Miller (Miller, 1983)[7] and we have used extensively the psychodrama of J. L. Moreno (Moreno, 1977)[8] with children and adults, both individually and in groups. For groupwork we have also drawn on the work of Yalom (Yalom, 1985)[9] and Jennings (Jennings, 1986).[10] Virgina Axline's seminal work on play therapy has also been an influence (Axline, 1969).[11] Many others have undoubtedly influenced our work but it is our own experiences that shaped the work.

Most team members joined us with a good knowledge of child sexual abuse but again this is something we have shared in order to widen our field. Because research is constantly updating our knowledge there has been no feeling that we are experts, since we are always learning something new. We have realised, however, that unless we are extremely well informed about all aspects of abuse we will be unable to help clients effectively and our intervention may even be damaging. No treatment can be applied without a full knowledge of what we are treating. One theoretical model which we have found helpful is that proposed by Finkelhor and Browne

(Finkelhor, 1986).[12] They suggest that understanding powerlessness, stigmatisation, betrayal and sexualisation is vital in the treatment of those who have been sexually abused.

POWERLESSNESS

One of the difficulties about using words like treatment or therapy where child sexual abuse is concerned, is their connection with sickness and the potential powerlessness of sick people towards those who seek to heal them. Although a very small percentage of abuse perpetrators may be diagnosed as mentally ill and a small percentage of abuse victims may also have symptoms of psychiatric illness, the majority of those caught in the aftermath are not suffering from an illness. The survivors of abuse, however, may have survived at great personal cost and their capacity to experience life fully may be seriously impaired. The main difficulty is often a feeling of powerlessness and this can be exacerbated in any therapeutic relationship which does not offer some control for the client.

Following the child's agenda, working at the child's pace, placing boundaries rather than controls, are essential parts of our work. It follows then that we would never 'break through resistance', with any child or adult, but we may try to 'harness the resistance', bring it to the client's attention, and help the client to bring it under control themselves.

Another element of control is the abuse of gender, race or class in the therapeutic relationship. Adult clients may be offered a choice of therapist, male or female, for instance, but how far children can give informed consent or make choices is problematic and therapy can even reflect the abusive situation unless we take positive steps to acknowledge and understand this.

Sometimes groupwork for women survivors, with women leaders, may be the best way for an abused woman to understand the power of gender. In such groups that we have run we have often found that the first few weeks or even months of a group is preoccupied with group members seeking to exert their power in a very covert way, and with the leaders showing vulnerability and therefore abdicating some of their power because they are anxious not to abuse it. This can then evolve into the leaders putting themselves into the victim role and the women feeling more in control but being unable to do anything with the power that they had because they were stuck. We have now learnt that it is important for leaders not to slide into the victim role, but to keep boundaries and use power assertively, when necessary.

A mistake we have sometimes made is not to realise the strength of survivors. We have to realise why we use the expression 'survivors'. It is because they have lived through appalling experiences in which someone has sought to destroy their own inner integrity. They have survived these experiences, sometimes against all odds. A survivor will, therefore, look for whatever she can out of any relationship. Her expectation of others may be low, her expectations of herself even lower, perhaps, but her automatic response is protection. It is therefore difficult to trust anyone who is in the position of a therapist, although it might be easier initially to trust a female if the client has been abused by a male. To learn that a woman in authority need not abuse her power and to feel one's own power as a woman and as a group of women may be a good start to understanding wider abuses of power in society. Through this a woman can understand her own power- lessness as a sexually abused child and be freed from guilt. This approach too, may help non-abusing parents whose children have been abused.

For children, too, groupwork can provide this insight into powerlessness, and gender is just as important a consideration here. A group that we ran for abused boys had male and female co-leaders so that boys could see good modelling of the use of power from both sexes. This group, and the groups for adult survivors and non-abusing parents are discussed more fully in subsequent chapters. Following our policy of skill sharing we sometimes share with colleagues in the Health Service as well as Social Services Departments and have found that the differing perspectives have added to our understanding. (See Chapters 4 and 5.)

Although we are a team of women we frequently work with men from other teams. If a child is brought to us for treatment we work closely with the referrer or carer. This may be a social worker or foster parent, for instance. We also supervise men who are running groups and ask men to supervise us regarding our group work. This sharing approach has been even more helpful in matters of race. We happen to be an all-white team but our practice has been enriched by co-operation with black colleagues. Sometimes we have needed advice on matters of culture, but it has been the insight we have gained into imbalance of power that has been of most help to us.

Class consciousness and the abuse of class power is an area that is not frequently discussed by teams working with child sexual abuse. On the training courses which we run we have often found reluctance to discuss the issues, although when differences are aired it is apparent that a great deal of class prejudice still exists in Britain. Like skin colour, accents are an obvious way of putting people into categories. In the North West of England where we work the variety of accents is rich and communication can easily be limited when therapists fail to understand what children are saying. Perhaps of more importance is the difference in values and expectations between classes which can lead to misunderstandings between therapist and client.

We recognise that all those caught in the aftermath of child sexual abuse will feel powerless, to some degree, but by addressing the dynamics of powerlessness that are likely to be already present in clients we can more easily assess the work to be done with individuals. In addition we can be alert to the potential that we have for increasing the powerlessness and endeavour to remove this.

During assessment we note behavioural problems which may be clues to understanding whether loss of power is the most overwhelming feeling for the client at that time. Children and adolescents may be truanting, running away, be involved in bullying (as victim or aggressor), or may be in trouble with the law. Nightmares or phobias, somatic complaints or depression may be a feature both in children and adults. Extreme feelings of powerlessness can lead to dissociation and some of our most damaged adult clients present in this way. Dissociation is a useful defence mechanism which the mind employs to escape an unbearable situation. The person may feel 'out of body', not feeling painful stimuli or apparently showing little emotion over traumatic events. People suffering from this may be judged 'hard' or 'stupid' by others and since this meets their own expectations such attitudes simply increase the powerlessness and the symptoms. Giving sensory stimuli and finding safe ways to express emotion are an important part of therapy.

STIGMATISATION

After powerlessness, guilt seems to be a key issue in our work. It goes without saying that we believe that no child is responsible for its own abuse. Those who have been sexually abused feel a particular stigmatisation that is not necessarily present in other forms of abuse. Although physically abused children often blame themselves ('she hit me because I was naughty') and try to conceal their injuries, when these are discovered the reaction of others is usually sympathetic to the child. The reaction of family members, and friends, to the disclosure of sexual abuse is often to blame the child, unless the child is very young. Disbelief is also a form of blame. Children are called liars, thus compounding their own view of themselves as worthless. In many classes and cultures the child is also stereotyped as 'damaged goods' and the pressure for secrecy adds to the feeling of shame.

It is part of our philosophy that we do not add to feelings of guilt or shame, that we understand stigmatisation but that we do not collude with unnecessary secrecy, which can increase shame. This is sometimes difficult in practice. We have a notice outside our door stating that we are the

'NSPCC Child Sexual Abuse Consultancy'. We try to make it clear that we do not feel it is shameful to have been sexually abused but that guilt lies with the abusers. We have clear rules about confidentiality, placing child protection before confidentiality, but always sharing our views and intentions with clients so there is no secrecy between us.

Because a therapist often acts as a 'safe container' for dangerous feelings shared by a client, confidentiality about those feelings is essential in the therapeutic relationship. Children, however, often ask us, when they are ready, to tell their parent some of these feelings in order to prepare the way for greater understanding between parent and child. It is at this point, when the child is ready, that work with parent and child together may begin.

Building self-esteem is also part of our general philosophy, in order to reduce guilt and shame. This begins even before we meet a client. Only in very exceptional circumstances do we cancel appointments, especially with children, and when children are brought in by carers or workers, we usually greet the child first, introducing ourselves and then waiting to be introduced to the child. All clients are asked permission if sessions are video-recorded and children are shown a little of the video tape immediately afterwards so they can understand what has happened. Respecting the need for a few week's break from therapy is important for children and adults, and we try to ensure that children have permission to recommence therapy if this is appropriate and possible.

Those clients for whom stigmatisation is the major dynamic often present with drug or alcohol problems, suicidal tendencies, or self-mutilation. Even quite young children can try deliberately to harm themselves with knives and scissors or simply by 'picking' at sores until their skin is damaged and bleeding. Sometimes children and young people can recover from feelings of guilt and shame quite quickly by re-enacting the build-up to the abuse so that they understand the 'grooming' that was deliberately carried out by their abuser. They see that the child sex abuser carefully prepared them to be abused by desensitising them and by bribes, threats or promises. They then realise that their own apparent 'consent' was inevitable and not because they were 'weak' or 'bad'.

BETRAYAL

One of the effects of betrayal is inability to trust, and since trust is at the heart of the therapeutic relationship this feeling can inhibit even the start of useful work. Building trust with someone who has been sexually abused means being sensitive to the fact that this client may be afraid of all men with beards or of all women in white coats for instance. Children are often ridiculed openly for such fearful feelings whereas a slow and careful desensitisation may be more appropriate. Being alone with a stranger can be frightening unless reassurance is given about familiar friends close by. On the other hand having two or three powerful adults in the room, even if one is familiar, can still be an ordeal for a child who has been betrayed. Sometimes this can be reminiscent of the abuse and other items such as cameras can also have unwelcome connotations. The impact of betrayal is often extreme aggression which can be just as frightening to the child itself as it is to the person on the receiving end. Boundaries and controls for such a child have to be clearer and firmer than with a client who is showing extreme grief and sorrow as a result of betrayal. Being allowed to express grief, to hold play rituals of death and dying, to act out funerals and scenes of destruction, are not simply morbid, but are natural ways of healing. It is unfortunate that in our society, we often 'shield' children from such feelings and thus unhealthily suppress their loss.

Adults who have suffered betrayal often have difficulty in intimate relationships or in relationships with their own children. Rebuilding trust is a slow and painful process but if the therapist can show complete acceptance, this model of a relationship can lead to a general improvement in family situations.

It is important for the therapeutic team to discuss the dynamics involved in betrayal because therapists are not immune to sexual feelings which can sometimes be aroused by the intimacy of discussing or re-enacting sexual incidents in a therapeutic setting. To betray that trust, with an adult client, would be to manipulate the relationship and so to repeat the abuse. If the therapist has been careful not to abuse power in the first place then this is a situation which is less likely to occur. The greater the power imbalance the more likely it is that the client will transfer to the therapist feelings which more properly belong to the abuser, and sometimes this can include ambivalent sexual feelings. (Theories of transference, basic in most psychotherapy, arise from the work of Sigmund Freud.) The therapist too must be sure that she has worked on her own childhood experiences, including any abuse, and also on her own sexuality.

A child's right is that adults will provide care and protection and if this is betrayed in the therapeutic relationship that, too, is repeating the abuse. All clients are vulnerable in therapy, and children even more so. They depend on adults to define the rules, to make and keep boundaries of behaviour.

SEXUALISATION

Keeping boundaries is sometimes very difficult with a child who has been traumatised sexually and who thus behaves in ways which are not according to sexual norms. By the age of five most children understand that grabbing the genitals or breasts of an adult is not acceptable but abused children may have been rewarded for such behaviour by affection, since this can be part of 'grooming' by the abuser. Abusers exchange affection or attention for sex so children learn to use this as 'currency'. Sometimes, of course, there may be a complete aversion to all sexual matters, especially if sex has been used as a punishment, which is very common in our experience.

The therapeutic team must be able to share with each other their own responses to overt sexual behaviour or confusion about sexual identity in clients. A therapist who becomes sexually aroused or, alternatively, feels disgust during a therapy session, must be able to contain that until she can discuss it thoroughly with a colleague. She will certainly feel guilty, especially by arousal, but it is comforting to know that it is not abnormal. Usually, as soon as this is shared openly the feeling does not recur. If it does it is a sign that the therapist still has some work to do on her own sexuality. This personal work will continue, ideally, as long as the therapist goes on working. We have found that it is common amongst workers, in the early stages of involvement with child sexual abuse, to discover aspects of their own attitudes which need to be resolved. These often include defensive or manipulative reactions to the four dynamics of powerlessness, stigmatization, betrayal and sexualisation.

THE INTERACTIVE APPROACH

Freud devised the therapeutic method of 'free association' where the relaxed client talked without intervention from the therapist so allowing the unconscious to express itself. Freud would then interpret this for the client. Jung felt that this was too simplistic, that the unconscious would become 'stuck' with what he called 'complexes'. He, therefore, used active intervention by the therapist, sharing ideas between therapist and client on the principle of 'two heads are better than one'. This is the basis of our approach, which we term 'interactive'.

Having been warned about the personal hazards involved in child sexual abuse work a therapist may be tempted to keep a tight rein on her feelings and try to work in an emotional vacuum, dispensing 'treatment' like medicine. We believe this is quite impossible since the therapeutic relationship itself is the key to success. We feel that the self is all we have to offer so we must make ourselves as available to our clients as we can. In groupwork each member of the group is potentially able to help one another, but it is still up to the group leaders to make the group safe enough to allow openness amongst its members.

The creative therapies, drama, art and music as well as play itself, can help to create an atmosphere of safety where feelings can be 'played out' symbolically in a non-threatening way. Children naturally express themselves through play and we will see in subsequent chapters, from case studies, many examples of this. Adults, too, although they may have forgotten how to play, soon respond to art, drama and music if they are presented with an acceptable, safe structure within which to work. Although it is common for severely deprived children to be unable to play in ways that are recognisable to adults, it is possible to nurture every sign of play behaviour in a deprived child so that she is encouraged towards more self-expression.

However, as Donovan states, in *Healing the Hurt Child* (1990)[13] there is a difference in 'playing' and 'just playing'. There is a difference too in self expression through art, drama and music and exploration of specific problems through these media with the help of a skilled therapist. All play, all artistic expression, can be helpful and therapeutic for a sexually abused person but it is the inter-action between the therapist and client, using the artistic or play medium that will really 'move the client on'. A child needs reassurance and encouragement that his play has been recognised and understood. Donovan quotes a child who stopped playing symbolically when pressure was put on him by an abuser because the child understood that the therapist could 'read' his play. Only very occasionally does a child need to be given an interpretation of play. The therapist should always be wary of offering interpretation and if she does so this must be done in a tentative, non-powerful way so that it can be easily rejected by the child if incorrect. Most children, however, seem to be closer to the use of symbolism and metaphor because of their familiarity with play, so any explanations from the therapist are superfluous. It is more valuable for the therapist to continue to look at the child's behaviour to confirm or disaffirm any interpretation of play.

Children often respond dramatically, in one or two sessions, so even assessments can be immensely therapeutic.

DRAMA

Adults too often respond more quickly and more completely to a creative therapeutic intervention than to more conventional methods. Roger Grainger, in *Drama and Healing* (1990)[14] gives four reasons why drama is a unique healing force: (1) *catharsis*, which is emotionally healing because it increases our courage to be; (2) *psychological integration*, which provides the link between our inner and outer reality; (3) *security*, which is provided because drama can manipulate aesthetic distance and so can foster personal boundaries, and (4) *validation*, making sense of an experience of life which is essentially nonsensical, arbitrary, self-contradictory or confusing.

Both children and adults may have cathartic experiences in interactive and creative methods of therapy. The catharsis can occur after permission is given to express anger, perhaps against mother, or extreme grief as loss of babyhood or childhood is experienced. Security, as we have already indicated, is an essential requirement for those whose boundaries have been violated, and dramatic or symbolic methods give the distance, the 'once removed' feeling that provides additional safety. A child may demonstrate clearly what he has experienced, but show this as happening to, 'the little boy, not me'. An adult may repeat 'forbidden' words or gestures because, 'this seems like an actor's script, not me'. But once the word or gesture is manifest, once the child re-experiences the feeling, the taboo is broken and the 'real' experiences can be confirmed.

The feeling of being validated is vital to someone whose mind and body has been discounted, whose feelings have been ignored and contradicted, whose soul has been raped. This validation frequently occurs in the re-enactment process. The therapist is alert to the client's body responses as well as to everything she says, she is given permission and encouragement to feel and those feelings are confirmed as the client understands why she felt them originally. A client begins to know who she is and is encouraged to explore her personality further. This in itself is a validation.

I have left psychological integration until the last because this is the ultimate aim and outcome of successful therapy. In addition to the model of child sexual abuse proposed by Finkelhor and Browne, which we have already explained is fundamental to our work, we also use a model proposed by Hartman and Burgess (1988).[15] They call this 'Information Processing of Trauma'. It explains how the trauma of child sexual abuse will have a different impact on each person because of factors such as the age of the child, its developmental level, the family structure, socio-cultural factors and any prior trauma. Then the nature of the abuse itself will be different in every case. How much control, secrecy, violence and coercion did the offender use? Each child will then cope in differing ways, by dissociation or denial, by repression and so on, and this will lead to distortion of cognition and perception. This is sometimes never satisfactorily resolved or occasionally it will be resolved on disclosure of the abuse. If disclosure is also a traumatic experience with the child suffering further from disbelief, blame, denial and so on, the distorted cognition and perception continues and often the child (or adult as they may now be) reacts with continuous and severe anxiety, or with avoidant, aggressive or delinquent behaviour. In extreme cases the personality may become seriously disorganised.

The aim is 'integration' and this is achieved by resurfacing the trauma, processing it, unlinking incorrect sensory, cognitive and perceptual information, and eventually transferring it to past memory. We believe that this integration process is most easily achieved by interactive, creative methods. The trauma is resurfaced in play, drama or art, it is processed through the same or similar methods (children sometimes jump from drawing to a dramatic enactment and vice versa), and the client herself then unlinks incorrect sensory feeling, cognitions and perceptions. An example is the client who stops mutilating herself by cutting because she is now able to feel the pain, she now believes that she does not deserve the pain, and she perceives that she no longer needs to do it because her inner pain can now be felt by her and seen by significant others. (See Chapter 7 for a further explanation of Hartman and Burgess' theory.)

PLAY

Virgina Axline (1969)[16] demonstrated the importance and effectiveness of play therapy over 20 years ago. More recently Linet McMahon (1991)[17] has shown how it can be used not only in one-to-one work with a therapist but in group and family settings, in nurseries and hospitals and for all kinds of problems, including sexual abuse. David Glasgow (1989)[18] demonstrates how play can be used in the investigative assessment of children who may have been sexually abused, and we ourselves have described how play can be healing for such children (Bannister, 1990).[19]

Children play not only to learn roles and practise skills but to repeat experiences in a safe setting so that they can make sense out of them, as in Grainger's experience of drama. Play validates a child but children need help with play if it is to be a full learning experience. Observe two children playing 'house' in a day nursery. One is mummy (or daddy if that is his role) making the dinner, bathing the baby, and brushing the floor. The other is the parent who goes out to work. All is well as the child plays at getting ready to leave for work, but as they leave the house they look bewildered, not knowing what comes next. This may be filled in by other children who have been to their parents' place of work or seen others doing the same job that they know their parent does, but unless there is this help from others the child has gaps in her knowledge which can be assisted by an adult playing with her. A child who has been abused has gaps of knowledge which prevent her from making sense of what has happened. She may have tried to solve it in play, perhaps with another child, and been punished for it; to allow her to solve it in a safe play situation requires patience and encouragement. It also requires the worker to witness the child's confusion, pain and anger without trying to protect, and this can be difficult, especially for someone who is close to the child. It is not an easy task for a caring child protection worker either but, because she knows that the child is healing herself whilst playing out the uncomfortable feelings, she can cope more easily.

PSYCHODRAMA

We have also described how psychodramatic techniques can successfully be used with children who have been sexually abused (Bannister, 1991).[20] Psychodrama is a process where someone acts out personally relevant situations, usually in a group setting (Williams, 1989).[21] It was originated by Jacob Levy Moreno, a Viennese psychiatrist, over 60 years ago. It has been developed by his widow, Zerka Moreno, and many practitioners worldwide, especially in the USA, South America, Finland, Germany, Italy, and Australia, as well as in Britain. In his important work on psychodrama, *Acting In*, Adam Blatner (1973)[22] uses the expression 'growth-through-play' and points out that the essential elements of psychodrama are spontaneity, creativity, action and self-disclosure. He defines psychodrama as the method by which a person can be helped to explore the psychological dimensions of his problems through the enactment of his conflict situations, rather than talking about them. It is this essential 'enactment' that we use in our work with those who have been sexually abused in childhood.

A group psychodrama session consists of three parts, the warm-up, the action, and finally the sharing. The warm-up stage often consists of game-playing or psychological exercises to help the group to relax and get in touch with feelings. The expression 'warm-up' has been taken over to mean any beginning to a group session and indeed a group can warm-up to work simply by talking to each other and the group leader, or director as it is termed in psychodrama. Moreno was the originator of group psychotherapy and many others including Perls and Yalom have expanded his methods, adding their own creativity to form a different model. To Moreno spontaneity was of the essence so he surely would have approved of those who have extemporised upon his work. Our interactive work, 'Playback Theatre', and role-playing itself are all based upon his methods. To use psychodrama to its fullest extent, however, it is necessary to follow a structure; so groups which endlessly practise warm-up, without any follow-through will be less than effective, and may leave members feeling dissatisfied.

The action in psychodrama is usually a scene, or series of scenes, with the 'protagonist' at the centre, acting out his or her situation. Other group members, 'auxilliaries', play significant others in the drama. The psychodrama 'director' is the group leader who helps produce the experience and a satisfactory resolution of the drama. In the sharing session, group members express their feelings about their own participation or what they have witnessed and experienced. They do not give advice to the protagonist but may share similar experiences in their own lives.

Williams (1989)[23] states that psychodrama induces change in protagonists because they have, 'at last enacted roles that are inwardly truthful and appropriate to the original situation'. The spontaneity involved in the new interaction illustrates and changes the core dynamic of the original dysfunctional interaction and creates *new perceptions, responses, and interactional patterns.*

It will be seen that this technique, which is extremely powerful, provides exactly the sensory, cognitive and perceptual changes that the therapist seeks to make with a person who has been sexually abused. The writer, a qualified psychodramatist, began to use psychodramatic techniques with sexually abused children in the early 1980s. Therapeutic groups for such children were difficult to organise, especially for young children, and at that time the numbers were not sufficient to promote the setting-up of a group. She therefore used the techniques in one-to-one situations (known as 'psychodrama a deux') with children and young people aged from two to 17 years. More recently she has developed similar one-to-one psychodramatic techniques with adults who have been sexually abused. To help students to understand the structure of a therapeutic session she coined the phrase 'reassurance, re-enactment and rehearsal' (the three Rs) to describe the three stages. These three stages are also used by the team in investigative and assessment interviews (Bannister and Print, 1988).[24]

Following this three-part structure in therapy we seek to reassure clients with the philosophical background already described in this chapter. With children we take especial care not to ask too many questions. Background information can often be supplied by parents, carers or other professional workers. A careful history taking, however, is important, and with adults we often have a first session which we describe as a 'discussion', prior to therapy. Reassurances must continue, of course, through all the therapy but the time devoted to it in each session should get progressively less.

Re-enactment does not usually mean re-enacting the actual abusive experience. That would be abusive, especially if the protagonist was playing herself in the enactment. (Exceptions to this might be when working with those who have abused, to allow them to experience the victim role.) We have found, however, that children do sometimes want to re-enact the abuse, using dolls or puppets to play all the parts, with the child as director. This helps a child to make sense of a nonsensical situation and, of course, the child is fully in control since she is directing the action. A mother, whose child has been abused, may want to recreate other scenes which she now sees as leading up to the abuse. A sibling might want to re-enact their feelings of being ignored by the abuser or of being unable to protect the abused child.

We often use dolls or animal puppets to play auxilliary roles or to 'double' for or 'shadow' the protagonist. The abused person is assisted in the direction of the action by the therapist. The therapist must, however, remain fully sensitive to the person's needs, just as a director in a classical psychodrama must do. Children usually have no difficulty playing many roles and in changing roles frequently. After all we are constantly learning new roles throughout childhood and it is only in adulthood that we become more self-conscious about changing roles or taking on unfamiliar ones. The therapist helps the work along by suggesting role-reversals and by eliciting the feelings behind the words and actions.

Adults may be initially hesitant to use dolls or enact different roles. We start either with using tiny dolls (about 3 inches high) on a table, or by asking clients to draw or make diagrams. Most clients are happy to make lists illustrating, for instance, good and bad aspects of a particular behaviour which is causing them problems. It is then a small step to using drawings or small dolls to illustrate the lists. Other adults are happy to use larger dolls to enact non-threatening situations such as a work situation which is causing problems. From here we can move on to a similar family situation and continue to use the same dolls.

With other clients symbolism seems to be the obvious mode, either because the client has presented a problem symbolically through a drawing or a poem, or because her language, when describing the problem, is full of symbolism, for example, 'I feel as if I have a metal shell around me and I am afraid that others will remove it and find nothing within'. Then we might ask the client to become the shell and find out exactly how it has been constructed. She then gains control and realises that she can use the shell for protection if necessary but can discard it when she decides to do so. She may also be asked to become her own essential core, or centre of the shell and perhaps to play the different parts that make up this core. In this type of work the various roles are played by client and therapist, sometimes with chairs or cushions to represent parts of the self or significant others.

'Rehearsal' is our description for the time at the end of each session when the client practises future behaviour, discusses any practical changes that may be desirable and generally 'comes down' from the deeply felt enactment. Children, in particular, need to be reminded about current situations and about what is acceptable in the real world. Many children automatically have their own rituals when they are reminded that a session is coming to an end. They may ask for a story, or put toys into a certain formation, or generally tidy-up. We discuss whether anyone else needs to be told of anything that has happened in therapy. Sometimes it is decided by clients that parents or partners must be told certain matters and the mechanism and timing of this is shared and agreed.

We have described interactive methods with groups and in one-to-one situations. Of course, similar techniques can be used with siblings together, with parent and child, with parents together and with whole families. In child sexual abuse work, however, it is important that each person who is coping with the aftermath of abuse should be given space to work on their own difficulties and that they should be allowed to develop different coping strategies before work is attempted with several family members together. Proponents of family therapy (see Haley, 1987 for a basic introduction)[25] have found that if families are seen together in the early stages after sexual abuse has been disclosed it is impossible to change the power-base from which the abuser operates. Family therapy, which also uses techniques from psychodrama such as role-playing and sculpting, can be helpful at a later stage, to rebuild relationships with non-abusing parent and child, or between siblings. It should not be used in families where child sexual abuse has occurred until therapists and clients (including those who have had the least power) are convinced that they are ready to change relationships within the family.

CONCLUSIONS

This chapter has attempted to explain the long-term effects of child sexual abuse and the philosophy behind our methods of treatment. We have described the theories which have influenced our practice and how we have often adapted these theories to fit our own experience. We have described how our own approach to therapy draws on several disciplines and why we feel this approach seems to be especially suitable for those who have been sexually abused and members of their families. We believe that an eclectic approach is important, however, because of the complexity of child sexual abuse work. Subsequent chapters will describe aspects of our work in more detail and the work of others with clients who are sexually abused. Chapter 4 discusses our methods, and similar approaches, in relation to investigative interviews. The final chapter will describe the effects of child sexual abuse work on the workers themselves and how they, their colleagues and management can alleviate problems and provide support.

REFERENCES

1. Miller, A. (1987), *For Your Own Good* (Virago: London).
2. Winnicott, D. W. (1964) *The Child, the Family, and the Outside World* (Penguin: Harmondsworth).
3. NSPCC Child Sexual Abuse Consultancy (1991), *Child Sexual Abuse in Greater Manchester – A regional profile of child sexual abuse registrations*. From NSPCC CSAC, 175 Station Road, Swinton, Manchester M27 2BU.
4. Finkelhor, D. in Gail Elizabeth Wyatt and Gloria Johnstone Powell (eds.) (1988), *Lasting Effects of Child Sexual Abuse* (Sage Publications: London).
5. Winnicott, D. W. (1964) *op. cit.*
6. Erikson, E. H. (1977) *Childhood and Society* (Paladin: London).
7. Miller, A. (1983) *The Drama of Being a Child* (Virago: London).
8. Moreno, J. L. (1977) *Psychodrama: Vol. 1* (Beacon: New York). From British Psychodrama Association, 8 Rahere Road, Cowley, Oxford OX4 3QG.
9. Yalom, I. D. (1985) *The Theory and Practice of Group Psychotherapy* (Basic Books: New York).
10. Jennings, S. (1986) *Creative Drama in Groupwork* (Winslow Press: Oxford).
11. Axline, Virginia (1969) *Play Therapy* (Ballantine Books: New York).
12. Finkelhor & Browne, in Finkelhor D. (1986). *A Sourcebook on Child Sexual Abuse* (Sage Publications: London).
13. Donovan, Denis M. and McIntyre, Deborah (1990) *Healing the Hurt Child* (Norton: New York and London).
14. Grainger, Roger (1990) *Drama and Healing* (Jessica Kingsley Publications: London).
15. Hartman, C. and Burgess Ann W., 'Information Processing of Trauma' in *Journal of Interpersonal Violence* **3**(4) December 1988.
16. Axline, Virginia (1969) *op. cit.*
17. McMahon, Linet (1991) *Play Therapy with Children and Families* (Routledge: London).
18. Glasgow, D. in Wattam, Hughes & Blagg (eds.) (1989) *Child Sexual Abuse* (Longman: London).
19. Bannister A. in Bannister, Barrett & Shearer (eds.) (1990) *Listening to Children* (Longman: London).
20. Bannister A. in Holmes & Karp (eds.) (1991) *Psychodrama: Inspiration and Technique* (Routledge: London).
21. Williams, A. (1989) *The Passionate Technique* (Routledge: London).
22. Blatner H. A. (1973) *Acting In* (Springer Publications: New York).
23. Williams, A. (1989) *op. cit.*
24. Bannister A. & Print B. (1988) *A Model for Assessment Interviews in Suspected Cases of Child Sexual Abuse* Occasional paper series No. 4 (NSPCC: London).
25. Haley, Jay (1987) *Problem Solving Therapy* (Harper and Row: London).

2

CONFRONTING THE SHAME—THE INTERACTIVE APPROACH IN ACTION

Anne Bannister

> *I want my own voice.*
> *I want to reclaim my inner land.*
> *It is not enough to be the shell,*
> *In which the child can hide.*
> *We need to stand and speak as one.*

From a poem by a male survivor of childhood sexual abuse

One of the tasks which our Consultancy is often asked to undertake is to make an assessment of a family where child sexual abuse has occurred. The abuser has been removed from the family by this time, either to prison or hostel, or sometimes on a voluntary basis to friends and relatives. One or more children may be also away from home in the care of the Local Authority. The assessment is to assist the Local Authority and, ultimately, the Court, in making decisions about the future of the child or children. A therapist assesses each child separately to find out if the child's development has been affected and, if so, in what way. The level of the child's attachment, if any, to parental figures, is assessed as far as possible, and areas of work which need to be tackled in therapy are mapped out.

In addition if there is a non-abusing carer, she (it is usually mother) will be assessed by a separate therapist. Part of the assessment will be to assist her in comprehending what has happened and in helping her to understand her own needs and those of her children. She and the children may also be seen together, by both therapists, to look further at attachment and at work which needs to be tackled. Work with non-abusing carers is discussed further in Chapter 5, but this chapter will concentrate on work with children.

A thorough assessment may also lead to a judicial recommendation or Local Authority decision to provide 'treatment' for the family and we often undertake this treatment in the early stages. In keeping with our philosophy of sharing knowledge and responsibility, however, we consult frequently with the Local Authority staff who are the designated 'key workers' so that therapy can be continued by the field or residential social worker, or sometimes by a foster mother or other appropriate person. This may be the non-abusing mother herself if this is viable.

One such family was referred from a Local Authority outside Greater Manchester. They lived in a working class, rural environment and mother's family had lived in this part of the country for generations. There were four children, Marie aged 12, Stephanie aged 10, Ben aged 6 and Carl 4. They had been living with mother Jean, 30, and mother's brother, Uncle Frank, 37, who was employed as an agricultural worker. Their father had been killed in a road traffic accident when the youngest child was less than a year old. He was a lorry driver and by all accounts had not spent much time with the family. Stephanie had disclosed abuse to a teacher, a few months earlier, and Marie had confirmed the abuse of Stephanie and of herself. Uncle Frank had admitted abusing the two girls and was now serving a prison sentence. The initial investigation was not an exhaustive one, possibly because of the abuser's confession, and it has been decided that the two younger boys had not been abused. The girls had initially been removed from home and were now sharing some ambivalence about returning. The boys had remained with their mother. We felt we needed to assess all four children as well as mother and this we did, over a period of a few weeks.

During the assessment period the boys revealed that they too had been abused by Uncle Frank. Mother had refused to believe the children at first, then had blamed them for their own abuse, especially the girls. The two boys were, therefore, removed from home to be with their sisters, and the Court recommended that we continued to see the children for treatment. What follows is a description of the assessment and treatment of each child in which it will be seen that although the abuse was similar for each child, the way in which they were affected was vastly different.

MARIE (AGED 12)

Marie and Stephanie were brought to the first session together, with their workers. They were to see separate therapists and the sessions only coincided two or three times. In appearance Marie was much bigger than her sister although there was only 18 months between them. She was tall and considerably overweight. Her figure was well developed but she was obviously embarrassed about this and kept her coat on throughout the first session. She seemed docile and obedient, looking without apparent interest as we showed both girls our playroom and the video equipment, and explained the procedures. She clung to her worker in the manner of a much younger child and seemed pleased when we suggested that the worker viewed the session on the video monitor. We explained to both girls that we knew they had been hurt and we were here to listen to their feelings about that. Although Stephanie looked hostile and suspicious, Marie seemed accepting and resigned to whatever might happen.

In the playroom Marie spontaneously played with the dolls house, again rather like a younger child. She used furniture and small figures to set up her own home and the people in it. She became confused when she picked up a small doll to represent Uncle Frank saying she didn't know where he was going to sleep but that she and Stephanie would go to their room and 'share secrets'. Marie moved easily between the small dolls, puppets and larger anatomically correct dolls. The latter were fully dressed on a chair at the edge of the room. She declared that a fluffy, appealing-looking animal puppet was her friend and she spent some time, with the puppet on her hand, explaining how much she needed a friend. This is typical behaviour and we encourage this, using the 'friend puppet' throughout the session. She selected a large 'mother' doll to be 'Mummy' and, using the friendly puppet as her voice she addressed the mother. 'You didn't believe my friend when she told you what had happened.'

Marie and Fluffy, the puppet, looked at the doll. The doll seemed to stare back. Marie turned away, in despair. Her hand in the glove puppet drooped. For the first time in the session the therapist intervened with a question that moved the action on. 'Who can help Fluffy with this?' she asked.

'He needs lots of friends', Marie replied, moving over to the pile of animal puppets and selecting three. She put one on her other hand and instructed the therapist to put her hands in the other two. The four puppets faced 'Mummy'. 'You should have believed my friend', she told the mother. 'I'm mad at you.' Marie's voice was louder, she seemed a little surprised. The doll stared back.

Fluffy poked 'Mummy' in the face, tentatively. 'She didn't tell lies, you're a naughty Mummy, you should have believed my friend.'

Fluffy hit harder and Marie's other puppet joined in. She motioned the therapist's two puppets to help her out and the mother doll was thumped and bitten by the dragon puppet on Marie's other hand. The therapist intervened again. 'What should the Mummy have said?'

'I believe you', answered Marie. She contemplated her reply. Suddenly she dropped the puppets and clapped her hands. 'We can change things', she cried. She picked up a 'grandmother' doll and held it in front of her, facing the 'mother'.

'You should believe your children', she told the mother, in a 'grandmother' voice. 'You were naughty because you didn't believe what Uncle Frank did.'

Marie picked up a 'girl' doll. 'This is Marie', she explained to the 'mother'. 'Tell her you believe her.' The therapist picked up the 'mother' doll and held it in front of her. 'I believe you Marie', she said simply.

Marie looked satisfied. There was a silence then she turned to the drawing materials on the table behind her and quickly drew a rabbit with large ears. She handed it to the therapist still sitting behind the 'mother' doll.

'That's for you', she said. The therapist placed the drawing on the mother doll. Was Marie telling mother or the therapist to listen? Perhaps it was both and Marie was warning the therapist (who was in appearance a 'motherly' figure) that she must not behave like her own mother.

It seemed that already, in this first session Marie knew what she needed to heal her. She needed supportive allies, 'friends', and she needed her mother to believe what had happened. For Marie to express this in a session was therapeutic in itself but later in the same session she showed the therapist how likely she thought this was.

She turned again to the small dolls in the dolls house, selected one to be 'the Uncle' and another to be 'the little girl', she placed Uncle's hand between the girl's legs. Picking up the girl she carried it over to the mother doll and said, 'Uncle Frank's been touching me.'

'All right', she replied, as mother. 'Get in bed with me, I'll tell him off tomorrow.' Marie held tightly to the little girl doll, tears filling her eyes.

'What can she do?', the therapist asked gently.

'Tell grandma', Marie whispered. She moved towards the grandmother doll but hesitated in front of it.

'It's no good', she whispered to the therapist. 'She won't believe either. Only the wise owl believes. He will have to tell the mummy and grandma that it's true and he will have to tell the Uncle he's naughty.'

Marie looked sad, but resigned. She was showing the therapist that her way of coping was to accept her victimisation as inevitable. She felt there was nothing she could do, only other, more powerful people could change things. As a young girl entering puberty her vulnerability was frightening. She had, however, in one session, shown the therapist her overwhelming feelings of powerlessness and betrayal. Her defence mechanism of accepting the victim role was clear, and she had shown what she needed to experience in therapy, in order to aid healing.

During subsequent sessions the therapist worked on improving Marie's self-esteem and allowing her to express some deeply buried anger. Marie had been stealing from other children at school and during one session she spontaneously told the therapist a story about a young woman who stole things. The therapist had merely suggested that Marie told a story about her drawing of a young woman. It was after telling the story that Marie felt able to express her anger and she spent 10 minutes hitting pegs through a child's peg board. It should be noted that when children express anger against certain people, e.g. their mother, and they hit dolls or puppets representing mother, they are always told afterwards that it is alright to be angry and to hit things in sessions, but that it is not alright to hit people outside the sessions.

In the early sessions Marie had insisted that she 'couldn't draw' but by the fourth session she was drawing competent pictures and using them to start stories or enactments with the dolls. Most of the stories were about feelings she needed to express. She became Cinderella, angry at her step-mother, and delighting in the admiration of the prince. She enacted a long scene about a little boy who, although telling the truth, had not been believed by anyone. He was believed in the end and she praised him for his persistence. With puppets she acted out scenes with a Tiger who was in prison (where Uncle Frank was) and by playing several roles ('good warder' and 'bad warder') managed to express her ambivalence. Her compassion and pain could both be stated clearly.

In psychodrama we give the protagonist an opportunity to express feelings by playing a role very different from their own. Marie did this instinctively, using the 'bad warder' to express some revengeful feelings. She still felt a lack of power, however, so she invented 'the manager', a very powerful figure who ordered the 'bad warder' to punish Tiger. Of course she also played 'the manager' herself and enjoyed the power of the role. In the sessions Marie was able to grow, to practise assertiveness and express some resentment. She moved from her victim role to one in which she was less vulnerable.

STEPHANIE

Although Stephanie was 18 months younger than Marie she was obviously much more grown-up in many ways and was used to taking a parental role. As soon as she entered the therapy room she took control of the therapist, ordering her to clean a drawing off a white board. The therapist declined to do so, obviously realising the dynamic that Stephanie was setting up. However, after about five minutes the therapist decided to allow Stephanie to have control, but only in a role-playing situation. Innocently, as Stephanie ordered her about, she asked, 'Are you the teacher then?' 'Yes', answered Stephanie, 'and you're the girl'. A school scene ensued with Stephanie playing a controlling and snappish teacher who occasionally became quite kind and helpful to her 'pupil'. If the pupil refused to follow teacher's instructions to the letter, however, she became abusive and was even more so when the 'pupil' introduced a doll to play 'mother' who had come to see 'teacher'.

Stephanie found it easy to play the controlling role, her anger was near the surface and she used her voice and gestures to emphasise it. This was familiar territory and she was reluctant to move from this position. As 'the girl' the therapist picked up a small, cuddly glove puppet. 'Hedgehog is feeling lonely and sad'. Stephanie looked interested. 'You can sit by that girl' she said kindly to hedgehog. Still in the role of 'teacher' she addressed the therapist. 'Hedgehog's uncle was naughty, he touched her and her sister. She's only little and he's very big. He's naughty.' The scene continued for some time. Stephanie found it difficult to show her vulnerability and was only able to do so by projecting it onto the hedgehog, whilst retaining her controlling 'teacher' role. She talked in detail about how the hedgehog felt when her uncle 'touched' her and when he hit her and said this had been going on, 'for ages, before hedgehog was old enough to go to school'.

At one point she changed her role to that of 'the girl' but only so that she could 'mother' the hedgehog and put her to sleep like a baby. Stephanie was indicating her need to be cared for, her intense need to be a child again, even a baby, but she found it difficult to relinquish the parental role in which she had been cast. This role was later confirmed by all the other children, including Marie, who treated Stephanie as a substitute mother, one who appeared to understand their needs.

As therapy progressed Stephanie tried out the more vulnerable role. She tucked the hedgehog into bed on a pile of cushions. 'How is she feeling?' asked the therapist. Stephanie lay down beside the puppet and curled up. 'Mm, nice . . .' she said tentatively. She closed her eyes. The therapist waited patiently. 'Time to get up', said Stephanie, reverting to the parental role and grabbing hold of the hedgehog. For a few moments, however, she had savoured the childlike role. They were moments she was to repeat often in the coming weeks.

Despite her apparent confidence Stephanie needed frequent reassurance that she was acceptable. She showed a talent for collage and the therapist fostered this, praising her for her artistic skill. Several times Stephanie showed her concern for 'unhappy children who had been hurt' but was reluctant to identify with them.

It took several more sessions before Stephanie could even mention her fear of Uncle Frank. She was setting up an imaginary party for herself and friends. She was clear that Uncle Frank would not be invited to the party. 'The children are afraid of him', she explained. 'All the children?' the therapist inquired. Stephanie picked up the doll playing herself and held it in front of her. 'Yes', she said quietly. 'She's frightened, very, very frightened.'

Eventually she was able to express her fears and worries about returning home and meeting Uncle Frank again. Although she had appeared at first less vulnerable than Marie, she was in fact less able to ask for help and therefore potentially more vulnerable. She had seemed to show more anger initially but in fact the true extent of her anger against mother and Uncle Frank was not revealed until she had dealt with her fears. She had coped with the abuse by becoming very controlling. This needed careful handling by the therapist and a thorough assessment of the controlling mechanism had to be made. If Stephanie had not been able to recognise her fear and to have it validated, then feelings of guilt and shame may have caused her to become even more controlling and possibly to become abusive of others.

BEN

Six-year-old Ben had already been assessed elsewhere as having learning difficulties. We were told that although he had been at school for nearly two years he didn't appear to recognise letters or numbers. We were told also that he was a quiet, obedient child who showed no behaviour problems in school. In the therapy room he moved rather restlessly between the toys. He picked up a puppet, looking at the therapist to check that he had permission to do so. He played for a few moments then picked up a small toy rabbit, gave it a cursory examination and then sat quietly for a few moments. 'I have a rabbit', he said. 'When it's frightened it goes to the back of the cage.' He picked up a pen in his left hand and began to 'write' on a wallboard. The 'writing' flowed in loops and twirls as he wrote from right to left. There were no discernible letters but there were breaks in the loops as if in a sentence. 'What does it say?' the therapist asked, naively. 'Be in charge', said Ben, quietly. Then he drew a rabbit, rather small, at the foot of the board. He was telling the therapist of his fears and how he thought he could conquer them. He didn't look very confident as he cleaned the 'writing' off the board. Then he drew a 'monster' with two large teeth. Beside the monster was a snake, upright and almost as big as the monster itself. The rabbit looked very small. Ben looked at his drawing and held his head in his hands, wordlessly. Within 15 minutes this 'learning disabled' child had communicated symbolically what seemed to be happening in his life and how he felt about it.

In this and the next session Ben showed the therapist quite clearly, using dolls, how Uncle Frank had physically and sexually abused him and his brother Carl. After Ben had shown this, the therapist asked, 'What does Ben do now?' (It is usual to work in the present tense so that the experience is re-enacted and feelings can be recreated accurately.) 'He tells his mum,' answered Ben, quickly moving the doll towards the 'mother' doll. 'She'll tell the uncle off.' He tried it out, reversing his role to that of the mother. 'You're naughty, Frank!' he shouted, with more energy than he had shown before. But the anger was shortlived and he reverted to the role of Ben, 'It's no good, she doesn't believe me', he said sadly.

He picked up a pair of scissors and some paper and, rather awkwardly, he started to cut out paper shapes. He grabbed at the paper with the scissors and caught his finger. He looked at the small cut, showing no pain, watching the blood appear. He picked up the blunt metal scissors again and would have jabbed them into his hand if the therapist had not intervened. In subsequent sessions plastic scissors only were provided, but Ben made several attempts to cut himself and he frequently picked at small sores on his arms and legs until they bled. Maybe Ben felt that if he could show how he was hurting outwardly, the therapist might see his inner pain. Another explanation of Ben's behaviour is that he had a feeling of unreality (common in sexual abuse survivors) and was drawing blood to reassure himself of his existence. Either way, the behaviour is significant.

Ben also used the scissors in the sessions to cut out a mask. He made several of these but they were always the same, a large round shape with two holes for eyes but no hole for the mouth. Whenever he felt that the work was becoming uncomfortable he would cut out a mask and hold it in front of his face, peering out wordlessly at the therapist. It was clear that when his mask was in place he could not talk, nor could anyone divine his feelings. He was safe, but lonely, behind his mask. As the work progressed he used the mask less often but it was a graphic explanation of the quiet, unfeeling, rather stupid personality which he frequently presented to the world.

The therapist felt that Ben had lived too long behind his mask and she tried to help him to express feelings. He enjoyed caring for a baby doll which he nursed tenderly during each session and sometimes tucked carefully into its cot. He desperately needed the tender nurturing which he was showing to the doll, and occasionally he would reverse roles with the doll and squeeze himself uncomfortably into the toy cot, asking the therapist to tuck him in. He also loved playing with the puppets, especially the more aggressive-looking ones. One day he picked up the tiger and, very tentatively, with the puppet on his hand, made some aggressive movements towards the large male doll. 'He looks angry', the therapist remarked, referring to the tiger. 'What is "angry"?' Ben asked. The therapist explained. 'Yes, he's angry', Ben confirmed, snapping the puppet repeatedly towards the doll. 'Tigers growl when they're angry', the therapist said, encouragingly. A small growl began in Ben's throat. His arm movements became stronger. The growl increased to a roar. He picked up the male doll and hurled it at the wall, roaring loudly. The tiger thumped the doll repeatedly. Ben turned to the 'mother' doll. The tiger looked at her, without roaring. Ben was panting breathlessly. The tiger slid off his hand and he went to pick up the baby doll lying safely in its cot. He picked it up and nursed it close to his chest, swaying rhythmically. 'Don't be frightened,' he said, 'the tiger won't get you.'

This experience was cathartic for Ben and soon he began to experiment with the dolls, trying out possible scenarios. Sometimes the 'little boy' told the 'uncle' that he was naughty and he would tell his mother. As uncle, Ben replied nonchalantly, 'Go ahead, she won't believe you'. Sometimes the mother doll thumped the uncle and told him to go away and on another occasion the mother sent the uncle to jail where he stayed for the rest of the session.

It soon became clear that Ben understood his own writing, even though no-one else did, and gradually the writing itself became more precise. He still wrote from right to left and soon it was realised that he was doing almost perfect 'mirror writing', where everything was reversed. His clumsy behaviour improved and he soon became quite dexterous, pouring orange juice into teacups in a competent manner. Life behind the mask had been difficult though and many of the feelings had still to be resolved.

One day he played with plasticine and made a beautiful flower. He took great care, moulding each petal gently and placing the flower head on a stalk. 'Where is the flower?' asked the therapist, 'Is it growing or in a vase?' 'Growing,' answered Ben, 'in a field.'

'Are there many flowers in this field?'

'No', Ben answered quietly. 'It's the only one.'

'Is it happy?'

'No, lonely.'

Ben was looking out of the window now and the therapist was gazing at the lone flower, on the corner of the table. There was a long silence, both Ben and the therapist were experiencing the dreadful isolation of the flower. Ben moved to the cot to comfort the baby whilst the therapist placed the tree she had fashioned next to the flower, protecting it.

Ben frequently seemed to take two steps forward and three back in therapy. There seemed to be a breakthrough when he cut out a large mask and then made a hole in the centre big enough to put his whole head through. He tried it on the therapist first before trying it on himself. His head looked rather exposed, sticking out of a white 'collar'. He looked at himself in a mirror then dragged the paper off quickly. He was rehearsing for the future but was not yet ready. Similarly he rehearsed feeling angry. After the catharsis with the tiger he seldom showed anger but occasionally asked the therapist to show him what she did when she was angry. He watched her as she hit cushions with a rolled up newspaper. It took many sessions before Ben was able to show his feelings spontaneously and directly.

CARL

Although he was the youngest child, Carl made more impression initially than any of the others. Like a miniature torpedo he projected himself into the first session, picking up a plastic sword and a rolled-up newspaper and making a great noise as he hit out at walls and cushions and at the therapist unless she moved quickly. He found a cloak and hat in the dressing-up box and spent five minutes impersonating the Lord of the Universe and ignoring the therapist except where she got in his way. He hurtled around at speed and soon became breathless and tired. He pulled off the hat and tried to remove the cloak. It was stuck. The Lord of the Universe quickly turned into a frightened four-year-old. 'Get it off,' he said to the therapist tremblingly. 'I can't.' This set the tone for several sessions, as Carl swung between aggressive, excessive control and babyish vulnerability. Of course these mood changes are not unusual in a four-year-old but Carl took each to its most extreme so that after the first session the therapist wondered how well she would be able to engage with him. In fact this little boy, already assessed by doctors as developmentally delayed, eventually proved to be the child who built the closest therapeutic relationship and who worked diligently and creatively throughout the treatment period. It may be that he quickly attached to the therapist because he seemed to show no other clear attachments with his family. We had been told that he had the closest relationship with the mother but although he slept in mother's bed, Carl never mentioned her as supportive or protective. It may well be that his father's death increased his mother's victimisation by her brother so that she was increasingly unable to protect her children.

Soon Carl initiated the 'Red Indian' game. This game ran as a constant theme through the sessions. He found two suitable headdresses in the dressing-up box and ordered the therapist to wear one while he donned the other. He mended fences which was noisy, energetic work. He banged a peg board with a wooden hammer. He ordered the therapist to 'make the stew' for when he came home. He picked up a tiger puppet which he said was his pet tiger. He growled loudly but the tiger role seemed to be that of a guard dog, to protect rather than attack.

He informed the therapist, whom he addressed as 'wife', that he was mending the fences to keep the horses in. He demonstrated by becoming a horse and breaking through the fence to leap about in the fields. 'Stop me, stop me', he begged. The therapist 'lassoed' him with an imaginary rope and with great relief he returned to the corral, reversing his role again to the fence mender. The worker asked whether the horse was happy out there and Carl shook his head vigorously. 'He's scared', he said authoritatively. 'He'd rather be here.' Carl seemed to know that many boundaries or fences had been breached in his life. He knew that the boundaries needed to be restated and the therapist was very clear throughout the sessions that Carl was never allowed to hurt her or himself or do great damage to property. He did try to hurt himself several times, sticking the pin of a badge through his fingers, but he responded well when the therapist laid down rules about his conduct.

One of the techniques in psychodrama is to ask the client to play the roles of significant others in his life. Many children do this without direction, and Carl showed great aptitude for this and tremendous insight for such a young child. The tiger puppet, who had been his friend in the early play, was soon given the role of 'the naughty person who hurts children'. Occasionally Carl slipped out of the metaphor and addressed the tiger as Uncle Frank, always correcting himself quickly if he made that slip. Tiger was frequently thumped and beaten and placed in prison by Carl and his 'friends', the other puppets. On one occasion he hurled himself into a corner saying that he was Tiger, in prison. The therapist took on the role of Carl and picked up the friendly puppets. 'Why did you hurt the children?' she asked. Carl changed from a fierce Tiger into a moaning, clingy animal. He spoke in an unpleasant, whining voice, 'Because they won't be my friends', he answered. 'It's not my fault', he said still whining. 'Let me out.' The worker agreed to let him out as long as he promised not to hurt children. Carl became himself again and picked up the Tiger by the scruff of his neck. 'He breaks promises', he said clearly.

One of the difficulties for children who are abused by a close family member is the ambivalence that children feel. Often the abuser has given them the only nurture and care that they have known, as well as exploiting them, sometimes at the same time. Carl demonstrated this by inventing 'good Tiger' who was 'bad Tiger's' brother and who was kind to children and advised 'bad Tiger' to stop hurting the children. In playing these roles Carl was not only sorting out the roles his abuser had played but perhaps also was looking within himself at his own good and bad feelings and checking that they were both acceptable.

Carl eventually asked the therapist to 'rescue' him in play situations. He seemed to be using her as a mother, asking her to protect and nurture him. It was difficult for the therapist not to allow Carl to become overdependent. He then may have settled for a victim role and ceased to use any of his own strategies for control. Gently she showed him that she could not always rescue him but that she could send other things to help him when he was in trouble. She sent in 'brave crocodile' and 'wise owl' and a 'magic stone' to give him strength. He used all these symbols, eventually settling for the (imaginary) stone which he kept in his pocket and said he would look at it when he needed it.

In the final session he played the 'Red Indian' game again but spent a long time as the horse who had leapt the fence and was gambolling playfully in the field. Eventually he came back to the therapist who was still the 'wife', or mother figure. He picked up a baby's feeding-bottle filled with orange juice and handed it to her. 'The horse needs a drink', he said. He sucked on the bottle greedily like a lamb taking milk. He stopped after a moment and went off over the 'fence'. As the horse he said, 'It was scary at first but I like it now.' Suddenly he fell down, shouting that he had fallen into a hole. He said he was dead and lay in a corner of the room quietly. He stood up, 'I wasn't dead,' he said, 'only asleep: I'm thirsty now but I want to drink out of a proper cup.' He picked up a teacup from the table and drank thirstily. 'You've grown up', the therapist remarked. Carl nodded and asked her to lie down while he covered her with cushions. She did so. He put on a cloak and asked her to give him 'the treasure'. She did so, ceremoniously handing over an imaginary gift. 'Thank you', he said. 'You can get up now.' Carl now had his own 'treasure' with which he could protect himself. He was not dependent upon the therapist.

SUMMARY

These sessions have not been presented to show a complete therapeutic intervention with any of the children. Indeed, their therapy continued for some time afterwards. This early assessment and therapeutic intervention is described to show how differently (and sometimes similarly) each child reacted, not necessarily depending upon age or sex. We have also tried to show how each child's agenda was followed so that work proceeded at a different pace and in a different direction for each. The assessment and early treatment stages each contained much reassurance (stage one of the interactive model) and very quickly, although at different times for each child, re-enactment (stage two) was introduced to explore feelings and to help cognition of what had happened. Rehearsal for the future (stage three) was a part of each child's treatment although for Stephanie, for instance, this was more difficult. We have, of course, not only changed the names, but also some details, including omission of some family particulars in order to protect the children we worked with. We would like to thank them and all the children we see for helping us to understand what they are feeling.

3

TO ALL THE FLICKERING CANDLES: DRAMATHERAPY WITH SEXUALLY ABUSED CHILDREN

Di Grimshaw

It is better to light a candle than to curse the darkness.

A Yiddish saying

An inspiring and hopeful image. During my experiences of working as a dramatherapist in the Child Sexual Abuse Consultancy, the struggle has been to hold onto hope, often at times when the anger, confusion and suffering of a sexually abused child threatens to annihilate it. I have learned that sometimes the child needs to catch hold of the therapist's hope like a person drowning at sea reaches for a lifebelt, except that sometimes children feel they do not have the strength or the belief that they actually want to survive.

Understandably, the work has caused me to look more closely at the impact abuse, and in particular sexual abuse, has on the vulnerable child. Sexual abuse is the violation and betrayal of a fundamental trust essential to a child's growth and development. Abused children learn that their value is to meet the sexual needs of an adult (James, 1993).[1]

The work has also given me the opportunity to use my skills as a drama and play therapist to facilitate the healing process. What I did not and could not know was the impact such work would have on my understanding of the society I share with these children, which creates the conditions for child abuse to exist.

The overall aim of this chapter is to tell some of the stories of their lives these children have shared with me, and of how they were able to use their own creativity through drama and play to bring about a healing in themselves. In addition, I have sought to place these children within the wider context of society. There is a sense, I believe, that as long as certain committed individuals and organisations endeavour to recognise and work with children who have been abused, then society can turn its collective back on the distressing business of child abuse, only needing to be outraged by such stories sensationalised in the media. It is easy to forget that children who are being abused can be living in any house and go to any school.

Within the context of this writing, I am not concerned primarily with the perpetrators of child abuse but with the recipients of it. I feel a sense of professional gratitude to those who have chosen to work with, and to understand better the complexities of child sex offenders. One colleague at the Consultancy, Eileen Gallagher, regularly challenged my own perception of perpetrators, for which I am very thankful.

I am not claiming to have *the answers*, and I may be naive in my understanding. Yet if we only ever say the things we understand we will never be creative.[2] If we lose our creativity, we lose our hope that we *can* make a better world for ourselves and our children. As a dramatherapist my attempt to contribute to this betterment is my own. Yet I hold the hope that other people share similar values, and collectively we can hold our candles to light the way.

The dramatherapy work undertaken at the Consultancy was largely post-investigative. However, the situation would often arise when a court case was pending for several months whilst reports were compiled. Fortunately, the Crown Prosecution Service is beginning to recognise children's need to address their experiences in a therapeutic environment; just as if someone was injured in an accident, treatment would not be withheld until liability was determined.

Before therapy can be considered, however, a child must be living in a safe environment. In many of the training courses facilitated by the Consultancy, social workers expressed varying levels of anxiety and relief on this particular issue. Often social workers feel under pressure to offer a child therapy or therapeutic intervention. A child in an unsafe place will be psychically and emotionally unprepared for therapy. Furthermore, children being offered therapy in such circumstances may believe that therapy is somehow to help them accept the abuse and that no-one can really stop it happening to them; that even professionals are powerless to protect children. It may even be that children feel the professionals are colluding with the abuser and that, in truth, the children are not being believed.

The social workers' anxieties seemed to be around denying these children *something, anything* to help them. In such cases, resources would be better used in providing a secure, abuse-free environment before therapy can ethically be considered. The ensuing relief seemed to originate from the social workers' own intuition which had somehow been silenced by the immediate demands and expectations made upon them.

Social workers, perhaps more than any other professionals involved in the distressing area of child abuse, are seen by society as buffers, protecting the public from the grim reality of a situation. When the system fails to protect a child, it is the individual social worker who is held responsible. Yet despite the detailed investigations and documentation following the tragedies that have befallen children in our society, it is still apparent that individual social workers are expected to carry enormous workloads.

As a dramatherapist I am responsible for addressing my own personal material to enable me to be emotionally present for the child. This journey of self-exploration and understanding is a relentless one (Grimshaw, 1995).[3] According to the British Association for Dramatherapists, clinical supervision of dramatherapy practice is regarded as an essential aspect of the work (1997).[4]

My theoretical orientation draws on several influences including the theories of Object Relations and Developmental Play and the work of Peter Slade.

OBJECT RELATIONS THEORY

First proposed by Melanie Klein (1932),[5] Object Relations is one theory of understanding personality development in the infant. This complex process begins when the infant, having taken in or *embodied* enough of the object, usually the mother as primary carer, allows for a separation from her. The separation creates a space between the two, a 'potential space' (Winnicott, 1971)[6] within which a relationship between the mother and infant has the opportunity to evolve. It is only with space between the two that there is a possible sense of 'I' and 'you'. Embodiment of the mother-object creates in the infant a belief and trust that he is not alone in the world. (See Jean Liedloff's fascinating and harrowing account of the world from the infant's perspective in her book *The Continuum Concept*, 1975).[7] Winnicott's 'potential space' is the place of play. He believed that the self may only be discovered through creativity, and that the ability to create comes through the process of play. Play is, by definition, a risk, for it exists in the interface between inner and outer realities; between the subjective and that which is objectively perceived (Grimshaw, 1996).[8]

Klein further proposed that the infant's first experience of the mother-object is actually split into two part objects, symbolised by the 'good' and the 'bad' breasts, representing comfort, nurture and love, and the denial of these respectively. The infant internalises the symbols of the 'good' and 'bad' breasts and his relationship with each. Thus, the 'good' breast creates in him a sense of well-being; he is cared for, loved and secure. The 'bad' breast creates in him a sense of anxiety and insecurity. From these two quite different experiences the infant begins to create an image of himself—in relationship to each.

Through the process of toleration it is believed that the infant gradually comes to understand that the two contradictory objects, the 'good' and the 'bad' breasts co-exist within the same object, the mother. The 'bad' breast which once threatened to annihilate all that is good is shown to be in relationship with the good. This process is internalised and mirrored in the infant's inner world, giving rise to ambivalence. Ambivalence is the co-existence in one person of opposing emotional attitudes towards the same object.

The developing child who has internalised the mother role in turn plays out this role. If the internalised mother role is *good enough* (Winnicott, 1971)[9] then the child will be able to establish a range of further good enough roles with others: other carers, siblings, friends and, later, partners. Alternatively, if the mother role is experienced as largely persecutory, indifferent, or critical, then it follows that future relationships will be similarly perceived.

Susie Orbach, Louise Eichenbaum and their colleagues at the Women's Therapy Centre, London[10] further developed the theory of Object Relations by increasing awareness of the mother's role. The mother, of course, is not an object, but a subject, bringing her own qualities and feelings into the relationship with the infant. She too has experience of being mothered. The nature of her actions and relationships is highly variable and dependent upon inner psychological factors as well as outer social and political factors (Landy, 1986),[11] as well as being influenced by the experience of mothering she herself received.

Rozsika Parker (1995)[12] explores ambivalent feelings experienced by mothers towards their infants. She challenges the views of idealisation or denigration projected onto mothers by society.

Children who have experienced sexual abuse from an early age are likely to have internalised and be skilled in playing a very sexualised role. Although this is just one of the roles in the 'repertoire' (Landy, 1986)[11] it may be a highly dominant one. These children have been 'taught' that in order to receive 'love' they must behave in a particular way. This sexualised role may be recognised by others as seductive, alluring and incongruent with emotional and physical maturity. This role not only makes these children vulnerable to the adult seeking inappropriate sexual satisfaction, but also to other children who are themselves susceptible to inappropriate behaviour. This can result in these children being ostracised and isolated by others, severely restricting their normal social development. Working with a child who is exhibiting sexualised behaviour can, even for an experienced therapist, be a challenging and at times, disturbing experience. However, it is essential that such children are not overlooked or ostracised, both for their own sake and for the sake of those they will encounter.

DEVELOPMENTAL PLAY

The developmental play model (Jennings, 1990)[13] comprises three stages; embodiment play, projective play and role play. Embodiment begins with the senses which begin to be experienced within the body shortly after birth. Exploration of bodily experience develops into a sense of self, creating a body image of the self. Through the process of engaging their senses, infants are able to relate to their environment and the objects they encounter therein. Physical sculpting with clay and Play-doh, finger-painting and sand-play are forms of embodiment play which are used in drama and play therapy to facilitate the development of a sense of self.

Once infants have experienced enough embodiment of themselves and their environment they are able to then project meaning onto external objects, both animate and inanimate. An early example of projection would be Winnicott's 'transitional object',[14] where feelings are projected onto an inanimate object such as a blanket or soft toy which is imbued with the same feelings of comfort and security once pertaining only to the mother-object. The transitional object allows the infant to create a separation from the mother, without forfeiting the good feelings experienced in relation to her. In drama and play therapy the clay sculpted figure may take on a particular meaning for its creator as feelings are projected onto and into it. If the figure is imbued with feelings of rage, it may become, to its creator, a monster. Other examples of projective materials in the therapeutic space may be dolls, puppets and visual images.

In Object Relations, the first external roles encountered by infants are those relating to the mother-figure. These are further developed through interactions with other carers, siblings and so on. Infants internalise these roles, and uniquely create their own roles in response to them: the role of the comforted in relation to the comforter; the role of the criticised in relation to the critic and so on. In Mead's terms (1934),[15] infants learn to act towards themselves as the others act towards them. In dramatherapy, the creator of the rageful clay monster may take on a particular role in relation to the monster. The role may be that of victim, at risk of being devoured by the monster. Alternatively, the creator's role may be that of a hero who outwits and slays the monster.

The three stages of this developmental play theory mirror the linear progressions in the very young infant's understanding and co-ordination. So to the child without sufficient satisfactory experience of embodiment play, moving onto projection and role play is likely to prove difficult. However, the stages are more cyclical in nature in that they are continuously revisited, beyond childhood, through all stages of human maturation.

Peter Slade (1954),[16] believed by many to have been the first person in Britain to have used the term 'dramatherapy' (1959),[17] distinguishes between two forms of play; personal and projected. Personal play engages the whole self and is typified by movement and role play. Projected play engages the mind but not the body so fully. It is more inner directed, relating to the individual's use of imagination. It is my understanding that Slade's definition of personal play encompasses both embodiment play and role play, whereas projected play relates directly to the projective play stage of the developmental play model.

Peter Slade (1997)[18] wrote:

> For endeavouring to discern whether abuse has taken place, one must test in both realms of personal and projected play—that is in physically active drama and in static play with dolls and objects. Results may be different. Only if unguided play in both realms reveals the same evidence can we begin to believe we are on the right track and are reading symbols correctly.

Children and adults with learning difficulties who have experienced sexual abuse will clearly have enormous obstacles to overcome before their abuse is recognised, particularly those who have not been able to engage in projected play, and especially those who are limited in their verbal skills. Furthermore, when there is a disclosure, these individuals are not given the respect due by the judicial system, as they are often deemed as 'unreliable witnesses'.

USE OF METAPHOR

Much has been written about metaphor and its therapeutic value. The therapeutic value of metaphor allows for the communication of internal experiences which are difficult to express (Noy, 1978;[19] Linden, 1985;[20] Rogers, 1978[21]).

Olney (1972)[22] defines metaphor as something that is either known and of our making, or something that we have chosen to represent and thus help us to understand something unknown or something not of our making. The child exposed to sexual activities prematurely, without free choice, by an inappropriate person, will lack the emotional maturity to accommodate and make sense of the experience. The therapeutic use of metaphor may be a very valuable tool in helping the child (or adult survivor) make sense of and come to terms with it.

Not only does metaphor establish a bridge between the inner and outer worlds (Shengold, 1981)[23] it also allows insight into, whilst maintaining a safe distance from, the original trauma (Caruth, 1966;[24] Jennings, 1990[25]), permitting change without destroying the defence systems (Cox and Theilgaard, 1987).[26] Metaphor, having its origin in the right hemisphere of the brain along with intuition and creativity, is the basic language of art and essential for dramatherapy (Grainger, 1990).[27]

It might be said that metaphor is the place where science and art part company with one another. Whereas science regards the metaphor as valuable as a means to an objective truth, art regards the metaphor as valuable in itself. Precisely where dramatherapy places itself upon this spectrum with objective truth at one pole and subjective truth at the other will be determined by a number of factors.

There has been an ongoing debate within the profession of dramatherapy for some time. One school of thought proposes that the dramatherapist works through metaphor with a client, trusting the method, staying with the chaos until such a time as the client finds their own meaning: that is, until the client consciously interprets the metaphor *for themselves*. Another school of thought proposes that the dramatherapist has a responsibility to facilitate the client in consciously interpreting the metaphor, looking for meaning and relating this to the client's own experiences. These two schools of thought are not mutually exclusive, particularly in the treatment of sexually abused children. The interpretive interventions the dramatherapist might make may be influenced by a number of factors. For example, the sole purpose of therapy might be to facilitate healing; or the agenda might include some element of investigation, with information gained in the therapy to be used during a civil court case. The child may be abuse-reactive, that is identifying with the abuser and going on to abuse other children. All of the above factors and others are taken into account during the referral and assessment stages, which collectively determine how, why and for how long a child is seen at the Consultancy.

The case studies below are illustrations of dramatherapy work with three children who had experienced sexual abuse. Each shows how metaphor helped the children to recognise and express their feelings and thus to gain insight into their situations.

OLIVIA

Olivia was four and a half years old when she first came to the Consultancy. She was tall, slim, and had very clear eyes, which seemed to watch everything, as if waiting for something to happen. Dark circles below her eyes were clearly evident. Olivia, together with her elder brother, sister and a number of their cousins had been subjected to ritualised sexual abuse perpetrated by their parents and several uncles, aunts and grandparents. Although Olivia had been preverbal at the time of the abuse, she was gradually able to give particular details of the abuse to her very supportive foster parents. Although the three children had been placed together, it was evident that Olivia's experience and understanding of the abuse were quite different from those of her siblings.

She had great difficulty sleeping, and the most distressing nightmares would ensue when she did eventually fall asleep. Olivia had been able to tell her fosterparents that before she went to live with them she would often wake up in a different place to the one she went to sleep in. The children had been transported during the night, in their sleep, to a rendez-vous where the abuse took place.

In the initial dramatherapy sessions Olivia busied herself creating paintings of bright suns, smiling children and colourful flowers. Together with the clay objects she moulded with her hands, they were made as gifts to her fostermother, Olivia's way of saying thank you. They were also Olivia's way of trying to portray herself as a happy, bright, carefree child. Momentarily during the sessions this was exactly how she seemed, yet her eyes betrayed her. Always watching and waiting. Olivia's engagement with the paints and clay seemed to be a way of coping for her. She was not using these media to explore and work through the immense trauma she had experienced, but as a means of protecting herself from the impact of the trauma. Perhaps this was why she suffered so greatly at night-time when she was unable to maintain the tight control.

One day Olivia burst into the play room, telling me that it was soon to be her fostermother's birthday and she *had* to make her a special card. She gathered paints, glitter, glue and card together and settled herself down. I decided to tell her a story whilst she worked and Olivia said she liked the story of Snow White. Although she made no comment at all during the telling I realised the story's resonances—this little girl who busied herself keeping everything clean and bright for others, who sang and whistled but who underneath must be feeling . . . hurt, frightened and confused. I noticed Olivia pause when I told her Snow White's plight of being taken from her home by the woodcutter into the terrifying forest; yet he was unable to kill her as the stepmother had ordered, instead leaving her alone and frightened.

As soon as Olivia had finished the birthday card she retreated to the pile of cushions and, curling up like a baby, asked for the story to be told again. Olivia spent the following three sessions curled up on the cushions, sometimes sucking her thumb, sometimes sucking a doll's bottle, listening to the story of Snow White. What felt very significant was that Olivia allowed herself to close her eyes whilst listening.

During the review meeting with fosterparents, Olivia was able to ask for her fostermother to tell her the story of Snow White at bedtimes. This request was granted. Gradually Olivia was able to allow herself to let go and resist fighting sleep. She was clearly exhausted as anyone would be surviving off so little and such disturbed sleep. The dark circles below her eyes slowly began to fade.

In subsequent sessions we explored Snow White's feelings when she was abandoned in the forest. Olivia told me how wrong it was for the 'bad mum' to do such a thing to a little girl. Snow White must have been very scared. The story of Snow White helped Olivia find a way of experiencing her own feelings in relation to the abuse she had suffered, with the traumatic memory of being taken to another place during her sleep.

EDWARD

A contract or agreement is always sought with a child during the assessment period of dramatherapy. The purpose of the contract is to establish a clear understanding between child and therapist of the work they intend to do together. It also serves to empower the child by giving her a voice that will be heard. Sometimes the contract is quite detailed and sometimes it is not. The contract can always be referred to throughout the therapy, and may be amended at any time. In the case of ten-year-old Edward, the contract was very short. It read simply, 'Him'.

Edward came to the Consultancy for brief dramatherapy work. He had been referred by his parents. Both parents were able and willing to co-operate with the Consultancy in supporting Edward through the trauma he had experienced. The decision to approach the Consultancy had been made by all the family.

Agreement to work for a short period of time was made during the initial interview with Edward and his parents, based in part on the fact that the child was very well supported in his home environment. Support networks outside of the therapy, and in particular in the home, are an important factor in determining the value and success of the therapy. A child's ability to cope with the effect of trauma depends on the quality of attachment to consistent, empathetic adult figures (Bowlby, 1969;[28] Miller & Boe, 1990[29]).

At the suggestion of making a story Edward clarified whether he *had* to write one about 'him'. He was clearly relieved to hear the story could be about anything at all.

The hero of the story was a horse. His task was to jump an enormous fence. The fence felt too big to jump and the horse was afraid he would collapse and break his leg. We established that the horse was very scared. At this point Edward sprang from his chair and exclaimed, 'I could jump it!' He promptly began building up a wall of beanbags and just as he was about to make the leap I gently asked him to stop for a moment. Was he sure that the landing was as safe as it could be? He created a soft area on the other side of the fence, and jumped! This was repeated several times before he was satisfied, then Edward returned to the story. We explored the choices available to the horse—he could run away, or he could jump, or he could simply do nothing. At that moment the horse was stuck, he simply did not know what to do. His rider, a little boy, understood his predicament and told him he was very glad he had let him know that he was scared.

Edward looked deflated. He said he did not know how to end the story. He wandered around the playroom glancing casually into the boxes of toys and chests of dressing-up clothes. His face lit up when he discovered a golden crown. The crown fitted him perfectly, and wearing it he walked around the room. His whole stature altered. Now he was moving with his head held high he looked powerful and stately, like a king. 'I am the King and these', pointing at the surrounding dolls, 'are my people.'

Edward had been the victim of a neighbour's inappropriate sexual advances. Although the neighbour had been questioned by the police, no charge had been made. The family were still living in quite close proximity to this neighbour.

In the first session, Edward was unable to name the perpetrator and referred only to 'him'. He described his fear that the man would damage the house because he must be so angry, that he would repeat the behaviour, and that he would attack Edward's mother. In the supervision which followed this session, I questioned whether Edward really was in danger and, if so, whether therapy at this time was appropriate: how was his fear meant to diminish if the threat to him was still real? It was agreed that the work would continue for another session, which would be followed by a meeting with the family, during which recommendations could be made. It was understood that should there be a recommendation that the family move house, then this would be acted upon.

Edward presented a crucial question at the beginning of the first session: why had this man not been arrested? We decided to bring this to the joint meeting for Anne Bannister, then manager of the Consultancy, to answer.

It was evident that Edward felt immobilised by his fear of this man and direct confrontation of these fears would have done little to facilitate his own resources. Yet he was happy to work through metaphor, and thus in the second session he created the following story.

For some time Edward embodied the characteristics he believed the King had. When the moment felt right I reminded him of the poor horse, stuck in his field and said, 'Kings are wise and strong men, I was wondering if the King could help out with the horse's problem?'

'Yes, I can!' he replied, 'The secret is he has to believe he *can* jump the fence.'

'Does the King believe he can? I'm sure it would be a great help to him if the King believes this is possible.'

'Oh yes, he does!'

We returned swiftly to the story. Edward, still in the role of the King, brought the story to an end, with the horse clearing the fence with great panache. Feeling relieved, he was about to take the crown off and let go of the King role but I asked if the King could stay a little longer. The King obliged. Together we walked around the room; our walk evolved into a march which felt energised and powerful. I introduced the subject of self-protection through the role-play. Sometimes even Kings need to protect themselves from bad people; was this King able to do this, and if so did he protect himself with the support of his loyal and trustworthy citizens? Thoughtfully the King agreed that there were bad people who wanted to hurt him, but he added there were lots of good people around who would take care of him. What happens when the King is alone? Could he protect himself then? We rehearsed different scenarios in which he practised looking after himself, and I reflected back the impact he had on me. The King was very proud and pleased that he could do this without anyone else around. We agreed that there were always dangers but rather than being afraid, which caused him to freeze and lose his power, he needed to be cautious. It is often believed that fear is a helpful thing. However, Diane Mariechild (1981)[30] argues that what is really needed is caution, not fear. It makes good sense to be cautious, to be aware of one's surroundings, and one's own limitations. Fear causes tension and panic and blocks energy. Letting go of fear does not mean letting go of good sense.

Before Edward said goodbye to the King he gave some advice for non-Kings. 'They can stand up for themselves and have courage.' With some time remaining in the session, I suggested he made a shield for himself. The idea of a person shield is based on the work of Ann Cattanach (1994).[31] I have used it often, with frequent adaptations, and have found it an extremely useful tool through which children can empower themselves. As Edward was wearing his school blazer he copied the design and created his own personal Shield of Power. Within the shield he wrote and drew his strengths and abilities: how well he got on with his classmates, his favourite subjects at school, the activities outside of school he enjoyed, his courage in telling his parents about the neighbour. Edward took his shield home with him as he wanted to show it to his parents.

During the joint session with his parents, Anne Bannister and myself, Edward was able to voice the question which he had struggled with, 'Why had the neighbour not been arrested?' Anne explained that the police had believed Edward and taken the matter very seriously. They had questioned the man, and his name had been recorded on their files. He would not get a second warning and he would be very stupid to behave this way again. The police, however, had decided not to bring any charges against him to spare Edward the distress of giving evidence in court. Edward seemed satisfied with this response.

Edward was able to express his wish not to move house. He liked his house very much and 'he' was not going to make them move away. Using small animal figures, Edward demonstrated his feelings. He showed how at first he and his parents had been so afraid, the fear symbolised by cotton thread wrapped around the figures representing his family. Carefully he untangled the thread and unceremoniously dropped it on top of the figure representing the neighbour. Edward had symbolically transformed his fear, and given his parents the permission to do the same.

The neighbour still lived nearby. Yet Edward's perception of the situation had changed. No longer was he fearful of this man, but cautious of him. Being a child, he would still need to be protected by his parents, of course, but they no longer needed to be unduly concerned for him. The abusive experience could be laid to rest in the past, and Edward and his parents had the opportunity to look to the future.

Several factors contributed to making this possible. Firstly, the perpetrator was not a significant figure in Edward's life. Had he been his father, brother, uncle or grandfather, then the situation, though not impossible, would have been quite different. Edward clearly felt able to trust his parents: they had believed and supported him and he seemed not to have felt betrayed by them. When Edward had shown anger, confusion and fear in response to the incident prior to therapeutic intervention, his parents were able to empathize with him.

A child, like Edward, who has been brought up in a loving environment and enjoyed acceptance and mothering/parenting that is, in Winnicott's words, 'good enough' (1964),[32] is not beyond the reach of pain and suffering. Such a child will struggle with these challenges and the situations which give rise to them, and with support and time, find some means of integrating the episode into their psyche comfortably enough to prevent lasting trauma (Grimshaw, 1995).[33]

SHAHIDA

I have had the opportunity to facilitate and to participate in training groups which included 'Asian' social workers. I apologise for the generalization of the term 'Asian'. It is a broad term which does not recognise important differences between the many cultures it encompasses. One of the purposes of the groups was to work towards a greater understanding of racial and cultural differences. Without exception the subject of racism very soon became one of the most uncomfortable and pressing topics of discussion. Literature on issues of understanding the impact of child sexual abuse within Asian communities is scarce (Mtezuka, 1990;[34] Wilson, 1993;[35] Little and Robbins, 1982[36]). Documentation of therapeutic interventions with sexually abused Asian children is even rarer.

The appropriateness of Western models of child sexual abuse in relation to the nature of abuse in Asian families is debatable. These models fail to recognise important structural differences such as the role expectation placed on Asian parents and their children; the financial dependency of extended families on the male wage earner; the stigma that will be attached not only to the child herself but to the whole family. The combination of these mean that it is the child who will maintain the silence and the child *who wishes she had remained silent* who will suffer the greatest. If she does disclose, she is likely to be condemned by her own community for betrayal. If she maintains the silence, tacit approval is given to the abuse (Wilson, 1993).[37] The racism which pervades white society is the evil which stands in the way of understanding the children of Asian origin who have become victims of child sexual abuse, and genuinely being able to offer them hope. In many cultures (and abuse and harassment of children and women transcend class and race boundaries) family members are understood to be the man's property (Wilson, 1993).[38] There is an underlying assumption which gives the man an unspoken assurance that he has a right to use his children to meet his own needs. Sexual abuse happens because some men want it to happen; yet the political, societal, cultural and religious attitudes which serve to undervalue the female, create a climate in which abuse can thrive. Professional response to the aftermath of child sexual abuse does not escape from patriarchal attitudes which pervade this society. It is a sad reflection that the professional response appears to perpetuate the inequalities of male power and status that are recognised as one of the underlying causes of child sexual abuse (see Chapter 5 by Print & Dey).

As a white female therapist I may be able to identify with some of these issues (as I, too, experience the patriarchial nature of this society), but it would be impossible to claim awareness of the psychic implications of these issues upon an Asian child in dramatherapy. Thirteen-year-old Shahida, a

Muslim girl whose parents had moved to Britain from Bangladesh, had the courage to disclose her experiences of sexual abuse by her father.

Shahida believed her father had been 'messing about' with her elder sister, Shajna, soon after their mother had died four years ago. Shajna is now eighteen and Shahida believes her to be in Bangladesh in an arranged marriage. Shahida disclosed her own sexual abuse to a teacher. To my knowledge, Shajna has never disclosed her own abuse.

Shahida also had twin sisters aged five. She had a strong emotional bond with both twins and had contributed much to their care. Since Shahida's disclosure, the twins had been removed from the family and placed for adoption. Shahida was not told where the twins were owing to fears that the children would be snatched by extended family members. Her only means of communication was by letter via the social worker. The social worker's role was not an enviable one.

Due to the scarcity of Asian foster families, Shahida was placed with a white family. Predictably, Shahida became intensely engaged in a cultural struggle. Placing a child in a white foster home, which bears little relationship to her own culture, is not regarded as helpful as the child is likely to be confused about her own cultural roots (Mtezuka, 1990).[39] Within the therapy, Shahida's continuing conflict between her own culture and 'the other one/yours/my social worker's/my school's/my foster family's' was clearly evident.

The intention of the dramatherapy work was not to uncover facts. Shahida had already given a written statement to the police, and although the case had not yet been heard in court, the Crown Prosecution Service had given permission for the therapy to begin. The purpose of the work was therefore not to investigate, but to facilitate healing.

Shahida appeared anxious and withdrawn in the first of three assessment sessions. She sat with her coat fastened and her hands buried deep in her pockets. In her second session we were able to complete the contract for our work together. Her first priority were the twins. She wanted to understand how her sisters came to be moved. Shahida was very clear that she did not wish to speak about her father. We clarified what this meant: was it that she did not want to make any reference to him at all, or was it solely in relation to the sexual way he had behaved towards her? 'Yes, in that way', she answered.

Using Babushka dolls, Shahida was able to show something of the relationships she shared with members of her family. Babushka dolls are the Russian-style wooden dolls that fit one inside the other. The truly traditional dolls might have in the region of 40 dolls all fitting inside each other. However, for use as projective tools in dramatherapy the ones I use have only five dolls of decreasing sizes. By using projective techniques children can externalise their inner world thereby allowing the therapist to gain understanding of that inner world, in a way a kind of 'snap-shot'. Shahida made a sculpt, a three-dimensional, moveable picture with the Babushka dolls which accurately reflected and supported the information she shared with me verbally about her family. The twins were close by the doll representing herself, Shajna was a little further away, and her father, represented by a wolf, was buried underneath a pile of cushions. She said she could not bear to look at him.

Shahida's insistence that she did not want to speak about the abuse was regarded as a positive sign that she was communicating her feelings and looking after herself. Why on earth should she share such personal details of her life with a stranger? It is vital that the child moves at her own pace, and that the dramatherapist conveys trust in the child that she will use this time to heal herself, if she feels 'the risk is worth taking' (Powley, 1993).[40] As the therapist, I had to accept that Shahida might never speak of the abuse.

Shahida's anxiety diminished when she chose to work through metaphor using stories. In the fourth session, Shahida created the following story:

'Once there was a cat called Sophie. She feels safe except for when the dog is around, then she feels unsafe.'

I interviewed Shahida in the role of Sophie. The unnamed dog was represented by a huge teddy bear. Similarities between the wolf representing her father in the earlier sculpt and Shahida's choice of dog in this story were noted, but not verbalized as we had contracted to work metaphorically.

'Sophie, what do you want to happen to the dog?'

'Lock him up for ever.'

Before the dog could be locked up, I asked if Sophie needed to find some protection from the dog. (Shahida's father had so far avoided prosecution. Shahida believed her father to be in Bangladesh. She had never been there herself and felt unable to imagine where he was. Sometimes it is easier to deal with the memory of a person if one can picture the person in a physical place. Shahida's father could have been anywhere and everywhere; he was free-floating.)

'Put him on a lead.'

Sophie led the dog into a shed (cushions) and locked the door. Keeping the key, she added assertively that it was *her* decision when he was released. She was not a cruel cat though, she made sure he had food and water. I made the comment that Sophie seemed a very fair cat.

'Now the dog knows he has done something to upset Sophie', she added. (A hope that her father might take responsibility for his behaviour and the consequences?) She told me the dog was mean and hated to say sorry. Sophie determined to keep the dog in the shed until he was sorry. Only when he said sorry would Sophie know he had changed, and if he did not he would stay in the shed for ever.

In the following session the dog was still in the shed. I asked Shahida in the role of Sophie if there was someone else with her when she was upset by the dog. Yes, there was someone else, another cat called Tiggy. Shahida in the role of Tiggy advised Sophie to stay away from the dog. Tiggy did not share what he/she had seen and this did not seem necessary. What did seem important was that Sophie had a witness in the story who was able to validate her experiences. Through the metaphor of the story Shahida had identified an inner witness for herself.

With Tiggy beside her, Sophie felt brave enough to open the shed door and lead the dog out. She was cautious in her actions. She set the dog a test. Could he be trusted not to bite? This she must know before she could consider setting him free and she actually needed to witness the dog *not* biting in order to *know* how she felt about this. In dramatherapy. Shahida had the opportunity to direct this scenario. Still in the role of Sophie, she identified a doll as a potential victim to the dog. He did not bite the doll and Sophie, the cat, found herself able to set the dog free. He was told, however, that if he should make any attempt to chase or bite, he would be sent back into the shed and there would be no second chance for him. In a second scenario, Sophie immediately intervened when the dog bit the doll. He was ordered back to the shed. We laughed about Sophie needing to speak loudly and clearly because the dog had cloth ears and very selective hearing. Shahida, still in role as Sophie, said, not without some satisfaction, that the dog was terrified of spiders and there were lots of them in the shed. The story was finished for the time being and the metaphor remained intact. Her father and the sexual abuse she had experienced were not named.

In the next session Sahida requested the Babushka dolls to make another family sculpt. Something had changed for her. This time her father, still represented by the wolf, was placed on the cushions rather than underneath them.

Margaret Mary Kelly (1995)[41] proposes that the course of therapy with a sexually abused child involves a succession of cycles in which the child repeatedly returns to three core processes: testing the therapeutic relationship, addressing traumatic experiences and undoing denial.

The story allowed Shahida to address metaphorically some of the trauma she had experienced. Shahida freely engaged in projected and personal play (Slade, 1954)[42] enabling her to explore themes of abuse of power, responsibility and appropriate use of power without feeling overwhelmed by her feelings. She expressed fear but also her potential to forgive, providing certain conditions had been met.

Shahida also recognised her own inner witness, a truly valuable companion to have. Often the therapeutic process is described metaphorically as a journey (Scott Peck, 1978;[43] Grainger, 1990[44]). The journey is untrodden.

Rowan (1983)[45] speaks of reaching the real self . . . it seems as if we almost have to die to get there.

There is a story told by the Besht Tellers, a Jewish theatre company, about an angel called Lila. Lila's task is to take souls from the Garden of Paradise whenever a child is conceived. She has to pull and pull the soul, understandably, because it does not want to leave paradise. Lila always has a struggle, but she always wins. Suddenly there in the womb is a light. The brightest, purest light ever. For the next nine months Lila whispers to the soul. She tells it all it will do, think, feel and experience. She tells it all the people it will meet and where. Everything. When it is time, and the whispering done, the child is seized and forced out into another world. The light is extinguished. The child, the person, remembers nothing consciously of Lila's words. Everything is forgotten. The person spends the rest of his/her life rediscovering the knowledge. Perhaps Lila is the witness along this journey of rediscovery.

The witness has the skill to guide the traveller safely through treacherous paths along the way. The witness is also the voice of encouragement; when taking another step feels impossible. It is the witness' voice that comforts the traveller when they stumble, and the voice of truth when it validates the pain and humiliation suffered. The witness is the narrator of *the* story. The presence of the witness in its many and wonderful guises, fundamentally signifies the presence of hope. Without hope, no amount of therapy will make any difference in a person's life. Long (1986)[46] describes the therapist as needing to have 'faith'; to be able to have faith in the child's own ability to solve problems and to grow.

Acting as another witness to Shahida's story I understood that these issues were likely to relate to the abuse Shahida had experienced. However, to close my mind to other possible interpretations would have been uncreative and anti-therapeutic. By consciously interpreting the drama, I may well have blocked the continuing process of understanding which is multi-layered and multi-dimensional (Jennings, 1990).[47] Furthermore, I am reminded of the psychodramatist Sandra Garfield's salient words, 'All interpretations are essentially self-disclosures' (1995).[48] The story of Sophie the cat remained in metaphor. Shahida was addressing manageable aspects of the trauma *in her own time* until she could accept the abuse in its totality (Miller and Boe, 1990).[49] It is not uncommon for a sexually abused child to regard therapy as another form of abuse (Haugaard, 1992)[50] and the therapist must be particularly mindful that her comments, interventions and interpretations are not reminiscent of the abusive experience. Making an interpretation in the therapy of an abused child is precarious when one considers the power the therapist has to direct and influence the child. Children generally try to please adults, and certainly to accommodate them. In the case of a thirteen-year-old Bangladeshi girl and a white dramatherapist the power imbalance is potentially greater. Shahida gained some understanding of the complex dynamics and sequence of events which led up to her sisters being removed. She continued to write to them, sending drawings she had made during the sessions. She acknowledged the reality of the situation, and could allow herself to feel the pain of losing them. Her attitude was one of hope. 'They will always be my sisters, and I hope that one day we'll see each other again.'

In subsequent sessions, Shahida spoke directly about the abuse she had experienced. She became the narrator of her own story, and the story, of course, continues.

SUMMARY

These case studies are not intended to show a child's complete therapeutic process. Rather, they have been excerpts, illustrating the healing these children were able to facilitate for themselves. Their therapy continued for some time afterwards, and it is highly likely that they may, particularly Shahida and Olivia, return to therapy at other stages in their lives. I have tried to show how each child's experience of the sexual abuse suffered was different, determined by the child's own understanding and her particular circumstances; and how her own agenda for healing was followed by the dramatherapist. Names and some details have been changed, of course, in order to protect the children's anonymity. I hope I have not done any of them a disservice in my translations. Finally, I would like to thank them and all the children seen at the Consultancy for allowing us to understand some of what they are feeling.

REFERENCES

1. James. B. (1993) 'The fallacy of children having power within an incest relationship: A response to Seligson's article', *Journal of Child Sexual Abuse*, **2** (1).
2. 'Science Today' (July 1997) *BBC Radio 4*.
3. Grimshaw, D. (1995) 'Shall I be mother? The development of the role of the dramatherapist and reflections on transference/countertransference', in S. Jennings (ed), *Dramatherapy with Children and Adolescents* (Routledge: London and New York).
4. Information Pack (1994, 1997) *British Association for Dramatherapists*.
5. Klein, M. (1932) *The Psycho-Analysis of Children* (Revised Edition) (Hogarth Press and the Institute of Psychoanalysis).
6. Winnicott, D. W. (1971) *Playing and Reality* (Tavistock Publications: London).
7. Liedloff, J. (1975) *The Continuum Concept* (Penguin Books: Harmondsworth).

8. Grimshaw, D. (1996) 'Dramatherapy with children in an educational unit: the more you look, the more you see', in S. Mitchell (ed), *Dramatherapy: Clinical Studies* (Jessica Kingsley Publishers: London).

9. Winnicott, D. W. (1971) *op. cit.*

10. Eichenbaum, L. & Orbach, S. (1983) *Understanding Women* (Penguin Books: Harmondsworth).
    Eichenbaum, L. & Orbach, S. (1987) *Between Women* (Penguin Books: Harmondsworth).
    Ernst, S. & Maguire, M. (eds) (1987) *Living with the Sphinx: Papers from the Women's Therapy Centre* (The Women's Press: London).

11. Landy, R. (1986) *Drama Therapy—Concepts and Practices* (Charles C. Thomas: Springfield, Illinois).

12. Parker, R. (1995) *Torn in Two: The Experience of Maternal Ambivalence* (Virago Press: London).

13. Jennings, S. (1990) *Waiting in the Wings: Dramatherapy with Families, Groups and Individuals* (Jessica Kingsley Publishers: London).

14. Winnicott, D. W. (1971) *op. cit.*

15. Mead, G. H. (1934) *Mind, Self and Society* (University of Chicago Press: Chicago).

16. Slade, P. (1954) *Child Drama* (Hodder & Stoughton: London).

17. Slade, P. (1959) *Dramatherapy as an Aid to Becoming a Person* (Guild of Pastoral Psychology).

18. Slade, P. (1997) Private correspondence.

19. Noy, P. (1978) 'Insight and creativity', *Journal of the American Psychoanalytic Association,* **26**(4).

20. Linden, J. (1985) 'Insight through metaphor in psychotherapy and creativity', *Psychoanalysis and Contemporary Thought—A Quarterly of Integrative and Interdisciplinary Studies,* **8**(3).

21. Rogers, R. (1978) *Metaphor—A Psychoanalytic View* (University of California Press: Berkeley, CA).

22. Olney, J. (1972) *Metaphors of Self: The Meaning of Autobiography* (Princeton University Press: Princeton, NJ).

23. Shengold, L. L. (1981) 'Insight as metaphor', *The Psychoanalytic Study of the Child,* **36**.

24. Caruth, E. (1966) 'Interpretation within the metaphor: further considerations', in Ekstein, R. (ed) *Children of Time and Space, of Action and Impulse* (Appleton-Century-Crofts: New York).

25. Jennings, S. (1990) *op. cit.*

26. Cox, M. & Theilgaard, A. (1987) *Mutative Metaphors in Psychotherapy* (Tavistock: London).

27. Grainger, R. (1990) *Drama and Healing: The Roots of Drama Therapy* (Jessica Kingsley Publishers: London).

28. Bowlby, J. (1969) *Attachment and Loss: Vol. 1. Attachment* (Basic Books: New York).

29. Miller, C. & Boe, J. (1990) 'Tears into diamonds: transformation of child psychic trauma through sandplay and storytelling', *The Arts in Psychotherapy,* **17**, 247–257.

30. Mariechild, D. (1981) *Mother Wit: A Feminist Guide to Psychic Development* (The Crossing Press: California).

31. Cattanach, A. (1994) *Play Therapy—Where the Sky Meets the Underworld* (Jessica Kingsley Publishers: London).
32. Winnicott, D. W. (1964) *The Child, the Family and the Outside World* (Penguin Books: Harmondsworth).
33. Grimshaw, D. (1995) *op. cit.*
34. Mtezuka, M. (1990) 'Towards a better understanding of child sexual abuse among Asian communities', *Practice*, Autumn/Winter, 248–260.
35. Wilson, M. (1993) *Crossing the Boundary: Black Women Survive Incest* (Virago Press: London).
36. Little, A. & Robbins, D. (1982) *Loading the Law: A Study of Transmitted Deprivation. Ethnic Minorities and Affirmative Action* (Commission for Racial Equality).
37. Wilson, M. (1990) *op. cit.*
38. Wilson, M. (1990) *op. cit.*
39. Mtezuka, M. (1990) *op. cit.*
40. Powley, D. (1993) Private communication.
41. Kelly, M. M. (1995) 'Play therapy with sexually traumatized children: factors that promote healing', *Journal of Child Sexual Abuse*, **4**, (3) 1–11.
42. Slade, P. (1954) *op. cit.*
43. Scott Peck, M. (1978) *The Road Less Travelled* (Century Hutchinson: London).
44. Grainger, R. (1990) *op. cit.*
45. Rowan, J. (1983) *The Reality Game* (Routledge: London).
46. Long, S. (1986) 'Guidelines for treating young children', in MacFarlane, K., Waterman, J. et al. (eds), *Sexual Abuse of Young Children* (Holt, Rinehart and Winston: New York).
47. Jennings, S. (1990) *op. cit.*
48. Garfield, S. 'The Healing Drama' Dramatherapy and Psychodrama Conference 1995.
49. Miller, C. & Boe, J. (1990) *op. cit.*
50. Haugaard, J. J. (1992) 'Sexually abused children's opposition to psychotherapy', *Journal of Child Sexual Abuse*, **1** (2) 1–16.

4

THE INTERFACE BETWEEN ASSESSMENT AND THERAPY

Corinne Wattam

This chapter will examine working practices at the initial 'formal' interview of a suspected child victim of sexual abuse in the context of the relationship between legal and therapeutic aims. My purpose is to restate some common ground between legal and therapeutic requirements and suggest that the interview could be more responsive to the child's immediate needs, yet retain the longer-term view of protection through the courts. What follows will argue for a redress of the balance between legal and therapeutic needs. The premise is that refining responses to meet what turn out to be narrow interpretations of legal requirements has had an adverse effect on both the quality of evidence and the child.

The argument, and the material used, is drawn from a research project begun in January 1988 *Disclosure: The Child's Perspective*,[1] which aimed to explore the actual methods used by practitioners during the process of disclosure. In the main, five sources of material were gathered and analysed: (1) that produced during periods of ethnography in a child protection team; (2) case files of all the child sexual abuse cases referred in the area over a two-year period; (3) interviews with social workers from social service teams within the area; (4) children who were reported to have disclosed; and (5) police and social work videotaped interviews.

The collaboration between police officers and social workers in child sexual abuse assessments is symptomatic both of the acknowledged difference between legal and therapeutic requirements, and also the need to combine them. The anticipated benefits of a joint approach have been outlined by Conroy *et al* (1990)[2] as: 'a reduction in the number of occasions children are interviewed; the establishment of a clearer understanding of individual workers' roles; increased co-ordination in the delivery of services; the establishment of group support for difficult decisions; and an increase in effective communication between professionals.'

Whilst joint working arrangements differ across the country, they have in common the anticipated aim that, by combining police officers and social workers, an optimum approach to the obtaining of evidence will be attained. Yet, apart from acknowledging the need for minimising the number of times a child should be interviewed, there is less than unanimity about how these joint interviews aim to meet the needs of children and their families. It is almost as if, by taking account of the needs of the pro- fessionals—which are for an improved mutual understanding of roles, increased co-ordination, and establishment of group support—the eviden- tial, child, and family requirements will all be met. It has been shown elsewhere that this is not the case. For example, Kelly and Regan (1990)[3] noted that the evaluation of the Bexley experiment did not show a better outcome for children and families.

Social workers and police officers have now been given a clear mandate from the government to work together (DHSS and Welsh Office, 1988)[4] and the objectives pertaining to aims relating to evidence and children need to be clearly outlined. The Home Office note that 'the welfare of the child is recognised as the overriding concern of all the professional agencies' (Home Office, 1988)[5] but unless clear aims and objectives are specified as to how the welfare of the child might best be achieved, it is likely to be glossed as a well-meaning intention largely taken for granted. The following excerpt from my materials, in this case an interview with a social worker about joint interviewing, exemplifies the practical complexity of combining the two kinds of requirements without addressing how the welfare of the child is met by doing so.

> . . . there are lots of things about obviously police interviews that make it really difficult for it to be a therapeutic interview for a child, and it certainly isn't the way in which anybody learns or develops skills with working with children . . . there are bits of it that are good, there are bits of it that maybe we're not quite as good at, in terms of helping the kids to be specific and to recreate something quite realistically by them having to be very very specific . . . in general I find them quite difficult for the children and quite difficult for us and quite an unnatural situation . . . I think at first we were quite thrilled by this relationship we had with the police and the way that we interviewed and the fact that we had relationships with the people we interviewed with and lots of that was good, but there were very obvious limitations to it which show up all the time.

I: Right, it's not just a case of putting police and social workers together and getting the ideal solution?
SW: No because I think we've maybe come almost as far as we can on that. I think inevitably (we've) just come to the point where the different agendas mean different things. I mean the interview and the police's need always remain primary on that.

This is one person's observation of joint working, which displays how legal requirements ('the police's need') are viewed as taking priority over and above the therapeutic needs of children. The point I want to make in this chapter is that this divide whilst patently present, actually mitigates against the aim to obtain the best possible evidence to enable child protection. There are points of consensus between legal and therapeutic aims which would further the progress of both and lead to a more sensitive and realistic response to children and families.

The use of video tape in respect of these interviews has been immensely consequential in shaping their content. Initially, videotaping was done for therapeutic purposes, to avoid several people having to interview the child, and allow for repeated analysis of the interview. However, it became clear that these video tapes may be useful as evidence and various projects, most notable that in Bexley (Metropolitan Police and Bexley Social Services, 1987),[6] began to record interviews for this purpose. The introduction of videotapes into the legal arena created problems, and practitioners were directed to examine their questioning techniques and recording practices to bring them within legal requirements. The therapeutic purpose of preventing repeated interviews and allowing further analysis remained, but the content of the interview shifted. Whether this content was therapeutic in the hands of the police and social workers became unclear, and the question arose as to whether these interviews could be therapeutic when their use as evidence was the guiding rationale.

In 1988 a working group, headed by Judge Pigot, was asked to look into the whole area of using pre-recorded video as evidence in criminal proceedings. One of the concerns expressed to that group by Douglas Hurd, the Home Secretary, was the effect of 'prospect of use' for legal proceedings on the interview and consequently the child (Home Office, 1989).[7] This question was inadequately dealt with in the report, likely as not because these tapes were currently not applicable to criminal proceedings and 'prospect of use' was not yet relevant. However, my research showed clearly that the 'prospect of use' as evidence was a key factor in determining how the interviews were structured, the type of questions asked and not asked, and the chances of a case being pursued or not. Thus we appear to have moved to the point where any therapeutic value of initial formal interviews becomes an incidental by-product given that its legal requirements become paramount. It is worth noting here that there is no other crime that is responded to in a parallel fashion; that is, where the victim is encouraged not to talk about the event until placed in front of a camera, and then cannot be helped by ordinary questioning techniques but must somehow volunteer all the information about the crime, albeit with guarded and circumspect encouragement. Imagine a burglary to your house dealt with in this way. At the very point when children are in need of skilled therapeutic intervention to encourage them to talk and to stop the abuse, they are often thwarted. This points to the way in which the practice of videotaping interviews has moved away from being of benefit to children and starts to act against them.

In Britain these initial interviews are variously known as 'disclosure' interviews, 'formal' interviews, or 'joint' interviews. All these terms refer to interviews conducted by the police and another agency, usually social services or the NSPCC. They may also involve an adult familiar to the child, such as a teacher or non-abusing parent. The interviews are convened by either agency after a referral indicates a possibility that a child has been sexually abused. Whether the interview is videotaped currently depends on circumstances at the time, such as; availability of video resources, an assessment of whether the case is appropriate for joint agency interviewing, the wishes of the child, or the parents who must consent and also, to some extent, the usual practice of the practitioner receiving the referral. With the introduction of the admissibility of pre-recorded video evidence in criminal proceedings, consideration needs to be given to when it is appropriate to video and when not, since *ad hoc* arrangements based on custom, practice and availability are not a sufficient rationale.

THE DEBATE BETWEEN LEGAL AND THERAPEUTIC PRIORITY

Formal interviews represent, to some degree, the areas of conflict and consensus for legal and therapeutic practitioners (Glasgow, 1987).[8] The legal response to child sexual abuse is founded on the principle that where it can be proved that a child has been harmed, or is at risk of harm, the child requires protection which is legally enforceable. In addition, the community has the right to be protected from perpetrators of abuse, who should be punished if their act constitutes a crime. People involved in the enforcement of the legal response are primarily police officers, social workers with statutory powers, solicitors, magistrates and other court personnel. From their point of view the videotaped interview is attempting to assess whether a child has been sexually abused and gather particulars of acts and events, with the focus on what, if anything, has happened. They will also be attempting to assess who perpetrated the abuse, and whether there is sufficient evidence to make a charge.

The therapeutic response is founded on the principle that the child who has suffered harm requires help to adjust to the consequences of that harm, so that he or she may resume functioning as a well adjusted and healthy child. Children are generally members of families (however loosely defined) and so it is often necessary to involve the people closest to them in this process. This is especially so where the perpetrator of the abuse is a family member. Perpetrators are considered on a continuum of untreatable at one end and treatable at the other. Therapeutic investment in perpetrators has as its primary focus the health of the individual, with a strong secondary focus of protection of the child community. People involved in a therapeutic response are likely to be social workers, probation officers, psychologists, psychiatrists, and other mental health professionals. Within the videotaped interview, the therapeutic practitioner will also be attempting to assess whether the child has been sexually abused, but will have as their focus the principle that the sharing of that knowledge is potentially therapeutic, as it is assisting the child to come to terms with what has happened to them. The focus is on effect and affect. In addition they, too, will be concerned that the child should be protected from further abuse.

Although there is some formal overlap between the aims of the legal and therapeutic responses to the interview, in practice their divergent emphases are substantial. Legal requirements stress detection and the sub-stantiation of suspicions, while the therapeutic side emphasises support of the child, its family and, possibly, the abuser. While both sets of require-ments acknowledge the importance of the other, their differential emphases can, on occasion, lead to conflict. Both legal and therapeutic practitioners will aim to act in the best interests of the child. However, because of the different emphasis of the legal and therapeutic aims—that is, child protec-tion and child health—there is likely to be conflict on occasions.

This debate is not solely an academic one of should a response be legal/ criminal or therapeutic? It is a practical exigency and child protection work is, in part, shaped and structured by it. In Europe there are a variety of responses which have evolved around respective judicial situations and salient therapeutic perspectives. In Holland, for example, there is the confi-dential doctor service where any child can go to report sexual abuse and receive therapeutic help. As in other countries there is the legal framework for prosecution, but services are set up to negotiate their way round the legal framework, using it when appropriate. Much as in the UK, 'Childline' offers a confidential service to children, guiding them towards statutory intervention when and where they can.

In assessing the nature of this divide between legal and therapeutic priorities it is helpful to take account of the need for confidential services. Or to consider why, even where mandatory reporting exists, cases fail to get reported (Finkelhor, 1984),[9] and why sexual abuse is under-reported by victims and their families. Confidentiality and the related phenomenon of under-reporting have much to do with the expected response, which is not anticipated as a positive experience. For example, a frequently given reason for not reporting is fear of not being believed (Waldby, 1985;[10] Wattam, 1990[11]). When the initial response is inherently and inevitably one which appears doubting and sceptical, which any thorough detection must necessarily be, this serves to reinforce the fear and mitigate against the giving of information. The *Cleveland Report* made it clear that no practitioner should embark on the investigative process with an opinion as to what has happened one way or the other. The term 'disclosure interview' was thus discredited since it presupposed the child must have something to disclose in the first place (Butler-Sloss, 1988).[12] If the problem becomes one of attempting to display whether something has happened, when it might not have done, in the context of legal requirements as they are perceived by police officers and social workers, the stance is inevitably a doubting one. The following extract from a pre-recorded video interview with a 12-year-old girl exemplifies this.

MPO = Male Police Officer; FPO = Female Police Officer; C = Child.

MPO: . . . If you can start, the thing is to start from the beginning, that's the main thing, alright?
C: It first happened when I were about seven, I'd been ill, I was sick and got in, like, me mum's bed, me mum and me dad, and a while later I couldn't go to sleep and then me dad started to kiss me and everything and then he started like rubbing his hands up and down me and I went to the toilet and was sick and got back in me own bed and he came out to me and he started kissing me and that, and I told him I didn't feel well and he goes, 'Oh well, we'll have to do something tomorrow', and he and then he left me and then if me mum went out or anything he'd start like kissing me and everything.
MPO: Can I just stop you there, can we just go back to what you were first saying, you weren't feeling very well. What was wrong with you?
C: I were just ill.
MPO: Just sickly ill?
C: Yeah.
MPO: Oh right, and you were in your mum's bed and your dad started kissing you. Is that wrong? There's nothing wrong with that is there?
C: No, but . . .
MPO: I mean I kiss my children.
C: Yes, but kissing like wrong, do you know what I mean?
MPO: Can you explain to me what you mean?
FPO: More detail than that.

It was clear from my materials that most children do not know what to expect, or what is expected of them in these interviews. However, they quickly learn that what they are experiencing is significant and very different from what they might have experienced before. The talk is not an everyday conversation, the child is the focus of the interaction, it is in an 'official' setting, adults appear not to know things that children could expect them to know, and so on. In these circumstances few children would have adequate reference points to understand what is expected of them. As King and Yuille point out (1987)[13] children who are placed in the artificial situations induced by experimental research are generally prepared, familiarised, with the task at hand. This is because experimental psychologists seem to understand that if an optimum performance is to be gained from the child, the child must understand what is expected of them. It would be interesting to see this concept applied to investigative interviews with children. The recall of information and the giving of evidence, that is, knowing how to display that information in the way required, are skills which could be rehearsed neutrally. For example, a pre-interview stage (still on video if appropriate) could comprise of a child being encouraged to talk about an everyday event such as teeth cleaning, in the kind of way that the interviewer (though not the child) knows will be required later of evidential information.

This approach could combine with the use of cognitive interviewing techniques in the interview (Geiselman and Fisher, 1989;[14] Westcott, 1991[15]) which focus on retrieval of details. This involves mental reconstruction of physical and personal contexts, recall from a number of different perspectives, requests to report everything (regardless of relevance—see below), and recall related to sequencing of events. The interactive approach employs some of these principles, particularly in relation to context.

One problem which underpins criticism levelled in Cleveland and subsequently, is the practitioner's knowledge that child sexual abuse can be difficult to talk about. While children may not indicate anything is wrong this does not necessarily mean that nothing has happened. My interviews with children endorsed this. They talked of situations, for example at school or with social workers, where opportunities were given for them to talk, but which they chose not to take up. It may be, as the *Cleveland Report* indicates, that practitioners have to accept this as something they can do nothing about. The message from Cleveland, and more recent controversies, is that practitioners cannot compensate for this feature in interviews. They cannot be seen to be challenging 'denial', or even encouraging in any overt and leading way. However, if a component of child sexual abuse is its secrecy, and fear of talking about it, how are practitioners to deal with it? I pose this question not because I have an answer, but to point to some practical implications. A well-publicised case, that of Elizabeth Morgan in

America, reveals one consequence. If, as in that case, the child cannot formulate what has happened to them in terms acceptable to the legal system, non-abusing parents and even practitioners may resort to 'alternative' measures. In the Morgan case this amounted to the child going 'underground'. The implication is that if the legal system cannot adequately protect children, the response should navigate it.

A problem standing at the heart of the legal/therapeutic divide can be illustrated by two views. One, that children should be legally (or otherwise) protected before they can be helped, and two, that criminalising child sexual abuse is a deterrent to helping children and families. Thus, if child sexual abuse were not a crime with all the attendant consequences, it might be easier for everyone to talk about it. Conversely, that child sexual abuse is a crime is recognition of the serious damage it causes, and that to decriminalise it would effectively licence sexual violence.

I do not want to enter into this debate here. However, it is important for every practitioner to be clear about where they stand within it. My materials indicated that there were individual differences in intervention response and the take up of joint working. This appeared to be related to how seriously the abuse was assessed by the investigator, and how adequately they felt they had prevented its recurrence without legal intervention. This was observable in past, rather than present, practice. However, guidelines are always open to interpretation, and always have to be implemented by individuals in particular circumstances. Thus, being aware of attitudes and beliefs that guide the implementation of policy guidelines and procedures is helpful. Furthermore, the practitioners' stance has some bearing on how they interview and carry out their assessment.

Finally, the debate between legal and therapeutic priority can result in conflict between practitioners at the evidence gathering stage. This conflict can arise where workers from either 'side' do not take sufficient account of the other. For example, when a police officer takes over an interview, asking questions to get a statement from the child, and ignores the social worker's attempts to handle the situation therapeutically. Or, alternatively, where the social worker interviews the child alone, and does not take into account the need for the police to be involved at a later stage. A joint interview between the child, a police officer and a social worker, requires a delicate balance which is often not talked about beforehand. It can be assumed that where social workers and police officers have had joint training, not necessarily together, they will achieve this balance. Sadly, this is not always the case. Hence, children still come out of interviews with much of their pain unresolved, or are subjected to repeated interviews by individual and 'joint' practitioners. Yet, the tragedy is that all adult parties to this could claim they were acting in the child's best interests.

The introduction of pre-recorded videotapes as evidence is likely to exacerbate this situation unless a serious attempt is made to address legal requirements in a way which is sensitive to the child's needs. It is a misconception to suggest that one must necessarily come before the other. As Glasgow (1987)[16] points out,

> It is absolutely essential that this situation is rectified and a consensus reached as to exactly how and by whom these assessments may be undertaken. The communication between child and investigator must be standardised, rigorous and carefully undertaken. It is also essential that assessment work is conducted in such a way as to both take into account the wellbeing of the child *and* anticipate the evidential demands of the forensic setting along with the likelihood of rigorous cross examination on the evidence presented. (pp. 26–27)

RECONCILING LEGAL AND THERAPEUTIC REQUIREMENTS

The social worker quoted above noted that one feature of the interview was helping children to be specific and recreate something realistically. From observations of interviews I can endorse that this is clearly a feature, and that the ability of the child to be specific gives credibility to their account. If children are not able to be specific they do not make good witnesses, nor do they provide sufficient information for corroborative evidence to be pursued. In terms of evidence the material facts must be established. But there is more to it than this. The evidence must show that the crime was committed by the person accused and in criminal proceedings this must be proved beyond all reasonable doubt. Furthermore, evidence must be relevant and legally admissable.

Therapeutically a focus on detail can also be important. During the course of the study a social worker who had been working for many years with adult and child victims in a therapeutic context stated,

> They all have something they want to get off their chests. It's a bit like when people are dying, they want to talk about some dark secret they'll go to hell for. It's very difficult when it might seem so trivial. Adults, when they get 'that bit' out in the open, they start to heal. A lot of it is to do with the actual physical description of the abuse. They seem to want to tell the details so it's not in their heads, their memories, and they've handed it over.
>
> One thing we mustn't do, we shouldn't console kids—shut them up and stop them saying what they've got to say 'Oh, well never mind, you're safe now'. We don't always let children talk about details, but they're usually not able to do it . . .

This comment indicates the therapeutic potential ('they start to heal'), though an acknowledged difficulty within it ('they're usually not able to do it'), of talking about detail. Difficulties in communication are characteristic of children who have been sexually abused (Summit, 1983;[17] Glasgow, 1987[18]). These difficulties must be taken into account and attended to if information is expected from the child. Attempting to get information in the very early stages of an investigation before these difficulties have been addressed is likely to reduce its quality, and thus its potential use as evidence.

The above extract from the interview with a 12-year-old girl acts as an example of the characteristic search for detail, and displays how difficult the task of obtaining it is when not being able to explain to the child just what sort of detail is relevant and why it is required. The child offers an account of what happened to her in terms of 'everything' or 'and that'. Whilst this would be sufficient in some context, to know something had happened; it is not sufficient for evidential purposes. This child, and many others, found talking about 'the nitty gritty' very difficult. Part of the problem was understanding what it was she should be saying—after all 'everything' can be seen as adequate, as could 'kissing like wrong'. This statement is focused on and the child is asked to clarify it more than once. She then offers 'like me dad kisses me mum', but this too required clarification. Eventually the social worker intervenes and asks a more specific question which the child readily answers.

> SW: . . . whereabouts was he kissing you?
> C: Like on me lips and all round me face and everything.
> SW: Anywhere else?
> C: and eh, no but he were like kissing me wrong do you know what I mean?
> SW: (Yes) were they sort of like longer kisses not just pecks on the cheek?
> C: Yes.

It is clear here that evidential needs are here being juxtaposed with the child's needs. The social worker is trying to help, without using leading questions, but in fact does end up using them. However, as Jones and McQuiston (1988)[19] point out, there is a difference between interviews that use leading questions occasionally and those comprised almost entirely of them. In addition, they also point to types of leading questions. There would be a difference for example between, 'Did your Dad give you long kisses?' and the option selected above, 'were they sort of like longer kisses not just pecks on the cheek?', in terms of evidential suitability, i.e. the degree of suggestibility that could be imputed to the questioner.

There is a general consensus that leading questions should be avoided (Vizard, 1991).[20] However, interpretation of what might constitute a leading question varies. Some practitioners have been so careful to interview within the perceived legal requirement of no leading questions, that as one social worker put it to me, 'they come out knowing no more than when they went in'. Given the level of criticism and debate surrounding these videos it is perhaps not surprising that this should be the case. However, attention is drawn to a citation from Spencer and Flin (1990);[21]

> Certainly there were some leading questions. Certainly there was questioning on an hypothetical basis. But has anyone, in this country or elsewhere, yet found a way of heading a child along without use of these methods? It is how it is done that matters, and then the interpretation to be put on the answers and reactions of a child. The fact is in this case that a good deal of what was elicited from A was spontaneous. (Latey J in C v C [1988] FCR 458, [1988] 1 FLR 462; p145)

The general rule is to avoid leading questions, but it is their positioning in the interviewing sequence which is of crucial importance.

RELEVANCE

Earlier, I refer to the predicament facing parents and practitioners where they can be convinced that a child has been abused, but where the child is not able to give an 'adequate' account of this, that is, adequate in terms of evidential requirements. Elsewhere (Wattam, 1991)[22] I display how such a situation is constructed, how parents or practitioners can believe a child '100 per cent' but courts fail to do so. One of the reasons for this is the way in which children's evidence is obtained, formatted and presented in different contexts. Many of the features which give truth value to accounts are (unintentionally) screened out because of perceived relevance. A key point of this chapter is that relevance should not be prescribed, and that taking a joint legal and therapeutic perspective to interviewing children offers one safeguard to this.

The issue of what is relevant evidence is central to an understanding of the divide between legal and therapeutic practitioners. As the above interview extract displays, in legal terms the focus is generally on what has happened. Thus relevant evidence is any information that contributes to displaying what has happened in as much detail as possible. Therapeutically, relevant information can be anything that the child talks about, not necessarily to do with the event itself, but also in relation to the effect. The effects of child sexual abuse are more likely to be considered appropriate to treatment which comes later, as are the effects of disclosure. What the courts want to know is as much as possible about events. However, a focus on what has happened, the event(s), seem to promote a narrow definition of relevance in practice, which is not reflected in legal principle.

A test for determining what is legally relevant is,

> that the matter under discussion should be cast into the form of a syllogism of which the alleged evidentiary fact constitutes the minor premise; it is then only necessary to consider whether the major premise is a proposition the truth of which is likely to be accepted by the person who has to draw the conclusion—in the case of a lawsuit, a reasonable man. (Cross, 1990)[23]

Thus, for example, if a man was seen running from the scene of a stabbing incident with a blooded knife and could give no adequate explanation for this, the syllogism would be: major premise; (1) people who have just stabbed someone and are in possession of blooded knives near to the scene of the stabbing, and who can give no adequate explanation for this are frequently found guilty, minor premise; (2) the accused was seen running from the scene with a blooded knife and he could give no adequate explanation; (3) therefore he could be guilty. This, of course, does not mean that the man is guilty, but it does mean that the evidence of someone seeing him there with a blooded knife is admissible. If this is transposed for the case of child sexual abuse, then the major premise is what 'a reasonable' person could accept as probable indicators of a sexually abusive act having occurred.

There are immediate and obvious problems here. Firstly, there are rarely definitive signs and symptoms of child sexual abuse, although there are many that can be associated with it (Glaser and Frosh, 1988).[24] However, just because a father gets in bed with his daughter, or the child has severe behavioural problems, or even lacks a hymen, it is not always the case that child sexual abuse is responsible. What tends to happen is that there are a number of probable symptoms or signs which, when pieced together, indicate the possibility of child sexual abuse. The assembly of such signs is not something that can be reduced to a checklist of symptoms which could, unequivocally or even always probably, add up to sexual abuse.

Secondly, there is a difference between a lay or public expectation about what would be symptomatic of child sexual abuse and that of professional knowledge. For example, a lay expectation is that child sexual abuse is not an enjoyable phenomena, and that children could be expected to resist, struggle, tell someone to stop it as soon as possible, as in the following example of a judge's summing up where the jury are asked to consider:

> ... circumstances in which the complaint was made, not one final significant attempt by (the defendant), it was her mother saying she would be put away ... over the last five years, possibly more, possibly less, and she has known for probably about two years what he has been doing was wrong

(pause) members of the jury why, why, why was there never a complaint to anyone . . . do you think there would not have been a single solitary piece of evidence . . . if it had happened as frequently of . . . screams, protests, marks, torn clothing . . .

One theme some years ago, when awareness of child sexual abuse was growing amongst professionals, was the attack of myths, such as 'it only happens in isolated rural communities', 'it doesn't happen in this country' and so on. It is sad to find a similar level of myth present today with regard to judgements about children. Children frequently give reports of submitting silently to the abuse perpetrated on them, and the term 'breaking the silence' has become a theme of survivors' accounts. As an example of the characteristic feature of silence the following is cited from a television programme which reported on institutional abuse in a special school (Yorkshire Television, 1991).[25] The boys in the school were being abused by the headteacher. When asked why they didn't say anything one boy said,

They daren't. They didn't know who they could turn to, who they could trust. That's my sort of thoughts, that they couldn't trust anybody at home, they've had the problems then they're the same problems. It's just you could tell little kids, the younger boys, just couldn't really they were scared of everybody.

Another said,

You'd want to tell someone. You could tell but they wouldn't believe you, they'd just laugh in your face. It was a waste of time, y'couldn't really tell no-one. You could tell your parents and they'd just laugh at you cos they'd think he's so great cos he'd put on an act while yer parents were there really so nice and pie to you, wouldn't shout at you nor nothing.

Another said,

It's hard to explain but Maurice had more hold over our lives at school, at home, the lot. He had us right where he wanted us, under his thumb. He was a very very convincing man.

Later the same child was asked what he said when the police began an investigation,

What I actually told them was Maurice is a lovely man and this is the best school I've ever been to. There was like countless other brainwashed misled little petrified boys that were telling them, y'know.

All this points to one crucial conclusion. If relevant evidence must be related to what can be accepted by 'a reasonable' person then a focus on effect, the feelings that would be anticipated (though perhaps difficult to accept—and this is another thing entirely—for example, where they are positive) and feelings in and about the context of 'telling', are a key feature.

THERAPEUTIC PRINCIPLES

Amongst the principles underpinning casework (Biestek, 1957)[26] is the value of allowing purposeful expression of feeling, acceptance, a non-judgemental attitude, client self-determination and confidentiality. All of these are compatible, to varying degrees, with the legal requirements in an assessment interview.

Expression of feeling tends not to be encouraged in these interviews. The emphasis, as I have pointed out earlier, is on the event, on what, if anything, has happened. However, as I also indicated, this leaves an important component out for those whose job it is to decide on the validity of a claim. Spontaneous expression of feeling is tolerated, and may even be hoped for. Police officers and barristers know that if a child breaks down it helps the case. But concentrating in an assessment interview on event *and* affect, and affect derived from effects and consequences of the event (including the assessment itself) was not evident in my materials. To ask how a child is feeling is traditionally considered to be the province of therapy, not assessment. If it is considered at all it is feeling about 'The Event', not for example about eating meals with someone who is about to abuse you, being left in the house with a particular person, and so on, even down to feelings about talking in the interview. In other words, there are a number of context relevant features which have affective components that could lend credibility to accounts but which, because they are not perceived as particular to the event, are not broached.

Acceptance and taking a non-judgemental attitude are linked. Legally and therapeutically they are crucial. It must be shown that the interviewers are not biased one way or the other, have no preconceived opinions regarding what it is the child has to say, and should never respond to a child in a way which could be perceived as biasing what they have to say next. They must therefore be accepting about what a child says and they should take a non-judgemental attitude. Confusion has crept in where interviewers may, in an attempt to compensate for the anticipated negative feelings children are likely to have, positively reinforce the child telling them they are 'good', 'brave', 'doing the right thing'. These are all judgemental, and have to do with imparting an opinion, however, it would be appropriate to accept feelings elicited from the child. Conversely, interviewers who remain silent in response when, normally, a response could be expected may also be perceived as judgemental by the child. Thus, an accepting response is crucial to encourage further disclosure. Where a child has not been abused, acceptance and taking a non-judgemental attitude are probably the clearest defences to secondary abuse and are safety measures against making the mistakes highlighted in Cleveland.

Client self-determination is also, and for similar reasons, relevant as a legal and therapeutic safeguard, as well as a therapeutic tool. A frequently recurring theme in the literature about child sexual abuse is its relationship to power on the part of the abuser and loss of control on the part of the victim. If children do not have a measure of control over the interview this replicates a dynamic of the abusive relationship and could be contributing to secondary abuse. This should include a measure of control about arrangements, duration, who attends, where it is held. This means that the child would be fully briefed as to the purpose of the interview, and fully informed about the intentions of the interviewers. There is no need to prejudice potential evidence in this pre-interview planning stage, since the content of what the child has to talk about would not be at issue, merely the organisation of the talking about it. This would necessarily include clear messages about the meaning of confidentiality and discussion on the use of information recorded in any medium as a consequence of the interview.

One fundamental principle of counselling is the importance of trust in the counselling relationship. An agreed principle of interviewing children for evidential purposes is that they should be accompanied by someone they trust. Legal interventionists have established that trust is an important component, and have a tendency to work it in by displaying their 'trustworthiness' and/or to include a known adult often to whom the child has first disclosed. For example, the following is an extract from the opening sequence of an interview,

> I am here because we are friends, Mrs C (the child's teacher) and I, we go back a long, long time. Now, I work in Oakley, that's where you live. I want to know what you have been telling Mrs C, I want to make a few notes and I am going to write a story about it . . .

The speaker attempts to formulate a link between herself and the other interviewer saying, 'I am here because we are friends' and to give depth to the link she says 'we go back a long, long time'. She then establishes a familiar link with the victim, saying that she works in the area in which the victim lives, thus establishing something they have in common. This could be construed as a 'short cut' to trust. The following extract from a file is another,

> . . . Agreed that we would attempt to re-interview Brian today at school on the basis that Brian originally disclosed to his classteacher on Friday. After the difficulties yesterday evening it seems more appropriate for the child to be interviewed in the presence of someone he obviously trusts and who can see him through any reactions he may have . . .

However, there is a clear distinction which needs to be made between being

interviewed in the presence *of*, or *by*, someone who is trusted. This may be
why in many files there are accounts of children disclosing far more information at a later date whilst attending therapeutic groups. In this limited
space I can only draw attention to the importance of timing and relationship
in terms of getting the best evidence. It may be that when a child first says
something, that is not the appropriate time, and there is no reason why in
terms of the child's protection and health this should present a problem.
Children do not have to give every detail in order to be afforded protection.
In terms of prosecution, the optimum timing may well be sometime (and
not necessarily a long time) later. The issue of coaching is one that needs
testing out, but it is the case that there have been successful attempts to go
back to court with further evidence at a future date for prosecution purposes. Considerations of timing also allow for considerations of how to
effectively establish a relationship of trust between the police officers/social
worker and child/family. Key factors would be establishing a dependable,
regular contact, with clear arrangements where help is agreed with the
child and the child is given a measure of control (Rouf, 1989).[27] Such an
approach fits readily with the principles underpinning the Children Act,
1989 and has all the resource implications attendant on it. However, if there
is a genuine endeavour to protect children in the community, and to pursue
the public interest, this may be the price to pay.

REFERENCES

1. Wattam, C. (1990) *Disclosure: The Child's Perspective*, Research Report (NSPCC:
   London).
2. Conroy S., Fielding N. G., and Tunstill J. (1990) *Investigating Child Sexual Abuse:
   The Study of a Joint Initiative* (Police Foundation: London).
3. Kelly, L. and Regan, L. (1990) 'Flawed Protection', *Social Work Today*, Vol. 21,
   No. 32.
4. DHSS and Welsh Office (1988) *Working Together: A Guide to Arrangements for
   Interagency Cooperation for the Protection of Children from Abuse* (HMSO: London).
5. Home Office (1988) *The Investigation of Child Sexual Abuse*. Circular 52/1988.
6. Metropolitan Police and Bexley Social Services (1987) *Child Sexual Abuse Joint
   Investigation Programme, Final Report* (HMSO: London).
7. Home Office (1989) *Report of the Advisory Group on Video-Recorded Evidence*.
   Thomas Pigot, Chairman (Home Office: London).
8. Glasgow, D. (1987) *Responding to Child Sexual Abuse*, Mersey Regional Health
   Authority, Marketing Department (available from author).
9. Finkelhor, D. (1984) *Child Sexual Abuse: New Theory and Research* (Free Press:
   New York).
10. Waldby, C. (1985) *Breaking the Silence: A Report Based Upon the Findings of the
    Women Against Incest Phone-In Survey* (The Honeysett Printing Group: Sydney).

11. Wattam C. (1990) *op. cit.*
12. Butler-Sloss, E. (1988) *Report of the Inquiry into Child Abuse in Cleveland 1987.* (HMSO: London).
13. King, M. A., and Yuille, J. C. (1987) 'Suggestibility and the child witness', in S. J. Ceci, M. P. Toglia and D. F. Ross (eds.) *Children's Eyewitness Memory* (Springer: New York).
14. Geiselman, E., and Fisher, R. (1989) The Cognitive Interview Technique for Victims and Witnesses of Crime, in D. Raskin (ed.) *Psychological Methods in Criminal Investigation and Evidence* (Springer: New York).
15. Westcott, H. (1991) *Introducing the Cognitive Interview—A Useful Tool for Social Workers?* (Submitted for Publication) (NSPCC: London).
16. Glasgow, D. (1987) *op. cit.*
17. Summit, R. C. (1983) 'The child sexual abuse accommodation syndrome, *International Journal of Child Abuse and Neglect*, **7**.
18. Glasgow D. (1987) *op. cit.*
19. Jones, D., and McQuiston, (1988) *Interviewing the Sexually Abused Child*, 3rd edn. (Gaskell: London).
20. Vizard, E. (1991) 'Interviewing children suspected of being sexually abused: a review of theory and practice', in Hollin V. T. and Howells, K. (eds.) *Clinical Approaches to Sex Offenders and Their Victims* (Wiley: Chichester).
21. Spencer, J. R., and Flin, R. (1990) *The Evidence of Children* (Blackstone Press: London).
22. Wattam, C. (1991) *Truth and Belief in the Disclosure Process*, Occasional Paper (NSPCC: London).
23. Cross R. (1990) *Cross on Evidence*, 7th edn. (Butterworth: London).
24. Glaser, D., and Frosh, S. (1988) *Child Sexual Abuse* (Macmillan: London).
25. Yorkshire Television, *First Tuesday*, May 7th, 1991.
26. Biestek, F. (1957) *The Casework Relationship* (Unwin University Books: London).
27. Rouf, K. (1989) *Working with Sexually Abused Children—A Resource Pack for Professionals.* The Children's Society.

5

EMPOWERING MOTHERS OF SEXUALLY ABUSED CHILDREN—A POSITIVE FRAMEWORK

Bobbie Print and Carol Dey

As the mother is the non-abusing parent in most cases of intrafamilial sexual abuse (Finkelhor, 1979;[1] Russell, 1983;[2] Wyatt, 1985[3]) she has a crucial role to play in helping her abused child. It therefore follows that it is to their mothers that most children will turn for support, reassurance and future protection. Their response has been shown to be critical to children's perceptions of events. (Adams-Tucker, 1981;[4] Fromuth, 1983[5]). By believing their children and taking appropriate steps to protect them mothers confirm to their children that they, the children, were not responsible for the abuse. Children who are not supported and believed by their mothers are more likely to develop serious and long-term effects (Goodwin, 1981).[6] It is essential that professionals, involved in work with families where sexual abuse has occurred, provide mothers with the support, understanding and assistance that will help them to respond appropriately to their children.

Generally in the UK there is a significant shortfall in services designed specifically to provide treatment and therapy for child sexual abuse victims and their mothers. This contrasts with growth in government and professional interest in the development of services for sex offenders in this country over recent years. A Home Office initiative aimed at establishing and evaluating treatment programmes for sex offenders is currently under way, and a number of community-based and prison treatment programmes are being established throughout the country. Work with perpetrators, the majority of whom are males, often involves a higher proportion of male workers than work with mothers or victims. For this reason perhaps it is given higher status by male managers. It is a sad reflection, however, that the professional response to family members appears to perpetuate the inequalities of male power and status that are recognised as one of the underlying causes of child sexual abuse.

There are, however, other reasons for the inadequate level of therapeutic and support services for mothers of sexually abused children. Despite theories from those working with sex offenders, which focus on offender functioning and characteristics to explain why adults abuse children (Abel et al 1981;[7] Salter, 1988[8]) there is still a tendency to regard mothers as in some way responsible for producing and maintaining the family circumstances which cause abuse to occur. They are also condemned for not protecting their children and colluding in the abuse which they 'must have known' was taking place. These attitudes reflect societal expectations and views of mothers as nurturers, protectors and emotional providers for their children. A mother whose child is abused is generally seen as having failed in her roles as wife and mother.

Systems theorists have suggested that intra-familial child sexual abuse is a product of family dysfunction. The abuse can be described either as a 'conflict avoiding' or 'conflict regulating' mechanism which the family employs to avoid the breakdown of the family. Implicit in this theory is the concept that each member of the family system is responsible for maintaining the dysfunction. 'In father–daughter incest the entire family is involved and each member is active in perpetuating the abuse' (Mayer, 1983).[9] Mothers are frequently described as being particularly responsible in that the dysfunction is largely due to their characteristics or failings.

Conte (1982),[10] in discussing the family systems approach to sexual abuse, pointed out the lack of empirical data to support such a theory and suggested that the multiple contexts in which sexual abuse occurs cannot be explained by such a theory. Others (Becker and Coleman, 1989)[11] suggest that family dysfunctioning could well be a consequence of abuse rather than a causal factor.

Systems theorists are not alone, however, in maintaining views of mothers as contributors to abuse. The report of the Cleveland Inquiry (Butler-Sloss, 1988)[12] for example, failed to distinguish between non-abusing parents and abusers but referred simply to 'parents' of abused children thus implying that they should be similarly regarded.

Such mother-blaming views are reflected in much of the literature on child sexual abuse. The mother in the family has been described as 'the most culpable individual either through default or through direct involvement' (McIntyre, 1981).[13] Blame for mothers is characterised by their failure as a wife, as a mother and as an individual. Studies that appear to support these arguments are open to question and interpretation. Most are retrospective and motivation for mothers' behaviours are often assumed when it is impossible to determine whether or not their behaviour resulted from the abuse in the family. If we examine the three points above we can begin to recognise that some of the mother-blaming arguments can be interpreted in different ways.

(i) THE BLAME AS 'FAILED' WIFE

Problematic marital and sexual relationships between parents in families where sexual abuse has occurred (James and Nasjleti, 1983;[14] Bander, Fein and Bishop, 1982;[15] Justice and Justice, 1979[16]) are often described in terms of the woman's responsibility, in that she is frigid, non-sexual or repressive in her attitude towards sex (Justice and Justice 1979;[17] Cormier, Kennedy and Sangowicz, 1962;[18] Finkelhor, 1979[19]).

Studies have shown that many mothers of sexually abused children were themselves sexually abused in childhood. Summit and Kryso (1978)[20] put the figure as high as 80 per cent, others such as Goodwin, McCarthy and Divasto (1981)[21] suggest a figure of 24 per cent. Women who were sexually, physically or emotionally abused in childhood may have lacked support, nurturing or suffered from low self-esteem. Consequently they may select emotionally inadequate partners (Cammaert, 1988;[22] Pincus and Dare, 1978[23]) or be vulnerable to selection by sex offenders who seek partners who are passive, emotionally vulnerable and dependent. Since women in our society are socialised to depend on others, normally males, and to be obedient within the family (Rush, 1980)[24] it is not surprising to find many mothers of sexually abused children adopting a passive role in the family. They are often dominated by their partner and see him as more capable, powerful and intellectually superior (Groth, 1982;[25] Finkelhor, 1979;[26] Stern and Meyer, 1980[27]).

Herman and Hirschman (1981)[28] compared the family histories of 40 adult female survivors of sexual abuse with 20 women who described their fathers as seductive but not sexually abusive. They concluded that the fathers who committed incest were more violent and dominating within the family and tended to isolate their families from the outside world to a greater extent compared to the non-abusive fathers. Server and Janzen (1982)[29] also noted a high degree of aggression or violence in the marital relationship whilst Sirles and Frank (1989)[30] found that 44 per cent of abusers physically abused the mother. These studies demonstrate the powerless position of many mothers and indicate that marital difficulties cannot simply be attributed to the characteristics of the mother.

Similarly it is inappropriate to assume that problems in the sexual relationships are the woman's responsibility. The presence of sexual problems in a marriage become irrelevant as we have recently learnt from those working with sex offenders that the non-availability of a sexually satisfying relationship with a consenting peer is not a causal factor in child sexual buse. Equally, many perpetrators continue to have sexual relationships with consenting adults during the same period that they are abusing children. Groth and Birnbaum (1979)[31] indicated that all of the male offenders in their study had the opportunity for having an appropriate sexually gratifying experience instead of abusing a child. Abel *et al* (1985)[32] have shown that most incest offenders began their abusive behaviour in adolescence and one-third fantasised about sex with children prior to marriage. These studies therefore suggest that an abuser's desire to abuse cannot be attributed to dissatisfaction with his sexual relationships with adults. It is also now known that many offenders have multiple victims both within and outside home (Abel *et al*, 1987)[33] which implies that a particular child is not selected as a substitute for an unsatisfactory adult partner.

(ii) THE BLAME AS 'FAILED' MOTHER

Mothers of sexually abused children have been described as the cornerstone of a pathological family (Justice and Justice, 1979;[34] Brandt and Tisza, 1977[35]). Their behaviour is described as neglectful, distant, sexually repressive (Cormier *et al*, 1962;[36] Finkelhor, 1979)[37] and that in many, if not all instances they consciously or unconsciously collude with the abuse of their children. (Kaufman *et al*, 1954;[38] Lustig *et al*, 1966[39]).

It is not difficult for a man who is intent on abusing children within his family to distance a child from its mother. His power in the family would allow him to effectively use physical or emotional threats. He may also 'groom' the child by offering special treatment or manipulate the child emotionally, for example by telling the child that his or her mother does not understand their special relationship or that she would place the child in care if she found out what was going on.

We should also consider what is expected of a mother who learns that her child has been sexually abused by a man she thought she loved and trusted. A woman who believes her child must accept the inevitable breakdown of her family. Professionals expect her to report the child's allegations to the authorities and thereby risk external judgement of her mothering, the removal of her children or husband, retaliation by her partner, social stigma, court appearances and loss of financial security. These possible consequences may explain why some women think twice before taking the steps regarded by many professionals as appropriate.

The still common misconception that most, if not all, mothers collude with, or at the very least ignore, abuse of their children has been disputed by the findings of studies such as those conducted by Bagley and Naspini (1987)[40] and Herman and Hirschman (1981).[41] The former found that in a sample of 44 mothers of sexually abused children only four had any knowledge that sexual abuse had taken place before the child disclosed and those four felt powerless to stop it. Thirty-eight of the women when informed of the abuse took immediate action to protect their children. In the latter study, 58 per cent of the adult survivors reported that they never told their mothers, and those that did so told them indirectly.

Despite the enormously difficult decisions facing mothers who discover that their child has been sexually abused within the family, recent studies highlight the 'myth' that mothers generally fail to believe or take appropriate action to protect their children (Sirles and Franke, 1989;[42] Pierce and Pierce, 1985[43]).

Mrazek, Lynch and Bentovim (1981)[44] reported in 1981 that 76 per cent of complaints to the authorities about child abuse 'were made by parents, primarily the mother'. Studies by Knudson (1982)[45] and Meiselman (1978)[46] have shown that a significant number of mothers took immediate protective action once they were aware of the abuse.

Very little information is available regarding women who protect their children by leaving their partners but do not go on to report abuse to the authorities. The accounts of adult survivors inform us that this is not an infrequent occurrence. The number of allegations of sexual abuse made during custody disputes, which had not otherwise been reported to the authorities, has increased considerably over the last few years. Research from the USA (Jones and Seig, 1988)[47] suggests that 70 per cent of allegations of sexual abuse made in these circumstances are substantiated. It must also be presumed that there are a large number of cases where there is no custody dispute, either because the abuser is concerned that the abuse would come to light or the couple were not married. In these cases, a mother would have protected her children by leaving the abuser but not reported the abuse to the authorities.

Another characteristic commonly discussed is the mother–daughter role reversal apparent in a number of families where sexual abuse has occurred (Herman and Hirschman, 1981;[48] Renvoize, 1982;[49] Forward and Buck, 1978[50]). It is often suggested that since mothers in these families wish to opt out of their family roles they effectively promote their daughter to take on caring and household responsibilities. The assumption follows that the daughter will also be viewed by the man as an appropriate sexual partner.

These suggestions are quite bewildering. First of all they imply that the mother simply decides to opt out of the family. They take no account of findings that show that a number of mothers of sexually abused children are ill, or disabled (55 per cent in the Herman and Hirschman study, 1981)[51] or burdened with many pregnancies and children (Julian and Mohr, 1980).[52] In such circumstances it would not be unusual for older children in the family to be called on to help with household tasks. Secondly, it is far too simplistic to suggest that males are sexually attracted to whoever undertakes the practical and caring tasks in the household, even if this is a child.

(iii) THE BLAME AS 'FAILED' INDIVIDUAL

Mothers of sexually abused children are characterised in much of the literature as lacking social skills and possessing a number of disturbed personality traits. These include: low self-esteem (Sahd, 1980;[53] Bennett, 1980[54]); intropunitive style of anger (Bennett, 1980);[55] experiencing psychosis (Herman and Hirschman, 1981);[56] depression (Herman and Hirschman, 1981;[57] Harrer, 1981);[58] anxiety and suspicion (Fredrickson, 1981);[59] alcohol abuse (15 per cent, Herman and Hirschman, 1981;[60] 32.4 per cent, Julian and Mohr, 1980);[61] and attempted suicide (Goodwin, 1981).[62]

Given the physical, emotional and financial stresses previously described, it is not surprising to find that some mothers will exhibit the symptoms in the above list. Nor must we forget that abusers may seek partners whose resistance can be easily overcome. It is possible that these women were selected by the abuser because their illness or disabilities significantly reduced their ability to protect their children.

The argument that mothers absented themselves from the home for periods and so provided the opportunity for the abuse (Summit, 1983)[63] is also unacceptable. It suggests that mothers should watch over their children 24 hours a day and never leave them in the care of their fathers. By implication these views also condemn working mothers for not adopting traditional roles and remaining at home with their children.

THE IMPLICATIONS OF MOTHER-BLAMING ATTITUDES

Whilst some mothers refuse to believe that their children have been abused and a few even collude with abuse, many act to protect their children in the best ways they see available to them. The obvious consequences of mother-blaming attitudes amongst professionals are that mothers will not be encouraged or actively supported in providing help for their abused children or in cases where, for whatever reason, their immediate response is not ideal they are unlikely to be understood or empowered to change.

Mother-blaming attitudes are also dangerous in that they dilute the responsibility of the abuser for what has occurred. Professionals, who themselves believe that mothers are in some way responsible, may well collude with an offender's excuses and thus reinforce his belief that he could not avoid his actions. Similarly an acceptance that a mother's attitudes or behaviour can be causal factors in child sexual abuse minimises the link between male sexuality and child sexual abuse and implies that it is something other than an abuse of power.

Many victims and survivors express anger towards their mothers for failing to protect them. If this view is reflected by professionals, the distance between mother and child is likely to be increased and children may ultimately find it difficult to accept that the responsibility for the abuse lies entirely with the abuser. Finally, mother-blaming attitudes are likely to stigmatise mothers who already inevitably blame themselves, consciously or unconsciously, for not having protected their children.

It is important that we recognise that mother-blaming attitudes are an endemic feature of our society. Where mothers are concerned we are all experts, each of us having personal experience of mother figures, each of us with expectations, disappointments and frustrations. The subject creates debate and emotive responses in both private and professional settings. Because practitioners' attitudes and beliefs can have far-reaching implications upon the outcomes for mothers and children, each of us has a responsibility to examine the degree to which we have internalised these 'universal truths' which although grounded in the mythological have become institutionalised over time.

Engaging in a process of self-awareness, either individually or in a team work-setting, is not an inward looking or self-indulgent exercise, rather an endeavour to develop a perspective which informs practice. In fostering philosophies which overcome mother-blaming attitudes we can hope to make more positive interventions on behalf of mothers and children so that children can be supported and protected in their own homes. This would result in fewer children in the care system, possibly shorter stays for those who come into care and, overall, a better prognosis for sexually abused children. By adopting a less judgemental approach the way is open to be more creative and develop more comprehensive methods of assessments.

ASSESSMENT

Fundamental to any assessment is a child's safety and wellbeing which must take precedence over any adult needs or considerations. In addition to this a clear theoretical understanding of the cultural, gender and power issues involved in families where sexual abuse has occurred would lead, in a high proportion of cases, to a view that the mother is a secondary victim of the abuser. This is not to suggest that the mother is without strengths, and it is important that an assessment process recognises and builds on these positives and indicates areas where a mother needs to develop other strengths in order to empower her further.

In cases of child sexual abuse the assessment process contains two distinct phases: (i) an immediate risk assessment, (ii) a comprehensive assessment. The former is likely to be based on details of the child's disclosure, known history of family members, the child's wishes and feelings and the reactions of other family members. The comprehensive assessment may take several weeks to complete and will be more detailed, encompassing the spectrum of practical and emotional issues.

The assessment should result in the identification of the therapeutic needs of the family members and plans for meeting those needs. Therapeutic work is aimed at resolving the emotional conflicts that may be present either within an individual or between family members, and continuous monitoring of progress is necessary so that plans may be adapted or changed as necessary.

Risk assessment

The aims of the risk assessment are to decide whether abuse has occurred, the likelihood of further abuse, the degree of available protection, the necessity for legal intervention and the placement needs of the child.

It is important to emphasise that there are several components in a systematic risk assessment. Whilst we have focused here on the issues involving the non-abusing parent this does not imply that these are the only factors. Details of the child's disclosure, the whereabouts and attitude of the abuser and the attitudes of other family members are also important aspects of the assessment.

In the aftermath of a child sexual abuse disclosure the mother will experience a whole range of feelings similar to those expressed by the abused child (Myer, 1985).[64] They include shock, disbelief, anger, powerlessness, guilt and betrayal.

Following disclosure, shock is a common reaction which can vary in it's intensity. Women use descriptions such as 'numbness', 'I felt dead inside', to describe their initial reactions. Given such responses we should anticipate that some women will find it difficult to make important decisions within short timescales. Yet it is often at this early stage that a mother may find herself in the position of having to make a choice between her child and her partner. Shock may then be further compounded by stress and anxiety and she may develop confused and ambivalent feelings towards the abuser and her child. Her feelings towards the abuser may be similar to the child's and MacLeod and Saraga (1988)[65] observe that, 'It is a common experience that children feel love as well as hatred or fear for their abuser'.

It is important that a mother is given as much time and support as possible to make decisions and that, in cases where she is unable to commit herself to believing and protecting her child, she is not dismissed or labelled as an unfit parent. Further support should be offered in order to help her to increase her awareness of her child's needs; a more positive response is then more likely to follow.

Women who do decide to separate immediately from the abuser are likely to face significant practical problems regarding alternative accommodation and financial support. Lack of available resources can result in children being placed in the care of the local authority. These practical difficulties bring sharply into focus women's relative powerlessness in property and financial matters, and underlines the importance of professionals undertaking an immediate assessment of needs and offering financial and practical support to mothers at such times.

It is also essential that a mother's abilities to believe, support and protect her children are assessed. The basis of this part of the assessment relies on focusing on the mother's strengths, skills and deficits in the following areas:

(i) *The mother's reaction to disclosure.* Mothers who believe their children and display appropriate anger towards the abuser are more likely to provide children with the necessary reassurance and protection. Mothers who are equivocal or inconsistent in their responses to the abuser or the child, or do not understand the consequences of the abuse will not be able to fully support or protect the child. However, with sensitive professional help they may be able to meet these needs in a short period of time. Mothers who are unable to believe their child or who choose to support the abuser are clearly not able to protect the child in the short-term but may be helped by therapeutic support to meet some, if not all, of the child's needs in the future.

(ii) *The mother's relationship with the abused child.* A mother who does not blame the child, has a close and nurturing relationship and who is able to communicate openly with her child, is likely to provide the child with the support the child requires. Mothers who have an ambivalent or difficult relationship with their child may not be able to provide a high degree of emotional support. In these situations, if the child is to remain at home, it is important to ensure that the child has an alternative concerned adult who can meet these needs. Many of these situations respond well to professional intervention aimed at improving a mother's understanding of her child and the relationship between them. In cases where a mother has a poor relationship with the child, and is unable to emotionally support the child at all, it may well be in the child's best interest to live away from home until such time as the relationship improves.

(iii) *The mother's dependence on the abuser.* Mothers who are able to confront the abuser and are able to exist independently from him are more likely to be able to effectively protect their children from further abuse. Those who are more dependent, for example financially or practically, or those who are afraid of the abuser will require considerable external support in protecting their children. Women who appear to be significantly emotionally dependent on the abuser are far less likely to be able to support and protect the child. In such circumstances the child is likely to require care and accommodation away from the mother although, once again, sustained work with the mother may improve matters.

(iv) *Other factors.* Other important factors which may affect a mother's abilities to meet a child's needs should be identified. For example, the nature and influence of the mother's support network through extended family, religious, ethnic or social contacts may directly affect her ability to provide for the child. A mother who suffers from alcohol or drug dependency, physical or mental ill-health may require additional support. For some, the severity of these problems may be such that they are not in a position to care for their children.

It is important that professionals conducting an initial assessment recognise that in many of the areas listed above a mother's abilities and performance may appear to fluctuate in response to the inevitable strains and pressures impinging on her. Thus an accurate assessment cannot be conducted in too short a timescale.

The results of the risk assessment in relation to mothers are likely to produce one of the following broad conclusions:

(a) The mother can protect and support the abused child (and siblings) and does not require further professional intervention.
(b) The mother can protect and support the abused child (and siblings) if provided with sufficient resources.
(c) The mother is ambivalent and the child's support and protection must be ensured by external sources, for example extended family and professionals who may require a legal mandate such as a supervision order or by the child's placement in care, either on the basis of accommodation or, if necessary, a care order.
(d) The mother denies the abuse occurred or is very dependent on the abuser and so is unable adequately to support or protect the child. In

these cases the child will require a placement in a safe setting with legal action to ensure security.

In (b), (c) and (d) further assessment and therapeutic work with mothers is normally required. In categories (c) and (d), a legal order is more likely to be necessary to secure the child's safety.

Comprehensive assessment

The principle aims of a comprehensive assessment are to identify problems in the family and changes that are required together with the abilities and motivation of those involved to achieve change.

The extent to which an assessment is comprehensive and accurate will depend to a large degree on the practitioner's skills in engaging the mother. In most cases this will require that the mother is allocated a different keyworker to the abused child or the perpetrator. Not only will this ensure that the mother's needs are identified, but many mothers and children would not develop the level of trust in a worker who was also engaged in direct work with another member of the family. A mother who feels angry towards the child, for example, may feel inhibited from sharing her feelings with someone who is also working with the child. It is equally important that all the professionals who form the core team working with family members have a shared philosophical approach and a clear understanding of what the aims, tasks and timescales are for the work. Frequent liaison and review meetings are essential to ensure that information is exchanged and that plans are adjusted as necessary.

The underlying philosophy of the Children Act 1989[66] requires professionals to work in partnership with parents and this concept is particularly important with mothers of sexually abused children even in situations where a legal order has been obtained. The purpose of work with mothers is to empower them by recognising and developing strengths and thereby increasing their confidence to support and protect their children. This cannot be achieved if professionals merely mirror the behaviour of the abuser by making decisions about the child without involving the mother. If a mother is to increase her confidence and take responsibility for her child's welfare she must feel, and be, fully involved in planning for her child's future. Even in cases where a mother has rejected her child, the supplying of information about the child is essential if positive links are to be maintained.

The partnership between the mother and her worker should be based on a mutually formulated agreement which outlines aims, timescales and methods and details the areas of work and tasks that each is to undertake.

This joint process will represent the first moves towards empowering the mother and enabling her to exercise some control, within the context of the child's best interests.

The issues that should be discussed and considered for inclusion in the agreement will include:

- the mother's feelings towards the abused child;
- the mother's ability to understand the offences and their effects on the child, siblings and herself;
- her ability to give appropriate emotional support to the abused child;
- the mother's ability to protect the child (and siblings) from the abuser in particular;
- the degree to which the mother is financially, emotionally or practically dependent on the abuser;
- the mother's support networks;
- relevant issues from the mother's past, for example if she has been abused herself, that may inhibit her abilities to support the child;
- medical and social factors that might be relevant.

A comprehensive assessment is a two-way process in that it involves the provision and receipt of information and will inevitably include a therapeutic component. It is often most productive to work with a mother in a therapeutic style and to involve techniques other than direct questions and answers. In this way a mother is not only able to focus on factual information but also to express her emotions and develop some insight into, and understanding of, her reactions and behaviour. The process also creates the opportunity to examine changes that are required and the degree of motivation to achieve change. An example of the benefits of a good assessment is offered in the case of Mrs J.

Mrs J presented as ambivalent following the disclosure to a teacher that her nine-year-old daughter had been sexually abused by Mr J, the child's father, for several months. Mrs J initially found it difficult to believe her daughter but agreed that her husband should move out of the home during the investigation. Mrs J remained in close contact with her husband and remained financially dependent on him, although both parents complied with the requirement that Mr J should have no contact with his daughter. Mrs J was allocated a social worker whose task was to support her and involve her in a comprehensive assessment of her child's needs and how best to meet them.

The social worker initially provided Mrs J with some practical assistance in organising the family's finances and supporting her in informing other members of the family of the situation. She arranged a number of individual sessions with Mrs J at a family centre where they had use of a room that offered privacy and comfort. Mrs J was initially very anxious but the worker's supportive attitude and respect for Mrs J's difficult position resulted in a reasonable degree of trust in the relationship. In an early session Mrs J indicated that she found it difficult to discuss and put into words her feelings. The worker therefore suggested that she could use some doll figures to demonstrate how she saw her family. Mrs J selected dolls to represent the members of her family and stood each one in relation to the others. She was very distressed with the three-dimensional picture of her family she produced since it reflected the isolation of the abused child and how her husband still remained the powerful figure in the family. During this exercise Mrs J began to recognise that her family had never been the way she wanted it to be. Her husband had always been closer to the child that was abused and she began to express some anger at the way in which she believed he had 'shut her out'. By developing this work in further sessions Mrs J was able to recognise many of the abused child's needs for support and the risk of the family reverting to the same unsatisfactory situation if her husband returned home before she and he had been helped to change.

On completion of the three-month assessment Mrs J was much more able to support her daughter and felt more in control of herself and the family. She was able to express clearly what she wanted for the child, herself and the family and was able to identify issues that still had to be resolved. Mrs J was keen to continue working with her social worker and to engage in dyad work with her daughter.

Mr J continued to deny his abusive behaviour and refused to engage in treatment. He resented his wife's involvement with professionals and eventually told her that he was moving to another part of the country. Mrs J decided that she did not want to move or to reunite with her husband unless he agreed to certain changes, which he was not prepared to make. She elected therefore to remain where she was and to instigate divorce proceedings. Mrs J continued to receive support from her social workers. Her confidence increased and she developed a close relationship with her daughter.

The purpose of the comprehensive assessment is not only to assess the needs of family members but also to construct a plan for the future of individuals and the family unit. In some cases the plan will be to evaluate the progress of individual and family work with a view to rehabilitating the family. This is only a realistic plan if all members of the family are motivated to engage in work with professionals, often for some length of time. Most recognised treatment programmes for sex offenders estimate that an offender will take approximately two years to complete a programme. For further details of the prerequisites for reunification of families see, for example, Server and Janzen (1982).[67] In a number of cases it will not be appropriate to consider a plan that aims to work towards reuniting the family. Bentovim *et al* (1987)[68] indicated those families which should be regarded as having a positive prognosis regarding reunification and those where the likelihood will be poor. In a number of cases the mother will decide that she does not wish to reunite with the abuser and it is essential that the abused child's wishes and feelings are always taken into account. A child who does not want the abuser to return to the family home should never have their views overlooked by a mother or professionals who otherwise consider that the abuser should return home.

THERAPEUTIC WORK WITH MOTHERS

The effects on a mother of the sexual abuse of her child are comparable to those typically associated with bereavement. This is understandable when as a consequence of the abuse a mother could lose her partner, her child or her home. The family will, at the very least, be restructured and mothers face the loss of the caring and trusting relationships that they previously assumed they had. They may also grieve for their child's loss of childhood and innocence. A mother may therefore experience a set of feelings which commonly start with shock and numbness, followed by denial, anger, guilt, resentment, isolation, sorrow, self-pity and finally acceptance. The ability of individuals to cope with the effects of bereavement vary from individual to individual and this is no different in mothers who have to cope with the knowledge that their child has been sexually abused by a man they thought they knew.

Those mothers of sexually abused children who have good personal coping strategies, supportive skills and networks will require little or no professional therapeutic help. However, many will require individual, dyad or family work. The assessment of the mother should have involved exploration of her history, emotions, strengths and weaknesses. The insight and subsequent changes developed from a sensitive and skilful assessment process can, in many cases, sufficiently empower the mother to protect and support her children. In other cases, assessment will have identified areas for which further help is needed. The range of help may vary from practical support to intense therapeutic counselling.

Therapeutic work with mothers aims to further the empowerment process commenced during the assessment by addressing specific issues. Continuing assessment is essential in order to recognise progress and to determine that work is still required. It is important that all therapeutic work is seen as having a beginning and an end. If therapeutic work continues beyond the point where issues are usefully being addressed, a mother could become disempowered and may consider herself unable to manage alone; dependency on the abuser might then be transferred to the worker and the professional system. It is particularly important that where statutory action has been necessary the requirement for others is regularly reviewed and they are discharged as soon as possible.

Additionally, therapeutic intervention will usually need to cover issues of jealousy, powerlessness and betrayal, many of which mirror the needs of the child. The principles and many of the techniques of therapeutic work used with children which can be adapted for work with mothers. A number of case studies reflecting the techniques and methods that have been found useful are given below.

Denial

Working with a mother who denies that her child has been abused can be one of the most frustrating and emotive situations facing practitioners. Many workers will have seen the pain that a rejected child suffers in addition to the direct effects of the abuse. The case of the K family characterises these issues.

Mr K sexually abused his 15-year-old stepdaughter, Amanda, over a period of four years. Amanda had told her mother of the abuse a year before the involvement of professionals. Mrs K had responded by remonstrating with her partner and the abuse ceased for a short period. When Mr K resumed his sexual abuse of Amanda she attempted to resist his escalating demands but finally suffered a severe physical assault and rape, following which she ran away from home. She was found in a distressed state by strangers to whom she disclosed and was taken to the police. Mr K was subsequently convicted and sentenced to a long period of imprisonment. Although initially Amanda remained at home with her mother, their relationship deteriorated rapidly as Mrs K refused to accept that Mr K was responsible for the abuse. She blamed Amanda for what had happened asserting that she had led her stepfather on. Amanda was removed from home by the local authority and placed with foster carers.

During the ensuing assessment the mother revealed that 25 years previously she had been the victim of sexual abuse by her grandfather who had also abused her brothers and sisters. She was the only one who had 'told' with the result that she was blamed for breaking up the family. She received no therapeutic support and was told by her mother to forget about the events and to put them behind her. Consequently she learnt to use denial as a coping mechanism and grew up with a multitude of unresolved feelings which she coped with by suppressing them and trying to forget. Her 'forgetting' was sometimes helped by sleeping pills, tranquillisers or alcohol. When her daughter's abuse came to light, her unresolved feelings and fears surfaced and she talked of being swamped by memories. Offers to help her with her own issues were rebuffed and she steadfastly maintained that her daughter was lying. She was unable to show empathy and could not use her own experience of abuse to understand her daughter's hurt in any positive way.

Mrs K rejected support from a variety of sources and eventually terminated the assessment as she found the work too painful. She was unable to meet any of her daughter's emotional needs largely due to the impact of her own unmet needs. She had spent her lifetime as a victim, using denial as a coping mechanism which she applied to many situations of crisis and threat. Her fear of facing these issues was, to her, far greater than the benefits to be gained by accepting offers of help which, in her view, were 'too little and too late'.

Guilt

As mentioned earlier, most mothers will experience feelings of guilt regarding the abuse of their children. Many will believe that they are responsible in some way for the occurrence of the abuse and for failing to recognise signs of the abuse which, with hindsight, might be more readily identifiable. Feelings of guilt are often deeply ingrained and difficult to overcome. Cognitive restructuring using factual and research information has provided one useful method of dealing with such guilty feelings. For example, the methods abusers use to manipulate and groom children (Conte *et al*, 1989)[69] can in many instances also reflect the abuser's behaviour with the mother. Using such analogies can help mothers understand and empathise with their children, particularly those who rationally believe and feel angry with the child that it happened and guilty with themselves for not preventing it. Although initially women who learn that they have been exploited experience mixed feelings, the benefits of understanding and making sense of past events can be instrumental in their ability both to recognise the power of the abuser and to conclude that the responsibility for the abuse is entirely his.

Ms D had lived with her partner Mr D for 10 years, together with her 14-year-old daughter, Jane, from a previous relationship and the couple's four-year-old daughter. The family owned a retail business which they found time consuming and necessitated them living on the premises. They shared the care of the children and took turns in minding the shop.

When Jane disclosed sexual abuse by her stepfather, Ms D confronted her partner, who denied the allegation and in order to 'punish' the family he moved out.

Mr D had on occasions been violent to Ms D but had always apologised afterwards and tried to make it up to her. He appeared to dote on his daughters and treated Jane as though she were his own child. He always insisted that she accompany them socially, even on special occasions when Ms D would have preferred them to have gone out as a couple. This led to Ms D feeling resentful and jealous of Jane.

By asking Ms D to recall how the various parenting and household tasks were allocated and who tended to make the decisions in the family, a process was begun which she described as 'pieces of jigsaw falling into place'. The guilt, anger and jealousy Ms D felt towards her daughter began to diminish as she recognised how Mr D had fostered rivalry between Jane and herself, for example, he bought Jane expensive clothes, elevated her to adult status and took her side in mother–daughter conflicts.

As her understanding developed, Ms D was able to examine her own feelings of powerlessness and betrayal and relate them to Jane's loss of childhood and damaged trust. The progress that Ms D made resulted in her achieving a better understanding of her daughter's needs and improving the communication between them.

Anger

Anger is often a powerful response by mothers of sexually abused children although in many circumstances anger may be displaced onto themselves, the abused child or those who try to help them. The release of anger is essential, as otherwise it may block the release of many other emotions. Some women, however, are so conditioned to suppress their angry feelings that they are afraid that by letting go they will release an uncontrollable torrent of anger.

Ms P was a single parent who believed her four-year-old son when he disclosed sexual abuse by his uncle, Ms P's brother. She immediately protected the boy by refusing all contact with the uncle, even though this isolated her from the rest of her family who did not accept the allegations. She also reported the matter to the police. The uncle denied the allegations and the police concluded that there was insufficient evidence to prosecute.

Ms P reassured her son that he was in no way to blame for what had happened but told him that he must forgive his abuser as he had lost control and was not really to blame either. Ms P's emotionally detached response to the events caused some concern for those working with the family. Whilst there was no question over her abilities to protect and care for her child, her reluctance to support the child in expressing many of his feelings led to an assessment of her ability to provide emotionally for the child.

During individual sessions with her worker Ms P disclosed that she had been abused in her childhood by both of her older brothers and that she had never revealed this to anyone before. She said that she had since forgiven them and thought she had not suffered any long-term effects from the abuse. She drew pictures of her family and childhood and depicted each of them with smiling faces. She said that apart from the abuse her childhood had been a happy one. Her father and her two older brothers were often out and this left her at home with her mother with whom she had a very close relationship.

Ms P showed little emotional response to life events except when talking of her mother who had died when Ms P was in her teens. This relationship was used positively as means by which she could express hitherto suppressed emotions. Her mother, a physically frail woman, was dominated by the men in her family, her vulnerability being a major factor in Ms P's decision not to disclose her own abuse. Although difficult and distressing, she was able to write a letter to her mother explaining recent events and was successful in alleviating some of her pain.

At a following session she undertook a role reversal exercise during which she was able to express deeply rooted feelings of hostility, blame and distress regarding the perceived culpability of the male members of her family in the death of her mother. She required considerable reassurance that her anger was understandable, normal and did not signify a loss of control.

In the work that followed these sessions Ms P expressed her deep and extreme anger towards all the men in her family and recognised that she could do so in a safe and supportive environment and whilst retaining self-control. Ms P described the release of these feelings as 'like the shedding of a dead weight that she had been forced to carry all her life.' She recognised that she had learnt to suppress her feelings and to excuse the behaviour of others. When her mother died she had been unable to shed any tears since she feared that if she began to release any emotions she would lose all self-control.

Through this work Ms P recognised the importance for both herself and her son of not denying feelings of anger. She was able to join in the therapeutic work undertaken with her son and supported him in expressing his anger towards his uncle. Ms P later joined a therapeutic group for adult survivors of sexual abuse and reported that she gained considerably from the mutual support and understanding provided by the group.

THERAPEUTIC GROUPS FOR MOTHERS OF SEXUALLY ABUSED CHILDREN

In many circumstances therapeutic groups for mothers can be a powerful supplement to individual therapeutic support. A group context can reassure women that they are not alone and provide a level of understanding that can only come from sharing with others who have had similar experiences.

Groups, however, rarely suffice as the only form of therapeutic intervention. Most women require individual work prior to, or in addition to, groups to provide opportunities to explore personal issues in depth. Sgroi and Dana (1982)[70] reported on a group established for mothers who were still in crisis and highlighted the difficulties they experienced in engaging the women in anything other than individual work:

Mothers   almost   uniformly   resisted   participation   in   other   treatment modalities . . . We speculate that their low self-esteem, lack of trust, isolation and fear of developing new relationships were powerful factors mitigating against their participation in anything other than a one-on-one relationship.

In 1988 we were involved in running a group for mothers who were past the crisis of disclosure and who had already been involved in one-to-one work. The group aimed to strengthen the women's skills, provide information and support with opportunities to work on issues that were important to them.

The group met each week for 20 weeks and the mothers set their own agendas for the meetings. The group leaders were responsible for organising each session and for directing the action-based exercises that were employed. These focused on the issues the women identified as important to work on. During the programme the women worked on feelings of guilt, anger, low self-esteem, assertiveness and the needs of their children.

Two-thirds of the women had been sexually abused in childhood and the group provided them with a safe and supportive environment in which to explore their feelings about their experiences. Many mothers gained considerable insight into the reactions and needs of their own children through the experiences of their colleagues who were survivors. In one session, for example, one mother was helped to talk to an empty chair in which she imagined her mother was sitting, who had died some years previously. She tearfully told her mother about the abuse she had experienced as a child and explained why she had felt unable to tell her at the time. The other group members reassured her that she was powerless to protect herself and they empathised with her inability to 'tell'. This exercise not only helped to relieve the tremendous burden of guilt and responsibility the woman had carried since childhood for not stopping the abuse, but it prompted more understanding amongst other members in the group about why their children had felt unable to tell them of their abuse.

The strength of the group was reflected in the mutual support they demonstrated and the powerful feelings that group members were able to express. For example, when working on their feelings towards their child's abuser the women worked together and drew an outline of 'an abuser' on a large sheet of paper. They were then asked to write on the sheet words that expressed their feelings. This was a powerful exercise and the sense of commonality and support enabled the women to express themselves fully. They elected to tear up their drawing which involved considerable physical activity and the expression of anger. The resulting sense of power, unity and relief was voiced by all the women involved.

Some of the women began to meet and offer each other support outside of the group. Upon completion of the programme they decided to continue meeting as a self-help group and discussed the possibility of establishing an out-reach service for isolated mothers with few support networks.

The group evaluations completed by the women indicated that the group had been very important to them. One woman reported that it was:

> only through attending the group that I learnt to live again. Up until then I had been dead. The abuse of my daughter destroyed not only her childhood but it suffocated the person inside of me too. The experience of being able to share some of these feelings with other women who knew exactly what I was going through. They helped me to realise that if some of them were able to cope then so could I. In the group I learnt how to laugh and to cry again. The signs that I was still alive were encouraged out and although I still have dark days I now know that there is a light at the end of the tunnel.

DYAD AND FAMILY WORK

Following work with individual members of a family where sexual abuse had occurred there is often the need for work between mothers and their abused children, mothers and their partners and other dyadic relationships in the family. It is important that this work is not rushed into and the timing should be right for all concerned. Particular attention must be given to the needs of the abused child and they should never be subjected to pressure to engage in work for which they are unready. Each of the family members involved in dyad work should be supported by their individual worker and the professionals involved should ensure that careful planning minimises any risks of inappropriate blaming, power dynamics or reinforcement of feelings of guilt. In many circumstances it will be necessary to include work on communication methods at the start of these sessions since one of the objectives of such work is to improve the accuracy and flow of information between family members.

In some cases, particularly those where reunification of the family is being considered, it will be necessary for some therapeutic work with the whole family to take place. The emphasis is likely to be similar to the work described for dyads, but additionally it will be useful if the professionals involved observe the family dynamics and ensure that their assessment of progress is reflected in the behaviour the individuals demonstrate in the sessions. Again it is important to consider carefully the timing of the work and to ensure that individuals agree to their involvement in the work.

CONCLUSION

Mothers of sexually abused children are the most significant people in an abused child's recovery. If we are to maintain seriously the view that the child's welfare is paramount then it is essential to recognise and support the importance of work with non-abusing parents. We should also recognise and confront the mother-blaming attitudes that exist in our society. If we choose to ignore the impact and influence of sexism, and power inequality which such attitudes stem from, we not only perpetuate the dis-empowerment of women but we also deny sexually abused children their right to appropriate protection and help.

REFERENCES

1. Finkelhor, D. (1979) *Sexually Victimised Children* (Free Press: New York).
2. Russell, D. E. H. (1983) 'The incidence and prevalence of intra-familial and extra-familial sexual assault of female children', *Child Abuse and Neglect*, **7**: 133–46.
3. Wyatt, G. E. (1985) 'The sexual abuse of Afro-American and white-American women in childhood', *Child Abuse and Neglect*, **9**: 507–19.
4. Adams-Tucker, C. (1981) 'Proximate effects of sexual abuse in childhood: A report on 28 children', *American Journal of Psychiatry*, **139**:1252–6.
5. Fromuth, M. E. (1983) 'The long term psychological impact of childhood sexual abuse', PhD thesis (Auburn University, Alabama).
6. Goodwin, J. (1981) 'Suicide attempts in sexual abuse victims and their mothers', *Child Abuse and Neglect*, **5**: 217–21.
7. Abel, G. G., Becker, J. V., Murphy, N. and Flanagan, B. (1981) 'Identifying dangerous child molesters', in R. B. Stuart (ed.), *Violent Behavior: Social Learning Approaches to Prediction, Management, and Treatment* (Brunner/Mazel: New York).
8. Salter, A. (1988) *Treating Sex Offenders and Their Victims* (Sage Publications: Newbury Park, USA).
9. Mayer, A. (1983) *Incest* (Learning Publications: Holmes Beach, Florida).
10. Conte, J. R. (1982) 'Sexual abuse of children: enduring issues for social work', *Journal of Social Work and Human Sexuality*, **1**: 1–19.
11. Becker, J. V. and Coleman, E. M. (1989) 'Incest', in V. B. Hasselt, R. L. Morrison, A. S. Bellack and M. Hersen (eds.), *Handbook of Family Violence* (Plenum: New York).
12. Butler-Sloss, Lord Justice E. (1988), *Report of the Inquiry into Child Abuse in Cleveland 1987* (HMSO, London).
13. McIntyre, K. (1981) 'Role of mothers in father–daughter incest: a feminist analysis', *Social Work*, **26**: 462–6.
14. James, B. and Nasjleti, M. (1983) *Treating Sexually Abused Children and their Families* (Consulting Psychologists Press: Palo Alto, California).

15. Bander, K., Fein, E. and Bishop, G. (1982) 'Child sexual abuse treatment: some barriers to program operation', *Child Abuse and Neglect*, **6**: 185–91.
16. Justice, B. and Justice, R. (1979) *The Broken Taboo: Sex in the Family* (Human Sciences Press: New York).
17. *Ibid.*
18. Cormier, B. M., Kennedy, M. and Sangowicz, J. (1962) 'Psychodynamics of father–daughter incest', *Canadian Psychiatric Journal*, 7(5): 203–217.
19. Finkelhor, D. (1979) *op. cit.*
20. Summit, R. and Kryso, J. (1978) 'Sexual abuse of children: a clinical spectrum', *American Journal of Orthopsychiatry*, **48**: 237–51.
21. Goodwin, J., McCarthy, T. and Divasto, P. (1981) 'Prior incest in mothers of abused children', *Child Abuse and Neglect*, **5**: 87–95.
22. Cammaert, L. P. (1988) 'Non-offending mothers: A new conceptualization', in E. A. Walker (ed.), *Handbook on Sexual Abuse of Children* (Springer: New York).
23. Pincus, L. and Dare, C. (1978) *Secrets in the Family* (Faber & Faber: London).
24. Rush, F. (1980) 'The sexual abuse of children', *Journal of Child Psychology and Psychiatry*, **21**.
25. Groth, A. N. (1982) 'The incest offender', in S. Sgroi (ed.), *Handbook of Clinical Intervention in Child Sexual Abuse*, pp. 215–39 (Lexington Books: Lexington, Massachusetts).
26. Finkelhor, D. (1979) *op. cit.*
27. Stern, M. and Meyer, L. (1980) 'Family and couple interactional patterns in cases of father/daughter incest', *Sexual Abuse of Children: selected readings* (National Center on Child Abuse and Neglect, Washington DC).
28. Herman, J. and Hirschman, L. (1981) 'Families at risk for father–daughter incest', *American Journal of Psychiatry*, **138**: 967–70.
29. Server, J. C. and Janzen, C. (1982) 'Contraindications to reconstitution of sexually abusive families', *Child Welfare*, **61**: 279–88.
30. Sirles, E. A. and Frank, P. J. (1989) 'Factors influencing mothers' reactions to intrafamily sexual abuse', *Child Abuse and Neglect*, **13**: 131–9.
31. Groth, A. N. and Birnbaum, J. (1979) *Men who Rape* (Plenum Press: New York).
32. Abel, G. G., Mittleman, M. S. and Becker, J. V. (1985) 'Sexual Offenders: Results of assessment and recommendations for treatment', in M. H. Ben-Aron, S. J. Huckle and C. D. Webster (eds.), *Clinical Criminology: the Assessment and Treatment of Criminal Behavior* (M & M Graphic: Toronto).
33. Abel, G. G., Becker, J. V., Mittleman, M., Cunningham-Rathner, J., Rouleau, J. L. and Murphy, W. D. (1987) 'Self reported sex crimes of nonincarcerated paraphiliacs', *Journal of Interpersonal Violence*, **2**(1): 3–25.
34. Justice, B. and Justice, R. (1979) *op. cit.*
35. Brandt, R. S. T. and Tisza, V. B. (1977) 'The sexually misused child', *American Journal of Orthopsychiatry*, **47**(1): 80–90.
36. Cormier, B. M., Kennedy, M. and Sangowicz, J. (1962) *op. cit.*
37. Finkelhor, D. (1979) *op. cit.*
38. Kaufman, I., Peck, A. L. and Tagiuri, C. K. (1954) 'The family constellation and overt incestuous relations between father and daughter', *American Journal of Orthopsychiatry*, **24**: 266–79.

39. Lustig, N., Dresser, J. W., Spellman, S. W. and Murray, T. B. (1966) 'Incest: A family group survival pattern', *Archives of General Psychiatry*, **14**: 31–40.
40. Bagley, C. and Naspini, O. (1987) 'Mothers of sexually abused children', Unpublished paper cited in Bagley, C. and King, K. (1990) *Child Sexual Abuse: the search for healing* (Routledge: London).
41. Herman, J. and Hirschman, L. (1981) *op. cit.*
42. Sirles, E. A. and Franke, P. J. (1989) *op. cit.*
43. Pierce, R. and Pierce, L. H. (1985) 'The sexually abused child: a comparison of male and female victims', *Child Abuse and Neglect*, **9**: 191–9.
44. Mrazek, P. B., Lynch, M. and Bentovim, A. (1981) 'Recognition of child sexual abuse in the United Kingdom', in Mrazek and Kempe (eds.), *Sexually Abused Children and their Families* (Pergamon: Oxford).
45. Knudson, D. G. (1982) 'Interpersonal dynamics and mothers' involvement in father–daughter incest in Puerto Rico', *Dissertation Abstracts International*, **42** (7A); 3305.
46. Meiselman, K. C. (1978) *Incest: a Psychological Study of Causes and Effects with Treatment Recommendations* (Jossey-Bass: San Francisco).
47. Jones, D. and Seig, A. (1988) 'Child sexual abuse allegations in custody or visitation disputes', in E. B. Nicholson (ed.), *Sexual Abuse Allegations in Custody and Visitation Cases* (American Bar Association: Washington DC).
48. Herman, J. and Hirschman, L. (1981) *op. cit.*
49. Renvoize, J. (1982) *Incest: a Family Pattern* (Routledge & Kegan Paul: London).
50. Forward, S. and Buck, C. (1978) *Betrayal of Innocence: Incest and its Devastation* (Penguin: Middlesex).
51. Herman, J. and Hirschman, L. (1981) *op. cit.*
52. Julian, V. and Mohr, C. (1980) 'Father–daughter incest: Profile of the offender', *Victimology: an International Journal* **4**: 348–60.
53. Sahd, D. (1980) 'Psychological assessment of sexually abusing families and treatment implications', in W. Holder (ed.) (1980), *Sexual Abuse of Children: implications for treatment* (American Humane Association: Englewood, Colorado).
54. Bennett, M. H. (1980) 'Father–daughter incest: a psychological study of the mother from an attachment theory perspective', *Dissertation Abstracts International* **41** (6B).
55. *Ibid.*
56. Herman, J. and Hirschman, L. (1981) *op. cit.*
57. *Ibid.*
58. Harrer, M. N. (1981) 'Father–daughter incest: A study of the mother', *Dissertation Abstracts International*, **41** (12B).
59. Fredrickson, R. M. (1981) 'Incest: Family sexual abuse and its relationship to pathology, sexual orientation, attitudes towards women and authoritarianism, *Dissertation Abstracts International*, **42**: 201.
60. Herman, J. and Hirshman, L. (1981) *op. cit.*
61. Julian, V. and Mohr, C. (1980) *op. cit.*
62. Goodwin, J. (1981) *op. cit.*
63. Summit, R. C. (1983) 'The child sexual abuse accommodation syndrome', *Child Abuse and Neglect*, **7**: 177–93.

64. Myer, M. B. (1985) 'A new look at mothers of incest victims', *Journal of Social Work and Human Sexuality,* **3**: 47–58.

65. MacLeod, M. and Saraga, E. (1988) 'Challenging the orthodoxy: towards a feminist theory and practice', *Feminist Review,* 2.

66. The Children Act 1989 (HMSO: London).

67. Server, J. C. and Janzen, C. (1982) *op. cit.*

68. Bentovim, A., Elton, A. and Tranter, M. (1987) 'Prognosis for rehabilitation after abuse', *Adoption and Fostering,* **11**(1): 26–31.

69. Conte, J. R., Wolfe, S. and Smith, T. (1989) 'What sexual offenders tell us about prevention strategies', *Child Abuse and Neglect,* **13**: 293–301.

70. Sgroi, S. M. and Dana, N. T. (1982) 'Individual and group treatment of mothers of incest victims', in S. Sgroi (ed.), *Handbook of Clinical Intervention in Child Sexual Abuse,* 191–214 (Lexington Books: Lexington, Massachusetts).

6

WORKING WITH ADULT FEMALE SURVIVORS OF CHILDHOOD SEXUAL ABUSE

Helen Sheldon and Anne Bannister

Incest ravages childhood.
For the child victim and the woman she will become, incest is more than rape
of her body. Because of her dependence on her abuser, incest is a rape of her
trust as well. In this sense, the sexual aspect of incest is secondary. Someone
the victim trusted, instead of giving her love, took what he wanted from her,
terrorised her, hurt her, humiliated her, controlled her, disgraced her, and
shattered the separateness of her.

Blume, 1990[1]

Although in her book, *Secret Survivors*, Blume was referring specifically to incest, the trauma experienced by a child who is sexually abused by *any* trusted person in a position of power and authority, is extremely likely to result in adverse long-term sequelae. Over the past few years, there has been a wide-ranging debate in the literature regarding both the prevalance of childhood sexual abuse and the likelihood of such abuse leading to significant problems in adult life (Sheldrick, 1991).[2]

The obstacles to reaching a consensus of opinion are manifold and are derived from such diverse factors as: the pervasive influence, far beyond the sphere of psychoanalysis and psychotherapy, of Freud's renunciation of the seduction theory in 1897 (Masson, 1984);[3] methodological research difficulties associated with the discrepant definitions of child sexual abuse employed by different researchers; and, most significantly, the complex layers of resistance to the acknowledgement of the very fact that sexual abuse occurred.

The building blocks of this resistance are composed of the defences of denial and dissociation so often essential to the sexually abused child's survival; the terror of speaking out, years afterwards, in the face of the abuser's continued wielding of power and control (in fantasy, if not in reality); and the continued subordination and oppression of women and children in a patriarchal society, in which the construction of masculine sexuality is based upon an inherent alienation from intimate relations and is bound up with competition, separation and power. Frosh (1987)[4] cogently argues that this link between masculine personality organisation and sexual victimisation implicates all men in the sexual abuse of children.

It is this last factor that underlines and permeates therapeutic work with adult female survivors of childhood sexual abuse in individual and group therapy. The feelings of fear, shame, disgust, humiliation and guilt that a survivor has to begin to confront and overcome in order to even arrive at the counsellor's, therapist's or agency's doorstep, are reinforced by collective societal defence mechanisms that unconsciously strive to maintain the 'myths' of child sexual abuse so vividly described by Nelson (1982).[5] These seek to deny the existence of such abuse, to minimise its impact, to locate responsibility for the abuse with the 'seductive child who wanted it' or the mother who was 'frigid', or to maintain that abusers are different from the 'ordinary man in the street/pub/workplace'.

In an excellent paper Lister (1982),[6] refers to possible responses by the therapist which reflect these still widely believed myths and can lead to a breakdown in communication between therapist and client. These include focusing on intra-psychic processes at the expense of attention to external reality, subtle insinuations that the client was responsible in some way, refusing to believe in the reality of our clients' experiences and avoiding material that relates to violence, threats or fears of violence. Such responses may be feared and anticipated by survivors; if such fears are realised in the therapeutic setting as Lister suggests, then the earlier abuse is re-enacted in the betrayal of the trust in, and dependency upon, a powerful authority figure, namely the therapist.

There have been recent indications in the literature that there is a higher prevalence of sexual abuse perpetrated by mothers than was previously recognised. Whilst not wishing to deny or minimise the impact of maternal sexual abuse, it is important to contextualise such abuse within the present-day structure of gender relations described above. The primary child-rearing role and responsibilities assigned to women, combined with their inferior subordinate status within our patriarchal society, can lead to sig-nificant difficulties for mothers in psychologically separating from their children (Dinnerstein, 1987).[7] Within the context of an enmeshed and poorly differentiated relationship with their children, the boundary between physical and emotional care and concern on the one hand, and exploitation of their children's dependency needs on the other, may be blurred and confused. Insofar as a psychological umbilical cord persists and the child continues to be perceived as an extension of herself, the nature and quality of maternal sexual abuse is distinguishable from sexual abuse perpetrated by fathers. Furthermore, recent research is beginning to indicate that a significant proportion of women who sexually abuse children within their family, do so under the influence of powerful, dominant and abusing males.

THE LONG-TERM CONSEQUENCES OF CHILDHOOD SEXUAL ABUSE

> Children are essentially a captive population, totally dependent upon their parents or other adults for their basic needs. They will do whatever they perceive to be necessary to preserve a relationship with their caretakers. If an adult insists upon a sexual relationship with a dependent child, the child will comply.
>
> Given this reality, it makes no sense to invoke the idea of consent. Consent and choice are concepts that apply to the relationship of peers. They have no meaning in the relations of adults and children, any more than in the relations of free men and slaves.

Ward, 1984[8]

The child's inability to comprehend or give consent is central to most definitions of child sexual abuse and in an earlier article, this author (Sheldon, 1987)[9] has argued that the sexual abuse of children is *not* fundamentally about the gratification of the perpetrator's sexual needs, but of the need to exercise complete authority, power and control over a dependent, vulnerable child who is never in a position to offer her consent. In violating the child's physical and psychological boundaries, the abuser is violating her integrity, the very essence of her being, and her separateness is denied.

Briere, in 1984,[10] was one of the first authors to comment on the similarities between the characteristic difficulties experienced by adult survivors which he defined as the Post-Sexual Abuse Syndrome and the diagnostic criteria of the borderline personality. He emphasised the significance of the child's global experience of violation, exploitation and powerlessness.

It is this global trauma, the trauma of the *theft* of their childhood that is subsequently expressed by a majority of survivors in therapy, which determines to a significant degree the extent and severity of the difficulties experienced by survivors in adulthood. The hotly debated issue in the literature of whether childhood sexual abuse is causally related to severe problems in later life is surely missing this crucial point—that violation and exploitation of a vulnerable, powerless child can only take place in the context of life circumstances which do not prioritise the developmental needs of the child. Gardner (1990),[11] having reviewed the literature, concludes that:

> the trauma of child sexual abuse is exacerbated by life circumstances that are deprived, inconsistent and lonely, and that the degree of trauma correlates with the degree of powerlessness experienced by the child during the sexual acts.

This powerlessness is surely reinforced by factors which prevent the child victim from being able to defend herself: a dependent relationship to the abuser; the child's age at the onset of the abuse; the inability to understand what is happening; the threat of, or actual, violence; physical and/or emotional isolation from other family members; the child's degree of self-blame; conflicting feelings over her love for the abuser and her need for his attention.

In this position, the child victim becomes a survivor through the process of developing defensive strategies which endeavour to protect her inner core. These strategies, or defence mechanisms, of repression, denial, detachment and dissociation will often result in the adult survivor not having access to memories of her sexual abuse. However, in adult life, these once adaptive defences create problems of their own for which survivors of childhood sexual abuse seek help. Gardner quotes Lindberg and Distad[12] who suggested in 1985 that the survivor theory, as applied to Vietnam veterans, accounts for the delay in symptoms; other authors have also drawn parallels between this syndrome, classified as the Post-Traumatic Stress Disorder, and the Post-Sexual Abuse Syndrome described by Briere.

The Post-Traumatic Stress Disorder is characterised by a period of repression, detachment and denial of the trauma which may last for years, followed by nightmares, intrusive recollections of the event, acting as if or feeling that the event is recurring in response to a situational cue, memory lapses, anxiety, problems with relationships and a feeling of detachment from others.

Thus, many survivors may seek help years after the abuse has ceased for a variety of complaints which are not recognised as being directly related to their sexual abuse (Sheldon, 1988).[13] These broadly fall into three categories:

1. Psychological problems with a psychiatric presentation such as depression, anxiety, sleeping difficulties, eating disorders, self-harm, alcohol and drug dependence.
2. Severe interpersonal difficulties characterised by feelings of isolation, alienation, distrust, fear of men, repeated victimisation in an adult relationship and difficulty in their relationships with their own children.
3. Sexual problems such as avoidance of sex, sexual anxiety and guilt, promiscuity and prostitution.

An understanding of the development of these problems will therefore need to take into account how the betrayal of the child's trust and the violation of her boundaries led to the fragmentation of her inner world; despairing and increasingly stringent attempts to maintain control; the development of extremely negative self-concepts derived from feelings of worthlessness; and a perception of herself as an object to be used by others, rather than experiencing herself as the subject of her own story. For it is her own story that has been silenced and that will be so terrifying, and so essential, to address in therapy in order to integrate the fragments of her inner world and achieve a sense of wholeness and security.

WORKING WITH ADULT SURVIVORS—THE CONSPIRACY OF SILENCE IS BROKEN

A survivor's decision to seek counselling or therapy may or may not have been triggered by an awareness of her childhood sexual abuse. In either case, she is once again entering into a relationship with a powerful authority figure, upon whom she will feel dependent for her welfare. There is consequently considerable potential for a re-enactment of the earlier relationship with the abuser and/or with the neglectful, unprotective parent(s) or caretaker figure(s).

It is thus essential for the therapist to be sensitive to the possibility of these dynamics developing within the therapeutic relationship. If they do develop before the therapist and client have established a therapeutic or working alliance (the capacity of therapist and client to work purposefully together), the whole process of working together may be undermined and jeopardised.

In working with survivors, it is necessary to understand that the journey upon which the survivor embarks is bound to be extremely distressing and painful, as previously entrenched survival strategies have to be identified, and deeply repressed inner conflicts worked through. These strategies, or defence mechanisms, of repression, denial and dissociation were invoked by the child in order to cope with the terror, pain, confusion, despair, guilt and ambivalence consequent upon the assault on her boundaries and integral sense of self. To deal with these overwhelming feelings, the child used such defences to deny their existence and these defence mechanisms remain intact into adulthood; it is as if 'the little girl inside' (a metaphor often used in therapy) has remained locked up inside the adult woman who paradoxically continues the role of gaoler where the abuser left off.

In order to understand how this paradox developed, we need to consider the little girl who was being abused. She would have been subjected to double messages about her sexuality and the responsibility for the abuse would have been foisted upon her by the perpetrator who placed inappropriate expectations upon her and treated her as an extension of himself. This inevitably led to intense feelings of guilt and self-blame which were compounded by the ambivalence sometimes felt towards the abuser when this highly exploitative and damaging relationship was nevertheless the only experience of attention or 'affection' from a supposedly trustworthy adult. This ambivalence was further reinforced when the child experienced physiological sexual arousal which was interpreted by the perpetrator and subsequently by the adult survivor as evidence that she 'wanted it'. The adult survivor attributes further blame to herself if she failed to stop the abuse, completely disregarding the power differential between herself and the abuser. It is therefore inevitable that her perception of reality became distorted, that she internalised the responsibility and blame in order to survive and in the process identified with the abuser/gaoler and kept 'the little girl inside' locked up. It is the control exercised by the image of the abuser, living on inside the adult survivor, that needs to be challenged through the process of therapy with the aim of allowing the 'little girl inside' to gradually and cautiously emerge, become recognised and accepted.

For the reasons identified above, issues of power and control are fundamental in both the abusive relationships and in the therapeutic relationship. This has important implications for both the assessment process and therapeutic technique, regardless of the therapeutic orientation and model that is selected. Assessment procedures should emphasise the mutual nature of the interaction; the client must be offered whatever information is necessary to help her to consider and assess any help that is being offered to her. If she feels able to make an informed decision, in conjunction with the therapist, about her capacity to work within a particular therapeutic orientation (e.g. psychodynamic) and mode (e.g. group), then she will have taken the first step on her journey towards empowerment, that is, the healthy use of, as opposed to abuse of, power.

Perhaps the most emotive issue related to the survivor's right to choose concerns the gender of the therapist. It has been suggested by some authors (e.g. Ganzarin and Buchele, 1986;[14] Mann, 1980)[15] that the presence of a male co-therapist in a group provides a different model of a parental couple and the experience of relating to a non-abusing male authority figure. In the opinion of this author (Sheldon) this position demonstrates a failure of empathy with the survivor, whose fear of being overwhelmed by the emergence of uncontrollable feelings may jeopardise her capacity to fully maintain a reality-based perception of the male therapist. (Also note that research has demonstrated the high prevalence of sexual abuse of female clients by male therapists: Davidson, 1981.[16]) This position also fails to attend to Frosh's contention that the potential to sexually abuse is inherently bound up with sexual-stereotyped masculine fantasies of the penetration and conquest of women. For these reasons, I consider the presence of a male therapist in a female survivors' group to be contraindicated; subsequent to individual or group therapy in which she has addressed her failed relationship with her mother and thus found the strength to confront her abuser, a survivor may choose to work on issues concerning her relationships with men. In this case the presence of a male therapist may be extremely helpful in working through unresolved issues and conflicts.

Finally, whether individual or group work is indicated as the most appropriate therapeutic option, it is important to ensure that the orientation employed by the therapist is governed by the survivor's capacity to work within that model. Although eclecticism can be used defensively in many situations to conceal therapist inadequacies, in working with survivors an eclectic approach, which is underpinned by a particular theoretical perspective but is responsive to the survivor's development needs, can provide a potentially non-abusive therapeutic space in which she can undertake her journey at her own pace.

THE USE OF PSYCHODRAMA IN INDIVIDUAL WORK WITH ADULT FEMALE SURVIVORS

As discussed in Chapter 1, psychodrama is a therapeutic perspective which is very adaptable and which appears to fit the needs of many survivors of sexual abuse. Although it is primarily a group psychotherapy, this author (Bannister) has, along with other practitioners, developed its use also as an individual mode of therapy.

One of Moreno's key concepts is that of 'tele', a process of interaction between two persons. It differs from empathy in that it is two-way. There has to be an equal pull between therapist and client. It is this egalitarianism which is essential for success in work with survivors. Tele differs from transference (which is discussed later in this chapter) in that it is a 'here and now' experience which does not have echoes from the past lives of either therapist or client. Tele contains trust and a belief that both participants can be creative together. Tele is produced spontaneously between two people who work together psychodramatically to produce a sensory and cognitive experience which throws fresh light on an old or familiar situation.

'Ms A' brought overwhelming guilt and feelings of stigma to her therapeutic sessions. At 40 she was a professional woman, married for several years, with a six-year-old daughter. At work she felt unable to press for promotion, feeling unworthy or less able than colleagues. At home she worried endlessly about her daughter, although her partner supported her and assured her that she was a 'good mother'. Ms A was convinced that she had caused her stepfather to sexually abuse her because she had, at four years old, welcomed him and his natural daughter into the home which she shared with her mother. She had, in her own words, 'lavished affection and attention on him', so grateful was she that his presence helped her divorced mother.

Ms A said she felt uncomfortable with role play and remained seated throughout the sessions. She was happy, however, to recreate past events, first with drawings and then with 2-inch-high miniature dolls. She created scenes which included her stepfather and older stepsister where she realised for the first time how sexualised their behaviour was already at the time she met them. She replayed scenes with stepfather and herself where she saw, in a moment of revelation, the 'grooming' process that her stepfather had begun as soon as he had entered her life. She saw how subtly he prepared her to be abused. By 'becoming' the small doll which represented her stepsister (reversing roles) she realised that she too had almost certainly been abused even before Ms A met her. In a catharsis of anger she exclaimed, 'He really was an abuser who would exploit any children that were available. I just happened to be there.'

Ms B was enthusiastic, energetic and creative. She described herself as 'promiscuous' and told of a string of broken relationships. She was keen to role-play scenes from these relationships in order to see 'what went wrong'. Mostly Ms B used an empty chair to represent a partner and the therapist asked her to reverse roles frequently into the 'significant other'. Soon a pattern emerged. Ms B recognised how deeply her self-cognition had been distorted by an adolescent abuser when she was a five-year-old. She had become sexualised, feeling, in her lonely childhood, that this was the only way to get affection. Using her abundant creativity Ms B was able to enact possible future scenarios where she broke the pattern of previous behaviour.

Ms C had been a member of a religious order but was now working in the community as a counsellor with substance abusers. She felt comfortable working with symbol and ritual. Her language was very expressive.

Ms C: I feel as if I'm locked in a tomb.
Therapist: Put your body in position in the tomb and describe what it's like in there.

Ms C: Cold, Lonely.
Therapist: What else are you feeling?
Ms C: Frightened. (She sobs quietly, like a little girl.)
Therapist: What are you afraid of?
Ms C: The grown-ups.
Therapist: Who can help you?
Ms C: No-one.
Therapist: Can you protect yourself?
Ms C: Yes, I can make a shell all around me. They can't get me because they won't know I'm here.
Therapist: Construct the shell.

Slowly, painstakingly, Ms C built a rigid hard shell, using steel chairs. The therapist invited her to step outside for a moment and look at the 'shell' which now surrounded a large doll representing herself.

Ms C (weeping): She's trapped, she's afraid.
Therapist: You can help her, you're her counsellor.

Ms C, no longer crying, looked at the problem professionally. Together with the therapist she looked critically at the separate parts of her 'shell' and devised a method whereby she could slowly replace some of the more rigid behaviours with more flexible reactions which she could use, as and when she chose. Gradually she regained power and control over her own defences which had been necessarily constructed when she had been abused.

In a final scene she surrounded herself with large cushions which now represented the more flexible 'shell' over which she had control. Slowly she pushed away one of the cushions and smiled with relief. 'I'm pushing away the stone from the mouth of the tomb', she said, thus breaking the silence that had closed her own mouth and imprisoned her in the tomb.

The foregoing case examples are reconstructed from an amalgam of several clients and do not represent individuals in any way. They are given to illustrate some of the many ways in which the therapist can use 'psychodrama à deux', or the interactive approach.

'Classic psychodrama' as developed by Zerka Moreno, the widow of Jacob Moreno, is conducted in a group setting. The therapist or director works with the protagonist and the group to enact a series of connecting scenes usually from the present into the past. The 'core scene', when working with survivors, is usually an abusive one. Care is taken not to recreate the abusive experience, but the protagonist often has a catharsis as feelings surrounding the abuse are re-experienced. Then director and protagonist together may choose future scenes to act out with the group, to make concrete the learning experience from the catharsis.

In our experience most survivors will require some individual work (counselling or therapy) before they feel ready to embark upon group therapy. This individual work may be two or three sessions or may take several months. Psychodrama is only one of the therapeutic modes suitable for use in a group of adult female survivors.

The powerful dynamics of survivors' groups persist, regardless of theoretical approach. An understanding of these dynamics is essential, not least to ensure the survival of the therapists and, of course, the success of the group.

GROUP WORK WITH SURVIVORS

Within recent years, group therapy for survivors of childhood sexual abuse has become increasingly recognised and valued as a helpful and beneficial therapeutic modality. Many authors (see p. 117) have described their different approaches, but all agree that group work is particularly suited to addressing issues of secrecy, mistrust, isolation, low self-esteem, shame and self-blame. Through the women's movement, a strong tradition of the value of women's groups has developed over the years, especially with regard to obtaining validation of one's own experience. Within a survivors' group, such validation can be more readily accepted from others who share similar past experiences, coping strategies and current problems.

This author (Sheldon) has co-conducted women survivors' groups for the past five years, in an inner-city NHS psychotherapy department. Although they have varied in their degree of structure according to the specific needs of each group, our understanding of the group process has always been informed by a psychodynamic theoretical orientation.

A psychodynamic orientation is based upon psychoanalytic theory, with its emphasis on the central position of the role of unconscious conflicts in personality development. Within a psychodynamic approach, the agent of change is the relationship between the therapist and client, especially the exploration of the transference and countertransference aspects. Transference is the process by which an individual experiences towards the therapist feelings and ideas which derive from previous figures in her life; the therapist is thus endowed with the significance of another, prior figure, such as mother. Countertransference consists of the therapist's emotional attitude towards the client, and is derived from responses that are specific to the client's transference and from responses that are specific to the therapist's own unconscious conflicts—hence the importance of therapists receiving supervision and preferably personal therapy, to minimise countertransference difficulties derived from the latter responses. Countertransference is useful in helping the therapist to understand the hidden meaning of the client's communications and thus to gain insight into their predicament.

In applying these concepts to our understanding of working with survivors' groups, we can anticipate the re-emergence within the group of
repressed, unresolved feelings towards members of each woman's family
of origin—the group in fact can be perceived in terms of re-experienced
feelings towards the whole family, with the therapists in the position of the
original parental couple and group members as siblings.

The group model

Much of the literature advocates a closed, time-limited small group, with a
maximum of eight women and two female co-therapists. Our groups now
consist of 20 sessions, with each session of one and a half hours duration.
Our first group, of 12 sessions, was too short to adequately address many
of the relevant issues; we entered the termination phase of the group whilst
we were still working on issues of trust and dependency, which made it
difficult for the group members to express their anger towards us
(Davenport and Sheldon, 1987).[17]

The advantages of a closed, short-term approach have been described
by Herman and Schatzow (1984)[18] and Goodman and Nowak-Scibelli
(1985).[19] This model promotes group cohesiveness; minimizes regression
and draws on the strengths of the individual; maintains a clear focus for
exploration and discussion and, in establishing firm boundaries, provides
a marked contrast to the ambiguous boundaries in the family of origin. In
contrast to some workers, we do not advocate concurrent individual therapy
during the life of the group; in our experience, this facilitates and intensifies
splitting processes, whereby the group is endowed with negative qualities
and members resist confronting painful feelings and issues in the group.
There is also the obvious parallel between the triangle of client/individual
therapist/group and the triangular relationships that existed in childhood,
without a forum for these dynamics to be explored.

The need for structure within the time boundary of each session, in order
to provide security and containment for intense anxiety, must be measured
against the need to respond flexibly to group dynamics. We have experienced great variations in the use and value of structured techniques, both
between different groups and within the lifecycle of an individual group.
As therapists, in structuring sessions, we are exercising our power and
control and this could easily invoke the childhood feelings of powerlessness
in relation to the abuser; what is offered as containment may be perceived
as control and domination. One group responded so intensely in this way
in the early phase of the group's life, that the group remained unstructured
thereafter, despite the considerable anxiety thus generated. This also highlights an example of how transference and countertransference exerts such

a powerful influence—the therapists were perceived initially as controlling abusers and subsequently as neglectful, abandoning mothers, whilst we felt trapped in a 'no-win' situation between being perceived as either abusers or bad mothers. The absence of structure, in our experience and that of Adams (1990),[20] facilitates and intensifies both transference and counter-transference aspects, stirring up violent and distressing feelings which the co-therapists must try to help the group to contain. This requires the co-therapy relationship to be cohesive, resilient and honest and the therapists to be able to accept, understand and comment upon the transference projections they are receiving. (The co-therapy relationship and supervision will be discussed later.)

We have found the use of structured techniques to be most helpful in the early phase of the group's life, when we are working towards the facilitation of group cohesiveness and identity. These structures have included paired introductions; the sharing of hopes, fears and expectations which recorded on paper and reviewed in the last session; the collective drawing-up and recording of the rules of the group, emphasising the need for confidentiality and clear boundaries; the identification and sharing of current problems and difficulties; a regular period at the beginning of each session for feedback.

As trust and cohesiveness gradually develop within the group, the need for structure often diminishes as the threat of intimacy becomes less overwhelming. Nevertheless, projective art and drama methods have sometimes facilitated the expression of feelings, which may not have been accessible to verbal language.

Although it is vital to maintain clear boundaries for the group with regard to both maintaining a safe physical space (i.e. the same room, no interruptions) and punctuality with beginning and ending the sessions, we have always provided refreshments for group members after we have left at the end of each session. Although this can lead to a 'post-group group', with its inherent elements of secrecy and splitting, we believe it is important to acknowledge the ordeal experienced by each woman in the group and the difficulty of then facing the world outside. This is especially the case for women with children in a creche or women who subsequently have to go to work. We discuss the implications of the post-group meeting with the group members, especially with regard to secrecy and the possibility of splitting and encourage them to bring any group business that is discussed back to the following week's session. Although we have encountered difficulties, for example when one woman who was threatened by the post-group intimacy did not participate and then felt excluded, the benefits of mutual support and validation of their strength as survivors have tended to outweigh the disadvantages.

Selection of group members

The process of interviewing women for assessment forms an integral part of the group. In an NHS setting, a minority of women refer themselves specifically for a group but most women are referred by other professional workers. The preliminary interview(s) are conducted by one of the co-therapists with the aim of providing information about the group and exploring:

1. The client's motivation for attending the group. Does she positively want group therapy or has she been 'persuaded' that it would be helpful by family/friends/other professionals who feel powerless to help her or threatened by her emotional distress?
2. The client's ability to talk about her past experiences. Although the group focuses on feelings related to the abuse, would the prospect of sharing any details of her abuse with others feel like an insurmountable obstacle, once the group had established itself?
3. The client's ability to work in a group setting. Does she have a realistic degree of anxiety about being in a group, which she feels able to address or is she terrified at the prospect of becoming dependent upon others and exposing her feelings to them?
4. The client's capacity to manage and contain painful feelings. Will she be able to cope with distress between weekly sessions, without resorting to violence directed either against herself or others, or using maladaptive ways of dealing with her feelings such as alcohol or illicit drugs?

It is advisable to consider other approaches for women who are either in crisis, who do not have at least one supportive on-going relationship or who would find themselves isolated in the group by virtue of demographic factors, as the stress of the group super-imposed upon these concurrent stresses may severely affect the client's ability to function in everyday life.

Following the initial interview(s), each prospective member is offered an appointment with both co-therapists shortly before the beginning of the group. This enables the client to develop an, albeit tentative, relationship with both therapists and offers her time to reflect on her hopes and fears about the group, explore any difficulties that she may anticipate and obtain any further information she may require. In order to minimise the possibility of women dropping out of the group, we explain that the group will arouse painful feelings and ask each woman to make a commitment to regular attendance. Although some women have initially felt threatened or intimi-dated by the presence of the unfamiliar therapist, feeling that they were being observed and exposed, this can be addressed at the time thus helping them to deal with any similar feelings that will inevitably arise during the group. With this preparation we have had an extraordinarily consistent attendance with only one woman dropping out during the last three groups. This confirms our impression that women who were sexually abused are *survivors* whose courage and tenacity can be harnessed, respected and validated in their journey towards healing the wounds inflicted upon them as children.

Common group themes

During the life of a survivors' group, certain themes central to the original trauma are likely to re-emerge and be re-enacted in the group, with the opportunity of identifying and working through previously unresolved feelings and conflicts. Whilst these themes are inextricably interwoven and thus do not arise in a linear process, they will be briefly discussed below according to the pattern in which they commonly arise.

Trust, power and control. The betrayal of their childhood needs for trustworthy, dependable and loving relationships forms the core experience of all survivors of childhood sexual abuse. Thus, in initially seeking help and then in coming to a group, every woman has to confront a terrifying dilemma between her wish and need for dependency and her fear of being judged, shamed, violated and rejected. Learning to trust others in the group involves the painful process of acknowledging these feelings towards both her peers and the therapists, especially fears of the consequences of disclosing the secret, which had imprisoned her whilst simultaneously maintaining a 'special' relationship. This can feel particularly risky and painful when the abusive relationship provided the only source of attention for her as a child; this reinforces feelings of responsibility and guilt, causing the survivor to fear being blamed by other group members and/or unconsciously envied for having received something 'special'. Furthermore, feelings of isolation within the family and/or rivalry with envied siblings can generate anxiety about a 'hierarchy of abuse' within the group; confiding in other members carries the threat of being disbelieved, excluded or having one's experiences trivialised.

The development of trust between peers in the group may be facilitated by the sharing of information about current problems and past and present ways of protecting themselves within relationships, that is through processes of identification with each other. Learning to trust the therapists is much more hazardous; the initial engagement with the group occurs through the assessment process with the therapists, who may at first be idealised but subsequently are perceived as the abusing and/or neglectful parents of childhood. Frequently, 'splitting' of the therapists occurs with one therapist seen to be the 'good mother' or 'like one of us', whilst the other is feared as the abuser or neglectful, ineffectual 'bad mother'. The therapists' provision of consistent boundaries for the group as a whole, of non-judgemental responsiveness to feelings expressed by group members, and of a model of a united couple who can maintain appropriate boundaries and respect for each other—including differences between them, gradually enables group members to feel contained and secure enough to acknowledge and explore their forbidden feelings and the existence of differences between themselves.

At this stage in the group, the metaphor of 'the little girl inside' and of 'the mask' may surface as group members begin to acknowledge their lifelong need to exercise control by denying to themselves and to others the existence of their hurt, vulnerable, needy, raging 'little girl'. Feelings of powerlessness which, accompanying the relinquishing of excessive control in the group, may give rise to defensive behaviour. This paradoxically exerts an extremely powerful influence within the group, for example, through detachment by withdrawing from the group and/or reverting to silence, or through projection of powerlessness into the therapists who feel they have to minimise their own power in response to the 'little girl' who feels at their mercy.

Anger. A fundamental component of the childhood trauma of sexual abuse that leads to significant difficulties for an adult survivor, was the absence of a close, confiding, nurturing relationship with her mother. An all-female group (i.e. with two female therapists) generates intense feelings of anger towards mothers who failed them as well as fears that the therapist-mothers will not be able to contain and survive their hostile, destructive feelings. The group offers an opportunity for these feelings to be expressed and, in being contained and validated by the therapists and not punished and retaliated upon, the profound feelings of grief for the loss of childhood and of the desperately needed mother can at last find a voice.

It is the working through of these overwhelmingly painful feelings towards their mothers that creates a safe enough environment within the group of survivors to confront their abusers and relinquish their feelings of self-hatred and self-blame. Prior to the experience of having their needs and rage acknowledged, accepted and validated, such feelings were feared and condemned by the survivor as evidence of 'being just as bad as him', i.e. of identification with the aggressor. The recognition and acceptance of the previously repressed and denied grief of 'the little girl inside' leads to the development for the first time of a sense of entitlement to either murderous or ambivalent feelings towards the abuser which were formerly shrouded in a blanket of shame and guilt.

Sexuality. Although open acknowledgement of feelings about sexuality within the group is unlikely to occur prior to having worked through the feelings described in the above paragraph, the identification of sexual problems may have taken place during the problem-sharing stage and they may have been discussed with an absence of affect (emotion). Covert expression of their conflicts around sexuality may nevertheless have become manifest in dramatic alterations in appearance and dress, in curiosity about the therapists and in concern about their own children's sexuality. This concern may be based upon justified anxiety about the possibility of sexual abuse, but many survivors are also unable to recognise age-appropriate sexual behaviour in their children.

Concurrent with the growing sense of entitlement described above, there may develop an awareness of how their own childhood age-appropriate sexuality was deliberately abused and of how their adult sexual identity was based upon a self-identification as a sexual object, or on sex as a currency, to be used in an attempt to obtain affection. Sharing their feelings about sex is initially accompanied by shame and wariness about others' reactions, particularly those of the therapists. If this is overcome, a phase of mutual discussion follows which extends beyond the boundary of the group (out of sight of the 'parents') and is often accompanied by the humour associated with adolescent discussions of sexuality.

Loss. This theme, initially addressed in relation to the theft of childhood and the absence of nurturing relationships, powerfully resurfaces during the termination phase of the group. The therapists are frequently re-identified as abandoning, uncaring mothers and intense anxiety is felt about whether the group will continue to live on as a good experience inside each of them in the face of their anger about it ending. Acknowledgement and expression of their feelings about the impending loss of the group may enable each member to reflect upon and accept progress made and disappointments and frustrations endured. Also, through this process they may achieve a recognition of their individuation and differentiation from the group, resulting in more established self-boundaries and personal autonomy.

TRANSFERENCE AND COUNTERTRANSFERENCE ISSUES

As indicated earlier in this chapter, these issues are always present whether or not they are overtly addressed. The following chart briefly outlines the different dynamics commonly present during different phases of the group's lifecycle (with acknowledgement to Ms Lesley Mitchell with whom this was discussed).

PHASE	TRANSFERENCE	COUNTER-TRANSFERENCE
BEGINNING	(a) TO THERAPISTS: Idealisation of therapists, 'They can make it better for us', combined with fear of therapists' omnipotence, 'Will they abuse their power?'	(a) Powerful urges to protect, reassure and comfort them in response to the combination of idealisation and persecutory anxiety.
	(b) TO EACH OTHER: Emergence of peer/sibling rivalry: 'Who is the most/least abused?' Fear of isolation/aloneness: 'No-one can understand me.' The need to identify with other group members: 'We're all here for the same reason.'	(b) Anxiety about the group's capacity to negotiate the stage of basic trust: 'Will this group cohere, survive the first weeks?'
	(c) TO THE GROUP AS A WHOLE: Fear of trusting others in the group/the group as a whole. 'Is it going to be safe enough?' 'Can I trust this group?'	(c) Feeling the need to provide structure and containment for intense anxiety projected into the group as a whole by group members—both patients and therapists.
MIDDLE	(a) TO THERAPISTS: Unresolved feelings about mothers/fathers/abusers emerge, often in complex form. 'Do they really care, want to know?' 'Will I be criticised, rejected, ridiculed, if I express my true feelings?' 'Have they (therapists) been	(a) Struggling with feeling over-intrusive and abusive (identification with aggressor) or neglectful, powerless and incompetent.

PHASE	TRANSFERENCE	COUNTER-TRANSFERENCE
	abused, and if not, why are they doing this?' 'What are their motives, are they using/exploiting me for their own satisfaction?'	
MIDDLE	(b) TO EACH OTHER: Denial of difference, uniting together in the face of their negative feelings towards therapists leads to conflict about intimacy between them. As this is identified and explored there is a move towards acknowledgement of difference, which is feared. 'Will the little girl inside be accepted without the mask?'	(b) Pressure on the co-therapy relationship 'Need to provide a united front.'
	(c) TO THE GROUP AS A WHOLE: Identification with the group which is invested with significance and hope.	(c) Less preoccupation and concern with the differences between us—a flattening of the familial hierarchy and sisterly identification with the group members.
ENDING	(a) TO THERAPISTS: Focus returns to therapists as neglectful, uncaring and abandoning mothers: 'Are we going to be dumped when the group is over?' *and* as violating abusers: 'What are you going to do with our files?'	(a) Mirrors the group's transference to us as abandoning, uncaring mothers—powerful urge to 'hold on' to group members, partly in their interests 'they *do* need more time' and partly as a defence against their anger.

PHASE	TRANSFERENCE	COUNTER-TRANSFERENCE
ENDING	(b) TO EACH OTHER: Clinging to/dependency upon each other in the face of anticipated loss: 'Will our friendship survive after the group has ended?'	
		(b) and (c) Aware of the differentiation between group members —separation/individuation —being more aware of how they have developed and changed individually; cf 'Teenagers leaving home'.
	(c) TO THE GROUP AS A WHOLE: Difficulty in perceiving the group as a whole object with good and bad aspects— struggling to hold on to what they've gained/achieved in the face of their anger about ending.	

SUPERVISION FOR THE THERAPIST

In our experience, which covers statutory and non-statutory social work settings, as well as the Health Service, the provision of supervision for therapists working with groups is, at best, sporadic and patchy and, at worst, non-existent. Supervision is often seen as a privilege rather than a right and has to be fought for by the therapist. It often takes place in the therapist's leisure time and if it is inadequately funded (which it usually is) the therapist has to provide a reciprocal or similar service in payment. Thus supervision is seen as a 'treat', a gift to the therapist which she may or may not accept. This, of course, contains an element of truth since many supervisees describe supervision as 'something for myself' or 'something to replace the gap left after the group has taken from me'.

The violent, distressing, and sometimes horrifying images which are stirred up in a group for adult survivors naturally affect the lives of therapists as much as other group members. The conflicts and abusive situations which are common in all our lives, especially for women, are triggered and recreated by experiences in the group. It is vital that therapists should have a supervisor who can act as a 'safe container' for difficult feelings which can then be processed in the supportive calm of the supervisory setting.

The processing will often reveal transferences and countertransferences between therapist and client which can then be understood and worked with openly in the group. This will obviously not only benefit the therapist but also the clients. In addition the therapist's personal conflicts can be identified in supervision and subsequently addressed if necessary in the therapist's own personal therapy. Again this will ultimately help group members who will not be confused over an apparently illogical reaction to their behaviour.

A supervisor who is experienced as a therapist for survivor groups can also throw light on the issues of power and control which we have discussed earlier in this chapter. This provides reassurance and confidence for the therapist; both qualities are necessary in running a group of this nature.

One of the most important features of supervision is to provide a forum for working on the co-therapy relationship. As we have written, the group often project uncomfortable roles such as 'good mother' and 'bad mother' or 'abuser' or 'non-protector' on the co-therapists. Unless this is clearly acknowledged in the supervisory setting, therapists can sometimes continue the projections themselves and internalise negative feelings from the roles. Inexperienced co-therapists may blame each other for 'failures' in the group and so be unable to look objectively at the meaning behind such 'failures'.

Although it is therefore essential to the efficient conduct of a group that supervision is received by the therapists, it is also an intrinsic part of staff care. This issue is discussed at length in the final chapter of this book. To omit staff supervision is to leave a dangerous gap in the provision of services to those who have been abused. We have seen that a thorough understanding of our own potential for abuse, and sometimes our own unwillingness to take power, is essential for therapists working in this difficult area. Such objective understanding can only be provided by someone who is able to stand outside a particular therapist/client relationship. In this way the needs of the therapist and client will be equally well served.

Helen Sheldon wishes to acknowledge the support and work of Sarah Davenport, Sheila Cadman and Lesley Mitchell, with whom she has co-conducted survivors' groups since 1986. She also wishes to acknowledge the courage of the women who attended the groups, without whom this chapter could not have been written.

REFERENCES

1. Blume, E. Sue (1990) *Secret Survivors* (John Wiley & Sons: New York).
2. Sheldrick, Carol (1991) 'Adult sequelae of child sexual abuse', *British Journal of Psychiatry*, **158**(10), 55–62.
3. Masson, Jeffrey M. (1984) *The Assault On Truth* (Penguin: Harmondsworth).
4. Frosh, Stephen (1987) 'Issues for men working with sexually abused children', *British Journal of Psychotherapy*, **3**(4), 332–39.
5. Nelson, Sarah (1982) *Incest, Fact and Myth* (Stramullion Co-op: Edinburgh).
6. Lister, Eric (1982) 'Forced silence: a neglected dimension of trauma', *American Journal of Psychiatry*, **139** (7), 872–5.
7. Dinnerstein, Dorothy (1987) *The Rocking of the Cradle and the Ruling of the World* (The Woman's Press: London).
8. Ward, Elizabeth (1984) *Father–Daughter Rape* (The Women's Press: London).
9. Sheldon, Helen (1987) 'Living with a secret', *Changes*, **5**, (2) 340–43.
10. Briere, John (1984) 'The Effects of Childhood Sexual Abuse on Later Psychological Functioning: Defining a Post Sexual Abuse Syndrome', presented at the 3rd National Conference on Sexual Victimization of Children, Children's Hospital National Medical Center, Washington.
11. Gardner, Fiona (1990) 'Psychotherapy with adult survivors of child sexual abuse', *British Journal of Psychotherapy*, **6**(3), 285–93.
12. Lindberg, F. and Distad, L. (1985) 'Post-traumatic stress disorders in women who experienced childhood incest', *Child Abuse and Neglect*, **9**, 329–34.
13. Sheldon, Helen (1988) 'Child sexual abuse in adult female psychotherapy referrals', *British Journal of Psychiatry*, **152**, 107–11.
14. Ganzarin, Ramon and Buchele, Bonnie (1986) 'Countertransference when incest is the problem', *International Journal of Group Psychotherapy*, **36**(4), 549–66.
15. Mann, David (1980) 'Incest: the father and the male therapist', *British Journal of Psychotheraphy*, **6**(2), 143–53.
16. Davidson, Virginia (1981) 'Psychiatry's problem with no name: therapist–patient sex', in *Women and Mental Health*, Howell & Bayes (eds.) 141–48 (Basic Books: New York).
17. Davenport, Sarah and Sheldon, Helen (1987) 'From victim to survivor', *Changes*, **5**(3), 379–82.
18. Herman, Judith and Schatzow, Emily (1984) 'Time-limited group therapy for women with a history of incest', *International Journal of Group Psychotherapy*, **34**(4), 605–16.
19. Goodman, Barbara and Nowak-Scibelli, Donna (1985) 'Group treatment for women incestuously abused as children', *International Journal of Group Psychotherapy*, **35**, 351–54.
20. Adams, Mary (1990) 'The couple and the group: co-therapy with incest survivors', *British Journal of Psychotherapy*, **7**(1), 25–37.

REFERENCES: GROUPS

- Blake-White, J. & Kline, C. M. (1985) 'Treating the dissociative process in adult victims of childhood incest', *Social Casework: The Journal of Contemporary Social Work*, 394–402.
- Cole, C. H. & Barney, E. E. (1987) 'Safeguards and the therapeutic window—a group treatment strategy for adult incest survivors', *American Journal of Ortho-psychiatry*, **57**(4), 601–9.
- Gordy, P. L. (1983) 'Group work that supports adult victims of childhood incest', *Social Casework: The Journal of Contemporary Social Work*, 300–7.
- Hays, K. F. (1987) 'The conspiracy of silence revisited: group therapy with adult survivors of incest', *The Journal of Group Psychotherapy, Psychodrama and Sociometry*, 143–56.
- Swanson, L. & Biaggio, M. K. (1985) 'Therapeutic perspectives on father–daughter incest', *American Journal of Psychiatry*, **142**, 667–74.

7

YOUNG CHILDREN WHO EXHIBIT SEXUALLY ABUSIVE BEHAVIOUR

Carol Dey and Bobbie Print

This chapter examines the problem of prepubescent children (approximately 10 years of age and under), who are sexually abusive towards other children. Research into and recorded clinical experience of children who exhibit this behaviour are notably lacking in the current literature and consequently there are very few protocols or approaches to which practitioners can refer for guidance. A further difficulty is the lack of a common language. For example can we or should we refer to such young children as abusers? This terminology implies a set of characteristics which are identified with adult offenders who have developed abusive patterns of behaviour in order to gratify sexual and other needs. For most young children who exhibit inappropriate sexual behaviour such patterns cannot be readily identified. We must therefore be cautious in using defining terms which a child may carry throughout childhood and beyond. Whilst it is important that abusive behaviour must be recognised, identified and addressed it is essential that each child is regarded primarily as a child, with needs for affection, care and support. By employing such a perspective we are then able to label the sexually abusive behaviour as the problem rather than the child. For these reasons we refer throughout this chapter to 'children who exhibit sexually abusive behaviour' or 'children who abuse' rather than child abusers.

Studies such as those by Longo and McFadin (1981)[1] have demonstrated that a majority of sex offenders began their sexually abusive behaviours as early as seven years of age and that they progressed from less serious to more serious sexual offences. There is also a correlation between the seriousness of the offences committed by adolescent and adult offenders and the degree of abuse they suffered in childhood. Johnson (1988)[2] suggests that these findings should cause considerable concern about children who abuse:

> The high incidence of sexual victimisation in this population, . . . the seriousness of their offences, and their young age bring together a constellation of circumstances which may portend even more serious behaviour as they mature.

Our recent experience indicates a significant increase in the demand for consultation and direct work in cases of young children who abuse, some as young as four years of age. These extra demands are unlikely to reflect a sudden increase in the incidence of such behaviour. Rather, they result from the cascading effects of increased public and professional awareness of signs and symptoms of child sexual abuse. It appears, however, that this area of work presents practitioners and carers with particular difficulties and dilemmas. For example: How do we define abusive behaviour in children? How could we respond? Is it not better to allow the child to 'grow out' of the behaviour than to overreact? If we do respond, what therapeutic approaches and methods can be used?

A dearth of knowledge has resulted in a confused and haphazard response to young children who abuse. Professionals are unclear and anxious about how to respond and thus it appears that little therapeutic work is undertaken. The children's behaviour is often denied, ignored, or punished. Such responses can be costly in emotional and financial terms. For example, children in the care of a local authority who display abusive behaviour often experience placement breakdowns with many consigned to long-term institutional care due to the difficulties in finding suitable foster or adoptive homes.

The remainder of this chapter reviews some of the information that is available regarding children who exhibit abusive behaviour and uses case examples to demonstrate a preliminary framework we have developed.

RECOGNITION OF THE PROBLEM

Professional and public awareness and understanding of child sexual abuse has developed considerably over recent years and is reflected in the dramatic increase in professional training, joint working and arrangements for service delivery. The importance of therapeutic help for victims of abuse and their families is more widely recognised and work with adult perpetrators is now seen by many as a high priority. So far, however, there is no consensus on the approach to take with adolescent sex offenders. Whilst many professionals recognise the need for some form of intervention to try and prevent adolescent offenders from committing further abuse, there is some resistance to the idea of 'labelling' them as sex offenders and involving them in the criminal justice system. The argument that some, if not all, of these young people are simply experimenting sexually and will grow out of offending behaviour, is still a commonly held attitude. Such views are in contrast with research findings that show that many young sex offenders go on to commit further abuse in adulthood (Groth, 1979;[3] Abel *et al*, 1985[4]).

Given the difficulties in achieving a consensus as to how we should regard and respond to adolescents who abuse, it is not then surprising to discover that the increase in reports of prepubescent children who abuse has produced a variety of confused responses. (National Children's Homes Committee of Inquiry, 1991).[5] Understandably, professionals struggle to acknowledge the idea that young children sexually abuse other children. The idea that children can exhibit behaviour that produces such repulsion and anger when displayed by adults, causes considerable emotional turmoil for many people. The preliminary report of the National Adolescent Perpetrator Network (1988)[6] explained:

> In a society which denies all sexuality in childhood and attempts to repress sexual behaviour in adolescence, it is not surprising that we should minimize and deny sexual offending by children.

This denial together with a lack of knowledge regarding what is normal child sexual behaviour, a fear of overreacting and resistance to label children as abusers frequently leads to an apparent paralysis on the part of professionals. The result is that abusive behaviour is excused or ignored in the hope that it will go away, or more commonly, professionals' and carers' anxieties are raised but they often lack confidence in how to appropriately respond. An example of this involved David.

> At five years of age, David was referred by his headteacher because of his sexually aggressive behaviour towards other boys in school. David sexually abused two smaller boys in the school toilets by forcing them to touch his penis and put his penis in their mouths. He was found during this activity by a teacher.
>
> David was interviewed by social workers and disclosed that he and his three-year-old brother, Peter, had been abused by their paternal uncle. David's parents believed him and protected both their children from the abuser. A case conference recommended that David be offered therapy regarding his own abuse but no recommendations were made regarding his abusive behaviour.
>
> David engaged in a series of individual therapeutic sessions with a social

worker. These focused on reassuring him that he was not responsible for his abuse, helping him to express his feelings about his abuser and improving his self-image and self-protection skills. After six sessions, David's parents and his school reported that his behaviour had improved and he no longer presented difficulties. The social worker advised the parents on how to continue to reassure and support David and the case was closed. Six months later the family approached Social Services and requested that David be received into care as his parents had discovered that he had repeatedly sexually abused his brother, Peter, and the two-year-old son of a neighbour.

David's circumstances reflect a growing number of referrals to child protection agencies regarding young children who exhibit abusive behaviour and in our experience the response by professionals to David and his family is not uncommon. The professional system is geared to respond to young children who are victims of abuse rather than those who display abusive behaviour. Children who fall into both categories are likely, as in David's case, to be viewed primarily as victims, since there are no procedures to guide responses to children who abuse. In many cases, the expectation appears to be that work with children on their victim issues will positively impact on and prevent their abusive behaviours.

Experience derived from cases such as David's suggests that often this is not effective. Specific work that focuses directly on a child's abusive behaviour is also required.

EXPLORATION OR EXPLOITATION?

It is generally accepted within the range of normal behaviour that young children show curiosity and interest in each others genitals and participate in games such as 'I'll show you mine if you show me yours'. So at what point should we consider a child's sexual behaviour to be inappropriate or abusive and how should we judge what sort of intervention is required?

One of the greatest stumbling blocks in being able to answer such questions stems from our lack of knowledge regarding children's normal sexual development. An example of professionals' lack of agreement about 'normal' sexual behaviour in children is shown in Boat and Everson's (1986)[7] study of 6–12-year-old children's behaviour with anatomically correct dolls. This study showed that professionals generally agreed that staring at and touching the doll's genitals was normal, but there was less agreement when children engaged in other activities with the dolls. Police officers tended to regard any display of sexual activity with the dolls as abnormal, whereas demonstrations of penetration were seen as normal by many physicians. Professionals even failed to agree about whether using the dolls to show vaginal or anal penetration, or oral-genital contact, was normal for two to five-year-old children.

Ryan (1990a)[8] defined the range of sexual behaviour of children into four categories:

1. *'Normal'*—includes: genital or reproduction conversations with peers, exploratory games, imitating seduction (kissing or flirting), occasional masturbation, sexual language or jokes with peers.
2. *'Yellow Flag'* (some concern)—includes: preoccupation with sexual themes or masturbation, displays of inappropriate sexual knowledge, sexually explicit conversations with peers, attempts to expose other's genitals, mutual or group masturbation, simulated foreplay with toys or peers.
3. *'Red Flag'* (high concern)—includes: sexually explicit conversations with significantly younger children, touching genitals of others, simulated intercourse with toys, peers or animals.
4. *'No Question'* (clearly abusive)—includes: oral, vaginal or anal penetration of dolls, children or animals, touching another's genitals using force, simulated intercourse with peers with clothing off, any genital injury not explained by an accidental cause.

Although such categorisations are useful as initial indicators of situations which should cause concern, taken alone they are not often sufficient to fully assess an individual case where several factors must be considered in order to determine whether a child's behaviour is abusive. Work with adolescent sex offenders has led to the development of criteria which can be used to differentiate explorative behaviour from exploitative behaviour. The criteria most commonly applied are those of consent, equality and authority. Whilst these criteria can be useful when examining the sexual behaviour of younger children, they do require extension and adaptation.

It is commonly held that children are unable to give informed consent to sexual behaviour with adults since they are not sufficiently emotionally mature to fully comprehend the implications of that consent. However, when young children demonstrate sexual interest in each other we acknowledge their ability to consent to mutual exploration or experimentation. In some circumstances though, it is difficult to ascertain what form of consent was given. Ryan (1990b)[9] suggested that in order to determine whether 'consent' was genuine, informed and freely given, and not merely co-operation or compliance, it is important to determine: (i) that children understood what was being proposed; (ii) how this might vary from their 'normal' standards of behaviours, i.e. their cultural, familial or peer group standards; (iii) that they were aware of the consequences of their involvement, for example how their parents might react; (iv) that they had a true choice about whether to give their consent or whether the withholding of their agreement might have resulted in negative repercussions.

It is also important to determine the power relationship between the children involved. Inequalities in power are often identified by differences in age or size. Whilst it is likely that most children who abuse are older than their victims, in our experience it is not uncommon to learn that some children are abusing peers or those from an older age group. Pierce and Pierce (1987)[10] found a number of children who abused were younger than their victims. They commented, 'that defining an offence in terms of an age difference between the victim and the offender may overlook many offences.'

In addition to obvious inequalities of age and size it is also important to explore more subtle issues such as the power of peer status. For example, children who have status because of their popularity or because they are the leader of a game may be in a position to coerce others.

Ryan (1990a)[11] suggests that the range of coercion/pressure in children's sexual behaviour can be summarised as follows: normal behaviour—no coercion, no pressure, fun; yellow flag behaviour (concern)—manipulation, trickery, peer pressure, secrecy; red flag (high concern)—coercion, threats, bribes, secrecy; no question—physical force, weapon threat, violence.

It is also important to consider whether a behaviour is persistent. Normal exploratory behaviour tends to be short-lived whereas exploitative behaviour is often repetitive and interest increases rather than diminishes. Abusive behaviour may also escalate in its seriousness. Such behaviour is definitely not play. Weihe (1990)[12] in a study of sibling abuse reported that sexualised behaviour was often accompanied by violence.

Although young children playing sexually explorative games may do so in private and may be embarrassed if found, there is rarely an organised secrecy to their activities and they do not usually exhibit fear or high anxiety if discovered. In cases where one child coerces another into secrecy by use of threats or bribery it is indicative of an abuse of power and should be regarded as a symptom of abusive behaviour.

Complications in defining exploitative behaviour also arise in cases of non-contact sexual behaviour, for example, exhibitionism. This is often excluded or ignored. Whilst we should not identify a young child's uninhibited innocence and lack of embarrassment about nakedness with sexual behaviour, we must be concerned about children who repeatedly appear to expose their genitals for the apparent effect it has on others.

In summary we would recommend that in order to assess whether a child's behaviour is explorative or exploitative it is necessary to consider the following issues:

(a) Why has the child's behaviour caused concern and to whom?
(b) What preceded the behaviour? Was it planned or spontaneous?
(c) Was the behaviour age inappropriate?
(d) In what context did the behaviour occur?
(e) Did the other child give informed and true consent?
(f) Was the behaviour persistent? Has the abuser been confronted about his behaviour previously?
(g) What was the power differential between the children involved?
(h) Were overt aggression or threats used?
(i) Did the child attempt to ensure secrecy?
(j) What was the experience of and effects on the receiving child?
(k) What was the abusing child's reaction to what occurred?

CURRENT KNOWLEDGE

The development of a professional response to prepubescent children who exhibit abusive behaviour is hampered by many issues in addition to those outlined above. These include a lack of knowledge regarding incidence, causal factors, treatment methods and outcomes. Whilst information regarding adult sex offenders has pointed the direction for the development of approaches to work with adolescent offenders, it is much more difficult to make links with young children who abuse. The professional response to adult and adolescent sex offenders is based on the understanding that abusers engage in illegal behaviour in order to meet various needs including those for power and sexual gratification. Abusers are normally aware that what they have done is wrong although they need help to assume full responsibility for their behaviour. These issues are often much less clear with very young children who may appear to be simply replicating behaviour they have experienced or witnessed.

Incidence

Whilst there is evidence from studies of adolescent abusers that many commence their sexually exploitative behaviour at a much earlier age (Friedrich *et al*, 1986),[13] little is known about the incidence or characteristics of prepubescent abusive behaviour. In the UK, children under 10 years of age fall below the age of criminal responsibility and are not reflected in criminal statistics. Again, resistance by child protection agencies to label abusive behaviour in young children affects the accuracy of statistics from child protection registers. Thus, whilst there appears to be a growing demand from practitioners for information and advice about responding to very young children who abuse, we do not have reliable data concerning the incidence of the problem in the UK.

Studies conducted in the USA provide some information on incidence. Kelly *et al* (1991)[14] in their study of 16–21-year-old students found that 1 per cent of those who reported sexual abuse in childhood indicated that their abuser was another child. Pierce and Pierce (1987)[15] in a study of juvenile (6–17 years) abusive behaviour amongst siblings found that 30 per cent were under 14 years of age. Longo (1982)[16] evaluated 17 adolescent sex offenders and found that 76 per cent had committed an assault before the age of 12. Cantwell (1988)[17] reported that 3–4 cases per week involving alleged perpetrators under the age of 10 years were referred to the investigating authorities in Denver, Colorado.

There is an imperative need for further research into the incidence of children who exhibit sexually abusive behaviour. For example, we could find no reference in the literature to the gender of young children who abuse. Our clinical experience suggests that there is not a significant majority of boys referred for exhibiting sexually abuse behaviour, which is in contrast to the research and clinical experience of those engaged in work with adolescent and adult sex offenders. It is also essential that we increase our awareness of indicators which identify those children who are at risk of continuing their abusive behaviour into adolescence and adulthood.

The victims of child abusers

Although research on adolescent abusers indicates that a large majority of victims are not relatives (Becker *et al*, 1986),[18] Johnson (1988)[19] indicates that almost half the victims of the children who abuse in her study were siblings or extended family members. In a later study of female children who had abused (Johnson, 1989),[20] 77 per cent had abused children in their families. Johnson surmises that this may be due to the lack of mobility that younger children have. She points out that it is important that parents are made aware of the vulnerability of young siblings, cousins and other relatives who have unsupervised contact with a child who is known to have abused. She suggests that all young siblings in these situations should receive prevention training.

A further difference between adolescent and prepubescent children who abuse relates to the type of coercion used. Johnson (1988)[21] found that younger children tended more often to use verbal threats compared to adolescents who resorted more to physical aggression.

Child abusers' prior victimisation

Only a proportion of adolescent and adult abusers have been identified as sexually abused themselves (Seghorn et al, 1987;[22] Becker et al, 1986[23]). Our experience of work with approximately 20 prepubescent children who have abused is that they had all been sexually abused or had witnessed sexual abuse within their family. This finding is reflected in some of the available studies that addressed this issue. In a study of 47 male abusers, aged from 4–13 years, Johnson (1988)[24] found that 49 per cent stated that they had been sexually abused. The findings indicated that the younger the child the higher the rate of reported own abuse. Whilst a number of the older boys did not disclose their own abuse, staff working with the boys strongly suspected that each of them had been abused. A subsequent study by Johnson (1989)[25] of 13 young females who had abused found that all had been sexually abused by someone they knew.

Can we then assume that prior sexual victimisation or the witnessing of sexual abuse is a causal factor of sexually abusive behaviour in young children? There are a number of studies that indicate a correlation between a history of sexual abuse and subsequent sexual aggression (Finkelhor, 1979;[26] Ryan et al, 1987;[27] Friedrich, 1988;[28] Smith and Israel, 1987[29]). Our own clinical experience and the studies referred to above indicate that a large majority of very young children who have exhibited abusive behaviour have experienced or witnessed sexual abuse although the small samples involved in these studies are not sufficient to validate the findings. There is certainly a pressing need for further research on this issue. If, as we suspect, it is the case that most young children who abuse others have themselves been directly or indirectly sexually abused, then there are considerable implications for agencies who are responsible for child protection, preventative and therapeutic services.

The effects of prior abuse

If we accept early indications that most young children who demonstrate abusive behaviour have been abused then a number of questions are raised. Why do some young victims of abuse go on to abuse whilst others do not? How can we identify those who are at risk of developing abuse tendencies and what are the implications for therapeutic work?

Obviously the fact that a child has been abused does not necessarily lead to the conclusion that he or she will go on to abuse others. As far as we are aware, a vast majority of victims of sexual abuse do not abuse others. It follows therefore that whilst we can generalise about both the long-term and short-term effects of sexual abuse, a careful assessment of each abused child is essential to identify the needs of individual children. A number of factors are known to influence the degree of trauma suffered by children and the coping mechanisms they adopt. These include the nature and duration of the victim's relationship with the abuser (Groth, 1979;[30] Friedrich *et al*, 1986[31]), the response of adult care givers following disclosure (Sanford, 1980;[32] Fromuth, 1983[33]), the severity of the abuse (Wyatt and Mickey, 1988),[34] the opportunity to ventilate feelings (Silver and Wortman, 1980),[35] the level of previously developed coping strategies (Bulman and Wortman, 1977).[36] It is not clear exactly which of these factors, if any, relate directly to children's abusive behaviours but Friedrich *et al* (1986)[37] found that frequency, severity, sex of child and perpetrator were factors most associated with internalised (passive) behaviour. Externalised (aggressive or controlling) behaviour was determined by duration, perpetrator, time elapsed since the last assault and sex of child. A majority of male victims of sexual abuse externalised their behaviour whilst a majority of females internalised their behaviour (Friedrich *et al*, 1986).[38] Girls who do not follow this pattern tended to have a close relationship with their abuser and suffered a high frequency and more serious forms of sexual abuse. Friedrich in a later study (1988)[39] concluded, however, that the relationship between behavioural outcomes and abuse specific variables is not unitary or precise.

Hartman and Burgess's model of the 'Information Processing of Trauma' (1988)[40] indicates that there are several routes to both maladaptive and adaptive outcomes in response to trauma. The specific coping strategies adopted by a child may include dissociation, denial, repression and splitting. Some coping mechanisms tend to increase the risk of problem behaviours whilst others have a decreasing effect. For example, some children who cope by use of 'trauma reply', whereby they re-enact the abuse in their minds, may learn to identify with the abuser. Others may develop distorted beliefs or aggressive behaviour to cover feelings of vulnerability; such children may be at risk of displaying abusive behaviours towards others.

Other theorists suggest different explanations for some victims who develop abusive behaviours. Finkelhor's traumagenic dynamics model of child sexual abuse (1985)[41] suggests that an abuser's experience of sexual events in childhood may initiate the motivation to abuse. For example, 'Because of the rewards, sexually abused children learn to use sexual behaviour, appropriate or inappropriate, as a strategy for manipulating others to get their needs met'. La Fontaine (1990)[42] observed, ' . . . boys who are abused themselves, or know that their sisters have been abused by their father, have been given a practical lesson by an adult in the association between masculine power and sex'. Terry and Rogers (1984)[43] noted that the male victims of sexual abuse were more inclined than females to attempt to deal with their victimisation and gain mastery by over-identifying with the offender and modelling his behaviour.

It would seem, then, that abusive behaviour in young children is likely to be a learned response to the trauma of being sexually abused. Thus feelings of powerlessness, resulting from abuse, are mastered by externalising behaviour. The controlled seeks to control. The deviant sexual behaviour in which the children have been forced to participate, or made to observe, are accommodated in order for them to cope (Summit, 1983)[44] with the result that the child's cognitions are distorted by what Finkelhor and Browne (1985)[45] described as 'traumagenic sexualisation'. This develops into age inappropriate sexual behaviour, with powerful abusive and controlling actions by which the child attempts to mitigate its feelings of helplessness. These attempts at mastery take place within the context of an abusive milieu in which the perpetrator manipulates, coerces and controls within the bounds of secrecy. Ryan (1989)[46] aptly observes:

> The isolation imposed by secrecy supports the development of irrational thinking in the child, which may erode the victim's self-esteem and allow the guilt and confusion to grow without external feedback. Within such isolation, the victim feels most powerless, and anger may be translated into fantasies of retaliation in order to gain control. As fantasy becomes planning—whether consciously or unconsciously—the victim's aim is to regain the power and control that was lost in the experience of being a victim. Distorted thinking at this point may support a progression into functional coping style, negative behaviour, or criminal offending.

Prior victimisation is not the only factor that must be considered when assessing a young child who has abused. It has already been mentioned that the attitude of carers has important consequences for a child. Further risk factors identified in the literature include:

1. Abnormal sexual environments including families where sexual boundaries were too rigid or too relaxed. (Smith and Israel, 1987)[47]
2. Sexualised models of compensation where sex is seen as a comfort in difficult times. (Ryan and Steele, 1989)[48]
3. Parental history of sexual or physical abuse. (Johnson and Berry, 1989)[49]
4. History of drug or alcohol abuse in family. (Johnson and Berry, 1989)[50]
5. Inconsistent care. (Prentky, 1984)[51]
6. Parental loss. (Ryan et al, 1987)[52]
7. Lack of confidence. (Gilgun, 1988)[53]
8. Lack of social skills and maladaptive coping skills. (Ryan, 1989)[54]
9. Attention deficit. (Friederich, 1988)[55]

THERAPEUTIC WORK WITH YOUNG CHILDREN WHO ABUSE

As in all work with children, a therapeutic alliance is an essential structure. Within this context the practitioner must strike a balance between validating the child as a victim and addressing the sexually aggressive behaviour. It is important to be able to distinguish these two elements and bring a degree of clarity to this work. Just as therapeutic work with adult perpetrators differs from that with adult victims, practitioners need to be discriminating as to which of the therapeutic methods they choose. They must ensure that they are facilitating and validating without promoting unintended consequences, particularly reinforcement of the abusive behaviour. It is important therefore to address issues of trust, low self-esteem, guilt and anger whilst giving attention to the child's problem behaviour.

Therapeutic models

Ryan (1990b)[56] suggested that young children who have abused have developed similar cyclic patterns and thinking errors to adolescent offenders and therefore recommended a treatment model based on an abuse cycle. This has similar characteristics to the models developed for adult and adolescent sex offenders (Wolfe, 1984;[57] Ryan et al, 1987[58]). In our view, however, it is important to remember that there are significant differences between adolescents and young children who abuse. Treatment models for adolescent and adult abusers are underpinned by recognition that the abuser knows that what he did was wrong and that he must therefore accept responsibility for the abuse. Children frequently lack the maturity to consider or understand the effects of their actions. They may impulsively engage in behaviour with little or no thought as to the consequences and some very young children may not be aware of the 'wrongness' of their behaviour. Gordon, Schroeder and Abrams (1990)[59] demonstrated that sexually abused children, under seven years of age, had no greater under-standing of sexuality than non-abused children and may therefore be unable to discriminate between appropriate and inappropriate behaviour. Many young children who abuse are acting out learned experience and have internalised a degree of distorted thinking and rationalisation imposed upon them by their abusers. Thus in some cases the child may believe that such behaviour is normal, and in these circumstances children cannot be expected to take 'responsibility' in the same way that older offenders are. If they are confronted too harshly and punitively there is a risk that they will become further confused, anxious and as such may distance and dissociate themselves further from their behaviour. Young children who abuse should be helped to understand that their behaviour was wrong and there are negative consequences. They must be helped to recognise that they are accountable for their behaviour, but this must be done in an atmosphere of support and understanding, and this may take some time to achieve in view of the younger child's memory retention and cognitive ability.

A further difference between young children and adults who abuse concerns the motivation for their behaviour. Whilst it is accepted that young children who exhibit abusive behaviour are attempting to exert power and control over their victims, possibly in order to overcome feelings of powerlessness, confusion and low self-esteem, young children are rarely sexually aroused or gratified by their abusive behaviour. Johnson and Berry (1989)[60] described the girls in their study as generally not looking for orgasm or sexual pleasure as a result of their abusive behaviours. Instead, they were looking to decrease feelings of anger, confusion and anxiety. Although this association of abusive behaviours with stress relief may lead subsequently to deviant patterns of arousal in later life, most young children are unlikely to have developed such patterns and their motivation to abuse is therefore less complex.

A therapeutic framework

Since current professional knowledge of children who abuse is partial and incomplete there is a need for considerable further work and research before accepted models, methods and approaches can be identified and elucidated. In the meantime we have attempted to develop a 'preliminary therapeutic framework' based on our experience and the available literature. This is intended to provide an approach for working with this problem, and offers a basis for further discussion.

Almost all of the children who exhibited abusive behaviour we have seen have felt angry, confused and anxious. They have been physically aggressive with their peers and have few peer-group friends. It is important that these children are helped to understand their predicament, develop empathy for their victims, recognise appropriate boundaries, and to master new skills in problem solving, anger management and social skills.

The 'preliminary framework' is a multifactorial approach based on a range of theoretical perspectives and therapeutic techniques. We found that an important early step is to explore the child's experiences, feelings and confused or distorted thinking over a number of sessions. The information gathered, together with factual accounts provided by carers and professionals, form the basis of an assessment of the child's therapeutic needs and the priority of issues to be addressed.

Further sessions are then used to develop a strategy for meeting the child's identified needs. The factors to be addressed in the later sessions include: an educational component which involves the provision of accurate sexual information, limit setting, victim awareness and behaviour management. Our work with young children who abuse differs from that with young victims of abuse in that we are more directive, and only follow the child's agenda if it is appropriate to the therapeutic plan. It is essential to include the child's parents or carers in the therapeutic plan as their behaviour and responses are crucial to the child's progress.

Exploring the child's world

Initial therapeutic engagement with children who exhibit abusive behaviour is similar to the process adopted with child victims of abuse. They must be reassured that they are supported and understood. However, in cases where one child has abused another child it is not appropriate to accept unquestioningly their accounts of their abusive behaviour. Children who abuse may engage in denial in the same way that older abusers do. They may also exhibit distorted beliefs and attitudes about their behaviour. It is important that the practitioner does not collude with any denial but informs the child that they know of the problem behaviour and hope to be able to help avoid repetition of such behaviour.

It is through play that children express themselves best and the content of their play can often provide the practitioner with information regarding a child's experience, feelings, thoughts and fantasies. Careful attention should be given to the information a child gives in the initial exploratory sessions. Their feelings should be accepted and noted for further attention at a later stage if necessary, but negative behaviours should be addressed and the child helped to understand why such behaviour is unacceptable. Similarly, distorted thought patterns must be confronted and alternative perceptions offered.

In many cases it requires three or four exploratory sessions with a child in order to establish rapport and to determine the factors to be covered. The assessment process must be continued throughout the work with a child so plans and methods can be adjusted as necessary.

The sequence in which factors are dealt with will depend upon the needs of the individual child but generally information provision and boundary setting are likely to be high on the agenda in order that a child understands the context of their behaviour.

The factors that are generally included in a therapeutic plan are outlined below and case examples used to demonstrate methods and application:

Sex education and boundary setting. It is important that a child who has abused others is provided with sex education in a clear and direct manner. Children who are confused about their own and other's sexual behaviour often lack factual information about sex and related matters. They are unable to determine where the boundaries of appropriate behaviour lie. Children who have been sexually abused may develop highly sexualised behaviour but as Gordon *et al* (1990)[61] pointed out, they rarely have the sexual knowledge to place this behaviour in context and 'may need more information about sexuality than otherwise might be appropriate for young children'. The nature of the educational input will depend on what the child knows already and parental attitudes toward sexual matters. In most cases the involvement of parents or carers in this work will be necessary and helpful. Practitioners can make use of books such as *A Touching Book* (Hindman, 1985)[62] and *The Body Book* (Rayner, 1978)[63] to help in the education process, but they must be careful to avoid over-burdening a child with unnecessary information.

The following case example is used to demonstrate the importance of boundary setting for young children:

Kim was a four-year-old girl who had been sexually abused by her grandfather; this had not been reported to professionals. Instead, Kim's mother, a single parent, moved several miles from her father in order to protect Kim. Kim was later referred via her GP following her mother's concern about Kim's abuse of her two-year-old sister. Kim was found by her mother inserting pencils into her sister's vagina and although the mother did not reprimand or punish her, Kim became withdrawn and began masturbating to the extent that she made herself sore. When Kim started in therapy she was difficult to engage, preferring to spend much of the time during the initial session in a corner playing on her own or staring out of a window. By the third session, however, she began to accept the worker's involvement in some of her play. Kim was very controlling in her manner and would only take part in activities where she could role-play the adult and the worker played a child. It seemed that Kim was only comfortable if she made the rules and that by role-playing an adult she did not have to be concerned with complying with an adult's expectations.

By the sixth session Kim was eager to attend. She remained very controlling and began to verbally chastise the therapist if she did not comply. This continued until she reached such a pitch that she screamed at the worker telling her she was 'a very bad child' who never did anything right. After this outburst Kim became very apologetic and asked the worker if she wanted Kim to rub her 'wee-wee' (vagina) to make her feel better. The worker explained that she did not allow little children to rub her 'wee-wee' as it was a private part and it was not right that children touch grown-ups' private parts in that way. Kim then sat very quietly and although the worker was concerned that she may have made Kim feel hurt and rejected, she allowed her the time-out on her own in the corner. Kim eventually made an approach and asked if it was because her grandad had done that to her that her mummy had been so cross with him.

After this session the worker helped Kim to understand about the private parts of her body, appropriate and inappropriate touching and why she should not touch the private parts of other children. Her mother was shown that whilst it was important for her to support and reassure Kim it was also important that she should not be afraid of setting proper boundaries for the child. If Kim crossed these boundaries then she should be stopped and an explanation offered as to why the behaviour was inappropriate. Kim was helped to develop assertiveness skills and to ask what she should do in situations where she felt unsure. The improvement in her self-confidence became apparent in later sessions when she became happy to take on the child's role in games and appeared much more comfortable in allowing the worker to adopt the adult role.

For many young children the opportunity to express their confusion and to receive clear information about boundaries represents a significant proportion of their therapeutic needs.

Victim awareness. Young children who have received poor emotional care may find it difficult to empathise with others. For some children the special attention given by their abuser as part of the 'grooming' or preparation process may have been interpreted as a positive experience and in these circumstances the child may identify with her abuser. It is essential that children who have abused understand that one of the most negative consequences of their behaviour is the impact on their victims. In addition to providing a child with relevant information, their ability to empathise can often be enhanced by referring to the negative outcomes from their own abuse or other situations when they felt vulnerable. If a child is known to have been abused, it is often at this stage that the child's experiences and feelings of victimisation are fully explored and their coping strategies identified. It is of course essential that the worker empathises with the child regarding their victim experiences and reassures the child that he/she was not to blame for what happened to them. At the same time however, it is important not to collude with any distorted thinking or rationalisation the child presents and to continually compare and comment on their experiences as a victim with those of a child who has abused. It often requires considerable time and support to help a child understand that they should not feel guilt in relation to their own abuse but must be accountable for their own abusive actions.

Behaviour management and anger control. Friedrich *et al* (1986)[64] reported that victims of sexual abuse in the age range of 6–12 years demonstrated greater incidents of aggressive, antisocial and under-controlled behaviour than either younger or older victims. Ryan (1989)[65] points out that many teenage sex offenders report first practising offender behaviours and developing offender thinking during that same age span. From this we can assume that tackling these feelings and behaviours in therapeutic work with children who abuse is important in diverting them from becoming adolescent or adult abusers.

Techniques which allow expression of feelings such as anger and aggression are valuable and cathartic for victimised children who have internalised their emotions. Such methods, whilst generally accepted, do require careful planning, however, if used with children who have abused, who of course are already externalising their emotions inappropriately. Feshbach (1964)[66] and Goldstein (1987)[67] have demonstrated that expression of angry feelings by acting out aggressive behaviour is not always cathartic and is more likely to increase such behaviour than reduce it. Similarly, Terr (1983)[68] in her work with 'post traumatic play' has shown that re-enactment of the traumatic events can often reinforce feelings of anxiety rather than dissipating them. The 'interactive approach' should therefore be adapted to incorporate cognitive learning strategies so that problem-solving techniques and appropriate coping mechanisms are introduced and rehearsed. Opportunities to act out feelings and aggressive fantasies should be limited to the initial exploration sessions. In following sessions such behaviours should be confronted and the child helped to identify the origins of angry feelings, the negative consequences of aggression, together with alternative ways of coping. Danny's involvement in therapeutic work demonstrates these techniques.

Danny was a seven-year-old who had been sexually abused for several years by his father. He and his three siblings were placed in separate foster homes. Initially Danny settled well into his new home and he became very fond of his foster parents. The placement ended when Danny was found to have masturbated his younger foster brother and involved him in masturbating the family's dog. Danny was placed in a children's home where he received considerable support and caring but was advised to forgive and forget those who had harmed him in his past. Within a few months Danny had sexually abused young boys in the home and at school. Danny was said to be aggressive with his peers and had few friends. Therapeutic sessions with Danny commenced and initially involved play and observation. He avoided references of his family and focused intensely on acting out aggressive scenarios involving fantasy figures. He denied that he had sexually abused other children and was reluctant to talk about his own abuse. It was not until Danny was told that it was OK to feel angry with his father that he began to divulge the extent of his own abuse. He was informed by the worker that she knew of his abuse behaviour with other children and that it was important they talked about what had happened so that Danny could be helped to make sure he could avoid similar behaviour in the future. Danny's aggressive acting out was confronted and he was helped through role-play to consider the consequences for himself and others of his aggressive behaviour. Considerable work was required to help Danny develop victim empathy. This was achieved by encouraging him to think how the boys he had abused must have experienced similar feelings to those Danny felt when he was abused by his father.

Danny wanted to be accepted and liked by his peers. He described how he felt angry and upset when excluded or laughed at by other children. He was helped by use of story-telling and cartoon drawings to consider more appropriate ways of responding to his peers. He rehearsed new social skills suggested by the worker. These new skills were then reinforced by acting out stories where Danny practised assertive behaviour and more rewarding communications with peers. Danny also learnt to recognise how he could avoid risky situations when he felt angry and how thinking of consequences could lead to more appropriate responses.

Following several months' work with Danny and with the involvement of his residential key-worker Danny's behaviour in the home and at school showed significant improvement. He appeared to be more relaxed and his abusive behaviour towards others had ceased.

Parental responses and behaviour. On its own, individual therapeutic work with a child who has abused is rarely sufficient to effect significant change. The influence of attitudes and behaviour of carers on the child's behaviour is always likely to have a greater significance. Thus it is essential to involve the child's carers or at least keep them informed during the therapy. Sometimes separate sessions may be required with carers who are unable to provide their child with the necessary levels of understanding, support or appropriate role models.

The following case study, concerning Michael, describes the importance of involving parents in the therapeutic process.

Michael, a six-year-old, exhibited this confusion about his sexual behaviour. He was referred after his parents complained that he had sexually abused a number of peers at school and at home. He had asked classmates to touch his penis and had attempted anal intercourse with one boy. Michael had been interviewed by his headteacher, teacher, the police and social workers prior to his referral, but had consistently denied that he had done anything wrong. He was dealt with punitively by his parents and his school and received a warning from the police.

During initial individual therapeutic sessions Michael continued to deny his abusive behaviour and ignored all references to it. He appeared quite detached from the incident. He was a creative child and enjoyed the sessions, which in the early stages, involved trust-building and information gathering. His level of sexual knowledge was assessed and appeared to be age-appropriate, though he had very little knowledge of sexuality. Prior to the second session Michael's father reported witnessing Michael thrusting himself provocatively against a little girl his own age. Michael was punished by his father for the incident and appeared very sullen and withdrawn when he arrived for the next session. The latest incident was used as a point of discussion and although Michael was reluctant to do so, he was able to express his feelings about being chastised. This led on to Michael using drawings and puppets to talk about a fictional boy who had nightmares and who was afraid of monsters. He was reassured by the worker that it was OK to be frightened and not something to be ashamed of. Michael suggested that the little boy deal with the monster in an extremely aggressive way. His comments were reframed into helping him devise more appropriate ways of managing conflict. He was asked to identify a number of issues: Who could support the little boy; who could he trust? Who could he talk to when he was sad and unhappy because of the monsters? Michael went on to role-play telling his parents about the monster and the dreams and in the role-play the parents listened and were kind.

Following the session the worker discussed with Michael's parents her concerns about Michael feeling confused and isolated. She suggested that he had no understanding of his sexualised behaviour and that their punitive attitude might be compounding his confusion and apparent detachment. They were asked to view Michael as a child who needed their support rather than a 'bad' boy. The parents agreed to co-operate but were very concerned the behaviour might continue.

In the following session Michael disclosed that a neighbour's 12-year-old boy had been sexually abusing him over the past two years. The nature of the abuse was quite serious involving the older boy physically forcing Michael to submit to masturbation and anal penetration.

Michael's parents were able to support him in appropriate ways to which he responded. He was able to talk to them about the details of his own abuse and was reassured that his abuser's behaviour was wrong. Further sessions with Michael and his parents provided Michael with age appropriate information about sexual behaviour, appropriate play and children's rights to have control over their bodies. Michael responded well in these sessions. There was no reported repetition of his sexualised behaviour.

Michael's case demonstrates how too punitive a response to young children who abuse can exacerbate the problem behaviour. Children are likely to become dissociated from their actions and may feel inhibited from discussing anything that they feel will lead to further punishment. Their confused understanding of what is acceptable or unacceptable may increase their feelings of anger and powerlessness and they may fantasise about making themselves feel better by further abusive behaviour.

GROUP THERAPY FOR YOUNG CHILDREN WHO ABUSE

Current literature offers little guidance about group work with young children who have exhibited sexually abusive behaviour. The writers are not aware of any groupwork programmes in this country. In the USA the SPARK (Support Program for Abuse Reactive Kids) was established in Los Angeles in 1985 and described by Johnson and Berry (1989).[69] The programme is designed for 4–13-year-old children who have engaged in sexually aggressive activities with other children.

Treatment comprises of group, individual and family therapy with the emphasis on groupwork as Johnson explains, 'It is not our aim to have the child perpetrator be able to interact one-to-one with an adult but to be able to be with other children without being sexually inappropriate with them.' Separate group programmes are conducted for children who have abused, their siblings and parents, with families often in treatment for up to a year.

The group for children who have abused discusses sexual issues and helps the children to recognise feelings that precede abuse and how to avoid acting on these feelings. Issues of trust, betrayal, responsibility, victimisation, perpetration, blame, assertion/aggression, cognitive distortions and sibling rivalry are examined and the children are taught skills such as problem solving, impulse control, anger management and task completion. The siblings groups aim to decrease feelings of resentment, anger, confusion and jealousy which may develop from the attention given to the brother/sister who has abused. Prevention skills are taught and the children are encouraged to discuss their feelings and problems.

The objectives of the parents' group are to reduce feelings of isolation and improve self-esteem. The parents often need to explore their feelings of anger, denial and confusion. They discuss their personal histories and many are found to have been physically or sexually abused themselves; these parents are shown how their own experience of abuse may affect their relationships with their children. A 'human sexuality' programme increases parents knowledge of normal sexual development and emphasis is placed on teaching parents to be careful that they do not set their children up to repeat their abusive behaviour. Individual sessions and family therapy are provided when necessary.

VICTIM THERAPY

Ryan (1989)[70] recommended that in the light of knowledge which links sexually abusive behaviour with sexual victimisation in childhood, the traditional therapeutic approach to work with victims of sexual abuse should be adapted to incorporate a perpetration prevention programme. The idea seems to warrant further attention but, as far as we can establish, very few therapeutic approaches appear to have been incorporated into such prevention programmes. This may, once again, reflect professional resistance to classifying and treating children's abusive behaviours.

CONCLUSIONS

The summary of the Committee of Inquiry into Children and Young People Who Abuse (1991)[71] states that;

> What seems clear is that the knowledge and experience of working with children or young people who abuse other children is still at a very early stage . . . Almost all participants recognised the limitations of our knowledge and therefore the need to be cautious about making statements and claims for treatment.

We are still at an early stage in developing our understanding of children who sexually abuse others. Whilst it is essential that we do not allow this lack of knowledge to deflect attempts to address the problem we must recognise that any programmes, models and methods currently presented are based largely on hypothesis and therefore open to question. However, without such programmes and studies to test their effectiveness together with further research into the area of normal and abnormal childhood psychosexual development, we cannot properly extend or improve our response to the problem of children who abuse.

REFERENCES

1. Longo, R. and McFadin B. (1981) 'Sexually inappropriate behaviour: development of the sexual offender', *Law and Order*, Dec: 21–23.
2. Johnson T. C. (1988) 'Child perpetrators—children who molest other children: preliminary findings', *Child Abuse and Neglect*, 12: 219–229.
3. Groth, N. (1979) *Men Who Rape: The Psychology of the Offender* (Plenum: New York).
4. Abel, C. G., Mittleman, M. S. and Becker, J. V. (1985) 'Sexual offenders: results of assessment and recommendations for treatment', in M. H. Ben-Aron, S. J. Huckle and C. D. Webster (eds.) *Clinical Criminology: The Assessment and Treatment of Criminal Behavior* (M & M Graphic: Toronto).
5. National Children's Homes (1991) *Summary of the Views Expressed in a Series of Regional Consultations*, Committee of enquiry into children and young people who abuse other children.
6. National Adolescent Perpetrator Network (1988) Preliminary Report from the

National Task Force on juvenile sexual offending, *Juvenile & Family Court Journal*, **39**(2).

7. Boat, B. and Everson M. (1986) 'Use of anatomically correct dolls in the evaluation of child sexual abuse', Paper presented at fourth national conference on the sexual victimization of children. New Orleans.

8. Ryan, G. (1990a) 'Range of sexual behaviour of children', Paper presented at ROTA national conference, Lancaster University.

9. Ryan, G. (1990b) 'Understanding and responding to the sexual behaviour of children', Paper presented at ROTA national conference, Lancaster University.

10. Pierce, L. H. and Pierce R. L. (1987) 'Incestuous victimization by juvenile sex offenders', *Journal of Family Violence*, 2(4), 351–364.

11. Ryan (1990a) *op. cit.*

12. Weihe, V. R. (1990) *Sibling Abuse: Hidden Physical, Emotional, and Sexual Trauma*, (Lexington Books: Lexington).

13. Friedrich, W. N., Urquiza, A. J., and Beilke, R. (1986) 'Behavioural problems in sexually abused young children', *Journal of Pediatric Psychology*, **11**: 47–57.

14. Kelly, L., Reagan, L. and Burton, S. (1991) *An Exploratory Study of the Prevalence of Sexual Abuse in a Sample of 16–21-Year-Olds*, Child Abuse Studies Unit, Polytechnic of North London.

15. Pierce, L. H. and Pierce, R. L. (1987) *op. cit.*

16. Longo, R. (1982) 'Sexual learning and experience among adolescent sexual offenders', *International Journal of Offender Therapy and Comparative Criminology*, **26**(3), 235–241.

17. Cantwell, H. B. (1988) 'Child sexual abuse: very young perpetrators', *Child Abuse and Neglect*, **12**, 579–582.

18. Becker, J. V., Cunningham-Rathner, J. and Kaplan, M. S. (1986) 'Adolescent sexual offenders, demographics, criminal and sexual histories and recommendations for reducing future offenses', *Journal of Interpersonal Violence*, **1**, 431–445.

19. Johnson, J. C. (1988) *op. cit.*

20. Johnson, J. C. (1989) 'Female child perpetrators: children who molest other children', *Child Abuse and Neglect*, **13**, 571–585.

21. Johnson, J. C. (1988) *op. cit.*

22. Seghorn, T., Boucher, R. and Prentky, R. (1987) 'Childhood sexual abuse in the lives of sexually aggressive offenders', *Journal of The American Academy of Child and Adolescent Psychiatry*, **26**(2), 262–267.

23. Becker, J. V., Kaplan, M. S., Cunningham-Rathner, J. and Kavoussi, R. 'Characteristics of adolescent incest perpetrators: Preliminary findings', *Journal of Family Violence*, **1**: 85–97.

24. Johnson, J. C. (1988) *op. cit.*

25. Johnson, J. C. (1989) *op. cit.*

26. Finkelhor, D. (1979) *Sexually Victimized Children* (Free Press: New York).

27. Ryan, G., Lane, S., Davies, J. and Isaac, C. (1987) 'Juvenile sex offenders: development and correction', *Child Abuse and Neglect*, **11**, 385–395.

28. Friedrich, W. N. (1988) 'Behavior problems in sexually abused children: an adaptational perspective', in G. E. Wyatt and G. J. Powell (eds.) *The Lasting Effects of Child Sexual Abuse* (Sage: Newbury Park, California).

29. Smith, H. and Israel, E. (1987) 'Sibling incest: a study of the dynamics of 25 cases', *Child Abuse and Neglect*, **11**, 101–108.
30. Groth, N. (1979) *op. cit.*
31. Friedrich, W. N., Urquiza, A. J. and Beilke, R. (1986) *op. cit.*
32. Sanford, L. T. (1980) *The Silent Children: A Parent's Guide to the Prevention of Child Sexual Abuse* (McGraw-Hill: New York).
33. Fromuth, M. E. (1983) 'The long term psychological impact of childhood sexual abuse', PhD thesis, Auburn University: Auburn, Alabama.
34. Wyatt, G. E. and Mickey, M. R. (1988) 'The support by parents and others as it mediates the effects of child sexual abuse: an exploratory study', in G. E. Wyatt and G. J. Powell (eds.) *The Lasting Effects of Child Sexual Abuse* (Sage: Newbury Park, California).
35. Silver, R. L. and Wortman, C. B. (1980) 'Coping with undesirable life events', in J. Garber and M. E. P. Seligman (eds.) *Human Helplessness: Theory and Applications* (Academic Press: New York).
36. Bulman, R. J. and Wortman, C. B. (1977) 'Attributions of blame and coping in the "real world": severe accident victims react to their lot', *Journal of Personality and Social Psychology*, **35**: 351–363.
37. Friedrich, W. N., Urquiza, A. J. and Beilke, R. (1986) *op. cit.*
38. *Ibid.*
39. Friedrich, W. N. (1988) 'Behavior problems in sexually abused children: an adaptational perspective', in G. E. Wyatt and G. J. Powell (eds.) *The Lasting Effects of Child Sexual Abuse* (Sage: Newbury Park, California).
40. Hartman, C. and Burgess, A. (1988) 'Information process of trauma', *Journal of Interpersonal Violence*, **3**(4).
41. Finkelhor, D. (1985) *Child Sexual Abuse: New Theory and Research* (Free Press: New York).
42. La Fontaine, J. (1990) *Child Sexual Abuse* (Polity Press: Cambridge).
43. Terry, I. and Rogers, C. M. (1984) 'Clinical intervention with boy victims of sexual abuse', in I. R. Stuart and J. G. Greer (eds.) *Victims of Sexual Aggression: Men, Women and Children* (Nostrand Reinhold: New York).
44. Summit, R. C. (1983) 'The child sexual abuse accommodation syndrome', *Child Abuse and Neglect*, **7**, 177–193.
45. Finkelhor, D. and Browne, A. (1985) 'The traumatic impact of child sexual abuse: a conceptualization', *American Journal of Orthopsychiatry*, **55**(4), 530–541.
46. Ryan, G. (1989) 'Victim to victimizer: rethinking victim treatment', *Journal of Interpersonal Violence*, **4**(3), 325–341.
47. Smith, H. and Israel, E. (1987) *op. cit.*
48. Ryan, G. and Steele, B. (1989) cited in Paper presented at ROTA national conference, Lancaster University (1990).
49. Johnson, T. C. and Berry, C. (1989) 'Children who molest: a treatment program', *Journal of Interpersonal Violence*, **4**(2), 185–203.
50. *Ibid.*
51. Prentky, P. (1984) 'Childhood physical and sexual abuse in the lives of sexually aggressive offenders', Paper presented at the Second National Conference for Family Violence Researchers, Durham, NH.

52. Ryan, G., Lane, S., Davies, J. and Issac, C. (1987) *op. cit.*
53. Gilgun, J. F. (1988) 'Factors which block the development of sexually abusive behaviors of adults abused and neglected in childhood', Paper presented at First National Conference on Male Victims and Offenders, Minneapolis, MN.
54. Ryan, G. (1989) *op. cit.*
55. Friedrich, W. N. (1988) *op. cit.*
56. Ryan, G. (1990b) *op. cit.*
57. Wolfe, S. C. (1984) 'A multi-factor model of deviant sexuality', Paper presented at Third International Conference on Victimology, Lisbon, Portugal.
58. Ryan, G., Lane, S., Davies, J. and Isaac, C. (1987) *op. cit.*
59. Gordon, B. N., Schroeder, C. S. and Abrams, J. M. (1990) 'Children's knowledge of sexuality: a comparison of sexually abused and nonabused children', *American Journal of Orthopsychiatry*, **60**(2), 250–257.
60. Johnson, T. C. and Berry, C. (1989) *op. cit.*
61. Gordon, B. N., Schroeder, C. S. and Abrams, J. M. (1990) *op. cit.*
62. Hindman, J. (1985) *A Touching Book* (Alexandria Associates: Ontario, Oregon).
63. Rayner, C. (1978) *The Body Book* (Piccolo: London).
64. Friedrich, W. N., Urquiza, A. J. and Beilke, R. (1986) *op. cit.*
65. Ryan, G. (1989) *op. cit.*
66. Feshbach, S. (1964) 'The function of aggression and the regulation of aggressive drive', *Psychological Review*, **72**: 257–272.
67. Goldstein, A. (1987) 'New directions in aggression reduction', in R. Hind and J. Grobel (eds.) *Aggression and War: Biological and Social Bases* (Cambridge University Press: New York).
68. Terr, L. C. (1983) 'Play therapy and psychic trauma: a preliminary report', in C. Schaefer and K. O'Conner (eds.) *Handbook of Play Therapy* (John Wiley & Sons: New York).
69. Johnson, T. C. and Berry, C. (1989) *op. cit.*
70. Ryan, G. (1989) *op. cit.*
71. National Children's Homes (1991) *op. cit.*

8

THERAPEUTIC ISSUES IN WORK WITH YOUNG SEXUALLY AGGRESSIVE CHILDREN

Anne Bannister

The previous chapter looked at the problem of young children who are sexually aggressive. When that chapter was written, only a few years ago, professionals were just beginning to face up to the implications of this behaviour in young children. It is a reflection of the explosion of interest in and knowledge of child sexual abuse in the last decade, that in the intervening period there has been more research and more interest in the problems of treating sexually aggressive young children.

Dey and Print remarked that there was a lack of literature on the subject and many professionals were seeking guidance on treatment. There were already many research studies and much information on adolescent sexual offenders. See for instance: Ryan, Lane, Davies & Isaac (1987),[1] Kahn & Chambers (1991),[2] Davis & Leitenberg (1987),[3] Burgess, Hartman & McCormack (1987)[4] and Bagley & Sewchuk-Dann (1991).[5] Information from these studies and from studies of adult offenders (for example Waterhouse *et al* (1994)[6]) show that most sexual offenders start offending in early adolescence and even before. In our experience sexual aggression at a young age is largely ignored and it may well be that known offenders who have been first charged during their adolescence, may have committed earlier acts which had not been recognised or acknowledged.

Dey and Print provide a very useful model for assessing children whose sexually aggressive behaviour is causing concern and we endorse the use of this assessment procedure before any treatment is commenced. This new, short chapter will, therefore, build on the previous chapter by giving information from a research study which was conducted at the NSPCC Child Sexual Abuse Consultancy during 1995. We will also show, by case examples, how recent healing work with such children works in practice.

NEW KNOWLEDGE AND RESEARCH

In 1993 Gil and Johnson published *Sexualized Children: Assessment and Treatment*.[7] Both Eliana Gil and Toni Cavanagh Johnson are known for their interest and previous publications on this subject. They added weight to the current thinking that children who abuse need a firm grounding in both victim and offender dynamics, either individually or in groups. As Dey and Print pointed out in the previous chapter, the motivations of young children to sexually abuse are often different from those of adolescents. Gil and Johnson were clear that this, and the developmental difference between children and adolescents, made a different kind of treatment desirable.

At the Consultancy we had realised that this was imperative. When children were referred to us because of sexually aggressive behaviour we began work by assessing the children's behaviour as exploratory or exploitative as described by Dey and Print. Secondly, we assessed the children using Hartman & Burgess' model of the Information Processing of Trauma (see previous chapter) to discover whether a particular child was using 'control' as a coping mechanism. If so, a child was obviously at risk of re-offending. We included in a treatment plan strict boundary setting, exploration of children's feelings and therapeutic needs, an educative component egarding sexual matters, exploration of distorted thinking, victim empathy, and behaviour management and anger control. We also realised that parallel work with carers was even more vital with this category of children than with those who had not abused others. We found that Kee MacFarlane's publication *When Children Molest Children* (1991)[8] was helpful, particularly with regard to helping children to understand their behaviour and feelings immediately before an abusive event.

We realised that children who abuse others were in a situation which is quite different from adult or adolescent offenders. A young child is potentially powerless both within home and school. If necessary a child can be overcome physically by an adult, as well as being over-ruled on decision making. A child who is being or has been abused in any way (whether physically, sexually, emotionally or through neglect) will always experience extreme powerlessness and vulnerability until the abusive experience has been integrated. The sexually aggressive behaviour is an attempt to gain power or control but it goes alongside vulnerability which is always present. The adolescent or adult who abuses may also experience extreme vulnerability in certain areas of his life but he is likely also to have more control over some aspects of his own life.

It was, therefore, important that the worker was empathic and supporting to these children, whose experience of vulnerability was current, whilst not avoiding the issue of their dangerous behaviour. However, there were sometimes problems for the therapists in combining the more directive method necessary for such children with the interactive child-centred work on which we based our philosophy. We considered using two separate therapists for each child but decided that for some children this would collude with the 'splitting' which was already apparent in their own behaviour. Most of the abusing children whom we saw had suffered abuse themselves, at an early age, which had affected their development. We wanted to help them to integrate their own trauma, not to encourage further splitting.

THE RESEARCH AT THE CHILD SEXUAL ABUSE CONSULTANCY

We decided to carry out a small piece of qualitative research on children who were sexually aggressive. The research had three aims:

- To prevent further abuse by looking at each child's history to see if patterns could be detected which would alert us to other children who were at risk of committing abuse.
- To prevent further abusive acts in these particular children by looking at their offences to see if a behavioural sequence could be identified which might alert carers.
- To evaluate therapeutic interventions to see which were deemed helpful or otherwise by children and carers.

The details of the research are published elsewhere (Bannister & Gallagher 1996[9] and 1997[10]). Six children, half aged 11 and half aged 12 who had been referred to the NSPCC teams in the North of England because of their abusive behaviour were interviewed and in addition their social workers/ therapists and carers were separately interviewed. The interviews were repeated after six months. There were five boys and one girl in the sample. One child was African Caribbean, the others were white.

Preventing further abuse

This age group was at the upper end of our limit but we found a reluctance from social workers and parents to include younger children in the research. Adults feared younger children being 'labelled' as abusive, even though younger abusive children often told us that they were afraid of their own behaviour and wanted help in stopping it. This reluctance from adults to see younger children as abusive was not surprising. Dey and Print had expressed their own reluctance to identify young children as abusers, but we began to realise that unless the aggressive behaviour was stopped at this stage, there was a high risk of children beginning addictive cycles of abusive behaviour.

In this chapter I wish to concentrate on the way in which the research influenced our practice. However, it will be of interest to give brief information on the other aspects of the research.

As we had anticipated, five of the six children reported that they had been sexually abused, two since infancy. Three of the children had been physically abused and at least one had been seriously neglected. All the children had suffered other trauma as well such as abandonment by a parent, witnessing a parent abuse another child, witnessing domestic violence or feeling emotionally abused. With regard to the risk factors listed by Dey and Print we found that parental loss, lack of social skills and maladaptive coping skills and lack of confidence were the most obvious components of the children's histories.

This history is not particularly unusual in a sample of children who are referred to the NSPCC because they have been abused. What was different in these particular children was that they had all, without exception, exhibited angry behaviour in the past, including setting fires, running away, bullying, using racially abusive language and sexually abusive language to women. Often this behaviour had started below the age of five. Most of the children were also described as bullies, some had threatened adults with physical violence. Several children had also been bullied themselves.

It must be remembered that most of this seriously aggressive behaviour had occurred regularly and consistently in the children from an early age. The significance had not been realised and none had received therapeutic help in those early years. We felt that this finding justified us in taking seriously the aggressive behaviour of young children. We felt that it was possible that the sexually aggressive behaviour may have been prevented if they had received help with their anger over previous trauma.

Behavioural patterns

Our second aim in the research was to look at the sexually aggressive behaviours themselves. We were looking for patterns such as that described by Ryan (1989)[11] as a Dysfunctional Response Cycle. She describes how some children who are humiliated or rendered powerless, initially feel helpless and withdrawn but then become angry and attempt to control or blame others. These children then express their anger through sexual assault, exploitation, drug abuse or physical violence.

Our clinical work had already produced several referrals of children who were exploitative bullies or drug misusers and whose anger was undoubtedly triggered from their own experience of abuse or neglect. The children whom we interviewed in the research project seemed to react in similar ways. Some children were able to trace very clearly their fear and anger when parents were fighting, for instance, and their own subsequent sexually abusive behaviour.

This has implications both for carers and for the child. Parents and carers can try to be more aware of the affect of their behaviour on children, and children themselves can learn to understand their own reactions and how to control or divert them into less disastrous behaviour.

Implications for therapy

With regard to therapy, we endorse the comments by Dey and Print that allowing a child who was already exhibiting aggressiveness to act out aggression within the session could be counterproductive. However, as they pointed out, such expression of feeling is necessary in the early stages of therapy and can be safely confronted and can be a basis for helping the child to understand the cognitive distortion which often misdirects the anger.

The children in the research project most appreciated a therapist who 'really listened'. They also valued the power which they felt when the child and worker made an agreement about the therapy to which both had contributed. All the children in the research project had been seen individually for therapy and seemed to value this attention. At the Consultancy we had also seen children individually although we were aware of the apparent advantages of working with young abusers in small groups, following the ideas in the SPARK programme in Los Angeles, cited by Dey and Print. There are practical difficulties in running groups for pre-pubertal children of differing ages but, meantime, we became more convinced that individual therapy for these young children was the treatment of choice.

Although the desirability of peer group work with adult and adolescent sexual offenders has been demonstrated over many years, our opinion is that young sexually abusing children may find this mode of treatment difficult. The difference is that young children are still suffering acutely from their own recent abuse and work on this will play a very large part in their treatment. Adult abusers will spend much longer on breaking their addictive abuse cycles. In breaking addictions it has been shown that the support and power of a peer group is extremely effective (as in alcohol or drug abuse, weight loss, smoking etc.). Child abusers will have begun to form a recognised pattern to their abusing behaviour but it is unlikely to be as fixed or addictive as in adults. One reason for this may be that in young children the motivation to sexually abuse is less likely to include sexual pleasure or orgasm. Dey and Print cite Johnson (1989) as a source for this statement and our clinical experience endorses this, although we accept that young children can become sexualised by their own sexual abuse and this can lead to inappropriate masturbation and, sometimes, to sexual aggression with others.

The children in the research project had been seen by their workers for periods from six weeks (for extended assessment) to over six months. Most children (and their carers) felt that several months' work was necessary. We noticed that where the workers were known for their work with adult or adolescent abusers both parents and children complained that the children did not do enough work on their own abuse. Likewise, where workers specialised in working with abused children some worries were expressed about the possibility that the work had not been confronting enough.

However, the sexualised behaviours which the children were presenting were all reduced or eliminated by the therapy. One child reoffended during the period of the research and another, who had dropped out of treatment, said, 'I think I will need more help with this problem.' The two children who presented the most positive picture (with no reoffences after 12 months) were those who had been given a dual programme, covering both their own abuse and their abusing behaviour, for at least six months. In both cases their current carers were also particularly helpful and supportive.

The research helped us to formalise the work we were doing and gave us confidence to move forward. We always included the elements of strict control of abusive behaviour, work on the consequences of this behaviour both for the abusing child and for the victim, empathy with the victim, recovery from the abusing child's own abuse and on his/her own self-esteem and self-respect.

Case study (1)

Louise was a 10-year-old girl with learning difficulties. She had been referred because of sexualised behaviour towards a three-year-old foster sister, Jane. Some of the behaviour, such as asking Jane to touch her developing breasts, could be described as exploratory. However, the amount of coercion Louise used with Jane to play sexual games was unacceptable. Louise had been fostered since the age of five when she was taken into care because of physical and sexual abuse and severe neglect. It was known that from a very early age she had been used in sexual practices by her mother and other male and female relatives but the details of this were unknown.

Although Louise had very supportive foster parents she had never received any professional help with her early trauma. At a planning meeting with the worker, Louise and her foster parents, a three part plan was devised and agreed:

(1) The foster parents would keep strict boundaries to ensure that Louise was not left unsupervised whilst playing with Jane or other young children.
(2) Louise agreed to use drawing, which she enjoyed, to work with the therapist on her past in which, she said, there had been some 'bad things'.
(3) At this stage Louise was unwilling to talk about the abuse of Jane (which had been partly witnessed by the foster mother and confirmed by Jane). However, she agreed that she 'might talk about it sometime' and the foster mother and worker agreed that meanwhile some sexual education might be helpful for Louise and might also be a way of introducing the topic when Louise was ready.

Louise showed no resentment against the strict supervision at home, in fact she seemed to welcome the extra attention. The art work with the therapist soon revealed a disturbing story of ritualised, multiple abuse of Louise as a small child, the details of which had never been previously revealed. The therapist was able to help Louise to contain this and to understand it as far as possible. One feature of this exploratory work concerning her own abuse was that Louise apparently had no empathy or sympathy whatsoever with herself as a very young, seriously abused child. She drew herself as a 'bad girl' holding a knife over the wounded body of a baby. She said she was about three at the time. It has been our experience that children who have been seriously abused at an early age are often unable to visualise themselves as victims but see themselves in the role of the abuser, which is a safer place to be. Gradually the therapist helped Louise to realise that she had in no way deserved the abuse (and torture) which she had suffered. She began to express her pain and fear. The trust engendered in this work then enabled Louise to talk about her angry feelings, especially with regard to her birth mother. This suppression of anger meant that Louise had always been unable to express any angry feelings directly to her foster mother at times when she felt unfairly treated. According to our research, unexpressed angry feelings are nearly always an immediate prelude to the abuse of other children by children who have been abused themselves. Louise was helped to express these in a healthy way by stamping around and using her voice. The therapist then found it much easier to help Louise to have empathy with her foster sister Jane, whom she had abused. Just as she had no empathy with herself as an abused three-year-old, so she had been unable to empathise with Jane. Some joint sessions with Louise and her foster mother completed the work.

Case study (2)

Jack was a nine-year-old boy who had not been sexually abused although he had witnessed his two younger sisters being sexually abused by their father. His father had also physically abused him. Jack and his sisters had been in a foster home for two years and the foster mother had caught Jack trying to vaginally penetrate his younger sister. Jack was very open at the planning meeting and agreed to tight supervision of his activities at home and to exploration of his past through story telling, which he enjoyed. He was happy to discuss his abusive behaviour towards his sister, which he did not deny. It soon became apparent that Jack felt that he was like his father and to some extent he was fearful of this (mainly because his father had been extremely violent), but on the other hand he appeared not to fully understand why his father's sexual behaviour with his sisters was wrong.

He was encouraged to create stories, which he did with skill and enthusiasm. In the beginning the stories were full of violent and criminal activities. The therapist worked with Jack on the feelings of all his characters. He was encouraged to look at the consequences for his characters, of their deviant behaviour. Gradually the stories changed to ones where enterprising young men set up successful businesses. Working in this metaphoric way the therapist helped Jack to understand why his father's abusive behaviour was unacceptable.

Alongside the storymaking the therapist used worksheets to help Jack to track his 'steps to abuse'. This is a variant on the addiction cycle frequently used to help adolescent and adult offenders to anticipate and control their abusive behaviour. The abusing child thinks about events immediately preceding an abusive episode and identifies their own feelings. The 'steps to abuse' often start with feelings of rejection (being told off for misbehaviour for instance). In a child who has been frequently rejected in the past this feeling changes quickly into anger, in order to cope. The child feels 'it's not fair' and looks around for someone less powerful on whom to project the anger. Children who have been abused often then remember their own feelings of repressed anger at the time of the abuse. Deliberately they then plan and execute a sexually abusive incident. (See Kee MacFarlane 1991[8] for a fuller explanation of this theory.)

In a child who is at first unwilling to discuss his sexually abusive behaviour this technique can still be used by asking him to choose other physically or emotionally abusive incidents which he may have perpetrated. Invariably, at referral, a sexually abusive child who is denying or rationalising his actions, will have been involved in other similar incidents to which he may admit.

Jack's therapist encouraged him to identify his danger signals or triggers. His foster mother was also encouraged, with Jack's agreement, to identify the signs and to encourage Jack to use a less destructive release for his anger, such as using a punchbag.

Jack then worked on his self-esteem which was very low. He felt that he was bound to be a failure, as his father had been, and that this had been confirmed by his own abusive behaviour towards his sister. He felt extremely guilty that he had witnessed the sexual abuse of his sisters, and had sympathised with their distress, but had failed to prevent it reoccurring. Jack again created stories which featured a small dog which was unable to rescue some puppies which were being ill-treated by their owner. The stories eventually changed as the small dog liberated the puppies. This actually reflected Jack's experiences since he had been the person to tell about his father's abuse and so 'liberated' his sisters.

Summary

This dual approach appears to be more successful with children than treatment which concentrates only on changing their abusive behaviour or, alternatively, only explores the child's own victimisation. The duality of the approach also refers to the fact that the child's carer must be deeply involved and committed to the treatment for it to be successful. The carer (and sometimes the school also) invariably becomes involved in helping the child to set boundaries and even in 'policing' his/her actions. The parent or carer must also assist the child in stopping the 'steps to abuse' by identifying trigger experiences and diverting the young person to an alternative non-abusive action. The therapist and carer may also be jointly involved in providing sexual information or education for the child and, of course, in raising the child's self-esteem and respect for him/herself.

The following chapter on therapeutic intervention with young men who sexually abuse their siblings expands this subject and shows clearly the similarities and differences in treatment for young children and adolescents.

Acknowledgement

I am indebted to my colleague, Eileen Gallagher, the present Manager of the NSPCC Child Sexual Abuse Consultancy, for the outline of these two case studies.

REFERENCES

1. Ryan, G., Lane, S., Davies, J. and Isaac, C. (1987) 'Juvenile sex offenders: development and correction', *Child Abuse and Neglect*, **11**, 385–95.
2. Kahn, T., & Chambers, H. (1991) 'Assessing re-offense risk with juvenile sexual offenders', *Child Welfare*, **70**, 333–45.
3. Davis, C. & Leitenberg, H. (1987) 'Adolescent sex offenders', *Psychological Bulletin*, **101**, 417–27.
4. Burgess, A. W., Hartman, C. R. & McCormack, A. (1987) 'Abused to abuser: antecedents of socially deviant behaviors', *American Journal of Psychiatry*, **144**(1), 431–6.
5. Bagley, C. & Sewchuk-Dann, D. (1991) 'Characteristics of 60 children and adolescents who have a history of sexual assault against others: evidence from a controlled study', *Journal of Child and Youth Care* (special issue) Fall, 43–52.
6. Waterhouse, L., Dobash, R. & Carnie, J. (1994) Child Sexual Abusers, Central Research Unit, Scottish Office, Edinburgh.
7. Gil, E. & Johnson, T. C. (1993) *Sexualized Children* (Launch Press: Rockville, Maryland).
8. MacFarlane, K. (1991) *When Children Molest Children* (The Safer Society Press: Orwell, Vermont).
9. Bannister, A. & Gallagher, E. (1996) 'Children who sexually abuse other children', *The Journal of Sexual Aggression*, **2**(2), 87–98.
10. Bannister, A. & Gallagher, E. (1997) 'Children who sexually abuse other children', in J. Bates, R. Pugh, and N. Thompson, (eds) *Protecting Children: Challenges and Change* (Arena: Aldershot).
11. Ryan, G. (1989) 'Victim to victimizer: rethinking victim treatment', *Journal of Interpersonal Violence*, **4**(3), 325–41.

9

BROTHER NATURE? THERAPEUTIC INTERVENTION WITH YOUNG MEN WHO SEXUALLY ABUSE THEIR SIBLINGS

Simon Hackett, Bobbie Print and Carol Dey

INTRODUCTION

It is now recognised that the sexual abuse of children by young people is a widespread phenomenon, which is damaging to victims, their families and the community. Recent crime statistics indicate that people under the age of 18 years commit approximately one-third of all sex offences in this country (Home Office 1995).[1] Significant efforts are allocated to the management of sex offenders, influenced by an ever-growing, intense and frenetic socio-political preoccupation with 'paedophiles'. One concerning consequence of this attention is that the dominant view of sex offenders has become that of predatory males targeting children in the community. Sexual abuse within the family, and in particular the abuse of siblings by adolescents, continues to be less recognised (O'Brien, 1991).[2] The problem of sibling sexual abuse remains shrouded in an unhelpful level of societal, familial and individual denial, which is reflected in continuing gaps in theoretical material, policy and practice initiatives designed to promote change in those young people who abuse siblings.

In this chapter, our overarching aim is to contribute to the bridging of this gap by providing a framework for therapeutic intervention with young men who have abused their siblings. We acknowledge that to demarcate such young men as a sub-group of abusers is, to a certain extent, a false distinction and that there are many points of crossover between young people who sexually abuse siblings and young people who abuse other relatives and children outside the family. Nevertheless, working with those who abuse brothers and sisters includes a number of distinct themes which are central to the provision of a therapeutic intervention response aimed at promoting change and reducing the risk of further victimisation.

Throughout the chapter, we reflect upon our own experiences at G-MAP of working with young men who have abused siblings. G-MAP is an independent organisation offering a range of assessment and therapeutic services to children and young people who display inappropriate sexual behaviours, their families, carers and the professionals who work with them. The programme operates in association with the NSPCC and Salford Mental Health Services and has been established since 1988.

We refer to young 'men' as opposed to young people of both genders as males occupy the vast majority of our referrals. We believe that the sexual abuse of siblings by females is an important issue, which is in need of further attention. Whilst there has been an increasing focus given to women who sexually abuse recently (see for example Saradjian, 1996),[3] research relating to prevalence of young women who sexually abuse is as yet under-developed and evidence suggests that it is overwhelmingly young men who sexually abuse their siblings. To simply ignore this gender divide in suggesting that our intervention strategies apply equally to all young *people* would be short-sighted and tantamount to reinforcing the gender oppression which is so endemic in sexual abuse.

Within the chapter we describe a therapeutic approach to such young men and their families and suggest models to guide practitioners in their work. Importantly, we offer the example of young people and their families who have worked with us, shared their views, beliefs, pain and experiences. We have observed their personal struggles towards change and offer descriptions of their situations and work with us in the hope that their accounts will resonate for practitioners engaged in similar work.

COUNTERING THE MYTHS OF 'BROTHER NATURE'

Despite the increasing amount of literature relating to young British males who sexually abuse (for example, O'Callaghan & Print 1994,[4] Glasgow *et al* 1994,[5] Masson 1995,[6] Dolan *et al* 1996[7]), there remains a dearth of information on those who abuse siblings. Powerful myths continue to be associated with sexual abuse that occurs between siblings. These are widespread within society and, in our experience, often continue to be accepted by many professionals. These myths encompass views such as:

- Sexual abuse rarely takes place between siblings due to the notion of the incest taboo
- Sexual contact between siblings can be explained away as experimental
- Sexual contact between siblings can be explained away as consensual
- Sexual contact between siblings may be inappropriate, but is usually minor in nature
- Young men who actively seek victims outside of the home are more dangerous and have more problems than those who abuse siblings
- Sexual abuse between siblings will go away if left alone, it should be dealt with by the family or can be managed by simply pointing out its inappropriateness
- Sexual abuse between siblings is a symptom of an overly close sibling relationship
- Sexual contact between siblings has an erotic content
- Sexually inappropriate behaviour between siblings can happen, but is often a one-off, unplanned mistake, with no abusive intent.

The acceptance of these views can lead to oppressive or dangerous practice in some cases where victims fail to be protected. There is also the risk that responses can be inconsistent and iniquitous. For example, O'Brien (1991)[8] found that, whilst three-quarters of cases involving adolescents who abused victims outside of the family were referred to the courts, only 35% of those who had abused siblings received a similar response. The majority in the latter group was dealt with by the child protection system only. It was O'Brien's summation that the difference in response was largely due to the myth of sibling abuse as 'exploration' and less serious than abuse outside the family.

We offer the following information, from limited research available on adolescents who sexually abuse siblings, to counter these myths.

INCIDENCE

It has been suggested that although the most frequently reported type of incest is father–daughter (Meiselman, 1978,[9] Herman, 1981,[10] Russell, 1986[11]) the most common form of incest that occurs is between brother and sister (Weiner, 1964).[12] Finkelhor's study (1980)[13] of 796 undergraduates found that 15% of the females and 10% of the males had experienced sexual activity with a sibling and a quarter of those experiences were considered abusive. In our own study (1994)[14] 36% of the young people referred to G-MAP had abused siblings.

NATURE OF ABUSE

With regard to the nature of the abusive acts themselves, adolescents who sexually abuse siblings were found by O'Brien[15] to have committed more acts of abuse over longer periods of time than those that abused outside of the family. This is replicated in our own data and clinical experience, and is likely to be a reflection of the availability of victims within the family and the increased inhibitors on family members against disclosure. Becker *et al* (1986)[16] found that the 22 young people in their study of incest offenders had abused a total of 39 victims and that 21 of these young people had completed or attempted 199 offences. The remaining young man had committed a further 229 offences. O'Brien (1991)[17] found that 53% of those who had abused siblings had more than one victim and that they were much more likely to commit offences involving penile penetration (46%) than those who abused children outside the family (28%). This provides an important counter-balance to the myth that young people who abuse siblings engage in less serious acts.

CHARACTERISTICS OF VICTIMS

The evidence against simplistic and oppressive 'exploration theories' is clear. For example, in a study of 100 British adolescents who had sexually abused and were resident in a British secure unit, Richardson *et al* (1995)[18] identified that the younger the victim, the more likely he/she was known to their abuser. This suggests that victims abused by adolescents within the family tend to be younger children rather than peer aged or older siblings, confirming the power dynamics of the abuse. Finkelhor (1980)[19] found that the younger the victims of sibling sexual abuse the more extreme the lasting effects. Laviola (1989)[20] in a small study of four women who had been abused by older brothers in childhood identified that each had suffered significant and long-term negative effects as a consequence of the abuse.

FAMILY CHARACTERISTICS

Parental history of abuse

Kaplan *et al* (1988)[21] in a study of 27 adolescent incest perpetrators found that 27% of parents reported having been physically abused and 30% reported having been sexually abused during childhood or adulthood. In contrast, Smith and Israel (1987)[22] in a study of 25 families where sibling incest had occurred found 72% of parents in their study had been sexually abused.

Family dysfunction

Michael O'Brien (1991)[23] has compared a sample of young people who had sexually abused siblings and had been referred to his PHASE programme with young people who had perpetrated sexual abuse against children outside the family, and a third group of young people who had assaulted adults. He found that in 61% of families of adolescents who abused siblings, physical abuse had taken place and that 97% of the families were considered by professionals to be moderately (45%) or severely (52%) disturbed. Smith and Israel (1987)[24] found that the families in their study were characterised by absent fathers; emotionally distant parents; parental stimulation of sexual climate in the home; family secrets and, most significantly, extramarital sexual relationships (72%). They found that almost half (48%) of the young people who had abused had observed sexual activity, ranging from fondling to sexual intercourse, between their parents or one parent and another party.

CHARACTERISTICS OF YOUNG MEN WHO SEXUALLY ABUSE SIBLINGS

History of abuse

Pierce and Pierce (1987)[25] found that 62% of young people who had sexually abused within the family had been physically abused and 70% had been neglected. Bank and Kahn (1982)[26] suggested that sibling abuse is more likely to occur in families where there is a high level of parental neglect so that brothers and sisters turn to each other for comfort or as a means of expressing rage. There is also evidence that sibling abusers are the sub-group of sex offenders who are most likely to have been sexually abused themselves. O'Brien (1991)[27] found that 42% of adolescents who abuse siblings had themselves been sexually abused. Of this group, 33% had been abused by an immediate family member, in 19% of cases the perpetrator was their father. Pierce and Pierce (1987)[28] found that 43% of their sample of young people who committed incest had been sexually abused by a family member and that 60% had experienced more than one form of abuse within their family.

Behavioural problems

O'Brien's study (1991)[29] identified that young people who abused siblings were more likely than those who abused adults or children outside the family to have a history of involvement with psychological or psychiatric services. Almost half had displayed physical aggression at home, 21% had been involved in fire setting and 13.5% had displayed cruelty to animals. Becker et al (1986),[30] in a study of 22 adolescent males who had committed incest offences, discovered that 46% admitted to having committed sexual abuse outside of the family.

The brief overview of research above identifies the context in which we are aiming intervention when we work with young sibling abusers and their families. The message is clear: sexual abuse by young men against their siblings happens, it is serious in nature and is damaging to victims.

Below is a case example which demonstrates the escalating nature of sibling abuse and the ease with which a young person can manipulate and maintain a sibling's compliance in abuse:

> Andrew was 13 years old and lived in foster care with his half-brother, Christopher, aged seven, who had learning disabilities. Both boys had been badly let down by their mother, who had repeatedly placed them in and out of care establishments, as she changed relationships. Andrew had, in many ways, parented Christopher and spent a great deal of time looking after him. Drifting through different care establishments over a period of several years and with a fragile sense of personal identity through his history of boundary transgression and uncertainty, Andrew was highly vulnerable. In care, he was sexually abused by a variety of older male teenagers and also by a young woman. When this abuse came to light, Andrew and Christopher were moved to a further foster placement.
>
> Within the placement, Andrew was given a level of responsibility for his half-brother that mirrored the previous experiences he had at home with his mother. At the same time protective and resentful of his half-brother, but isolated and socially unskilled, Andrew entered puberty to be further bombarded by the bewildering mass of sexual and emotional responses associ-

ated with entry into adolescence. His own abuse, always present in his thoughts, took on new meanings. He began to imagine repeating the sexual acts he had experienced on his half-brother.

He ruminated on these thoughts, using his own flashbacks and introducing his half-brother into these, so that he moved from being the victim to the one in control, seeking mastery over the thoughts and memories which had caused him pain for so long. He battled against those voices in his head, which told him that to touch his half-brother would be wrong, by developing internal thoughts which supported the abuse and downplayed its significance and potential consequences. He later described this battle as 'like having a devil on one shoulder and an angel on the other.' His escalating thoughts were reinforced by a strong sexual response to these images. His masturbation to these images further served to strengthen the 'devil' side.

Given the nature of his relationship with Christopher, Andrew did not have to spend a great deal of time setting up situations to enable him to enact his thoughts. He engineered a game of hide-and-seek with Christopher upstairs in their house and, whilst hiding, masturbated to thoughts of sex with his brother. When Christopher found him hiding, Andrew took hold of him and indecently assaulted him by feeling Christopher's genitals over his clothes. Having touched his half-brother on this occasion he ensured silence by threatening his brother with the idea that they would both be in trouble if Christopher told anyone about what had happened. Andrew then began to increase the intrusiveness of the sexual acts he demanded, until he was regularly penetrating his half-brother.

DEFINING A SAFE AND APPROPRIATE THERAPEUTIC APPROACH

Within the field of sexual abuse, one of the most pronounced professional schisms has been that of 'victim versus offender' work. Historically, these two aspects of sexual abuse work have been viewed as diametrically opposed. There have been practice disputes as to the relative merits and efficacy of working with offenders and the impact of diverting scarce resources away from victim services in favour of work with abusers. Workers who intervene with abusers have been characterised as colluding with offenders by building therapeutic relationships with them. The accusations and counter-accusations, rationalisations and justifications that have ensued on both sides at times have mirrored those that have characterised the abuser's relationship with the victim in sexual abuse. A number of particularly dangerous consequences have emerged as a result of this professional polarisation.

Firstly, on a practice level, work with children and young people who have sexually abused or demonstrated sexually aggressive behaviour has been primarily influenced by the intervention methodologies which have guided work with adult sex offenders. Once a young person has sexually abused, invariably his position and needs as a child become subsumed by his status as an offender. Resultant intervention responses have therefore tended to stress confrontation, employing language such as 'tackling' or 'breaking down' denial.

Secondly, the confusion about how to define an appropriate intervention response can be seen in the lack of an agreed term to describe those young people who have sexually abused. Do we call them 'sex offenders', 'perpetrators', 'sexual abusers', 'sexually abusive', 'sexually reactive', 'children with sexual behaviour problems', 'victims', etc.? Do we call the process of working with such young people to address their behaviour 'treatment', 'therapy', 'offence focused work'? Is the notion of 'healing', so prevalent in the literature of work with victims, appropriate in the context of work with young people whose behaviour constitutes a chosen act? These linguistic dilemmas do not merely reflect differences in semantics, but are also a reflection of basic philosophical differences and practice confusions.

At G-MAP we have put considerable effort into developing a philo-sophical and anti-oppressive base to our intervention with young abusers. We are clear that our primary responsibility is to the actual and likely victims of sexual abuse and that the primary goal of our work is to prevent further victimisation. We view sexual abuse as a force of oppression. It is the sole responsibility of the abuser and never of the person who has been abused. At the same time, however, it is our belief and experience that it is impossible to meet oppression with oppression. Intervention responses that model anger and aggression on the part of the worker to the young person who has abused simply serve to reinforce the factors which have contributed to the abuse in the first instance. The challenge to us as practitioners is to develop a context to our therapeutic intervention, founded on support and understanding, which nurtures the child in the abuser, inspires acceptance of responsibility and promotes accountable and respectful behaviour. This has to be set on the basis of a non-collusive relationship which does not allow a young person who has abused to rationalise or minimise his abusive behaviour. A therapeutic response needs to be built within a context of appropriate 'control' which takes into account not only therapeutic bound-aries, but also child protection issues and the need for controls upon the young person's external life situation. The complexity of this challenge is not to be underestimated.

The concept of 'healing' the abuser assumes that he, as well as his victim, is damaged by the sexual abuse experience. Within the context of the sexual abuse field, this is a political, as well as a practice statement. We believe that young people who abuse, often themselves victims of sexual or other forms of abuse, are damaged by the experience of abusing. Many young people have told us of the damage they have experienced as a result of their abusive behaviour and their struggle to 'heal' from the experience. Moving away from abusive behaviour can be a painful and prolonged journey. Nevertheless, this is both quantitatively and qualitatively different from the struggle of the victim. The difference is illustrated by the following quotation, drawn from the feminist critique of the men's movement:

> *Oppression is what the slaves suffer; malaise is what happens to the slave owners whose personalities are warped and whose essential humanity is necessarily undermined by their position. Malaise and oppression are both painful, but they are not comparable. And the necessary first step in the cure for what ails the slave owner is to free the slaves.*
>
> (Starhawk, p.29 in Hagan, 1992)[31]

The notion of 'healing' for the abuser therefore has a set of interlinked connotations:

- Recognising the consequences of sexual abuse for victims, families and self
- Learning about control
- Developing the self-esteem, self-confidence and motivation to achieve change
- Making a determined decision not to abuse and acquiring the skills and resources necessary in order to put this decision into action
- Recovering from the damage to his self-perception and sexuality as a result of his abusive behaviour and experiences
- Respecting others' needs and rights, as well as understanding one's own needs and rights.

Setting out the above principles to underpin intervention is one step towards building an appropriate and effective therapeutic response to adolescents who abuse and their families. The second challenge is to define an appropriate intervention structure within which these principles can be given weight and put into practice. We have found that it is vital to be clear about therapeutic boundaries. Boundary transgression is a key feature of sexual abuse and we have frequently found that those young people with whom we work attempt to manipulate and distort our own boundaries. Additionally, we have experienced pressure on boundaries from parents, others in the family system or from those professionals who have commissioned the work or who are involved in the life of the family for other reasons. In the face of such potential pressure on boundaries, it is essential that:

- Child protection issues are addressed before any therapeutic intervention is offered
- Actual victim(s) are ensured of safety
- Potential victims are protected
- The abuser is not be placed in a situation which promotes continuance of the behaviour.

This means that we demarcate the following very clear boundaries around our own practice:

- We will not offer therapeutic work without a clear assessment of need and a resolution of child protection issues
- We will not offer work where there is no professional involvement by a responsible external agency, e.g. Social Services, Probation or Health Department
- We will not begin work with a young person who has abused siblings and who is still living in the same house as his victim
- We will not work towards family resolution without the victim(s) and the young person who has abused having been offered appropriate services
- The same worker(s) should not be involved in offering therapy to the abused child and adolescent who has abused.

We conceptualise this in the following way. In order for healing to take place within the family, there should be a series of concentric stages of healing (see Figure 9.1).

The notion of this model is that practitioners should consider 'healing' as working from the centre outwards. That is, in order to promote healing in the parents, it is first essential to ensure that the victim and abuser, in that order, have opportunities to heal. The model thereby places the victim at the core of all need. It is not meant to suggest that each element of the work needs to be done by separate workers, although we are clear that the victim requires a therapist independent of that of the abuser, given the power dynamic that will have existed between victim and abuser.

DEFINING A HOLISTIC INTERVENTION PROCESS TO SIBLING ABUSE WORK

Thus far we have set into context work with abusers and described the importance of clear and boundaried practice. In this next section we offer a model which seeks to build a holistic framework to therapeutic intervention with young men who have abused siblings and their families.

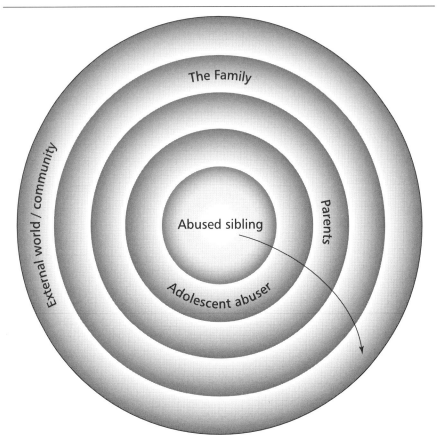

Figure 9.1

Figure 9.2 conceptualises three strands of work, each of which takes into one aspect of healing described in the above model of healing. This is not offered as a rigid, all-encompassing structure, for example, in some cases the parents may have severed all links and be unwilling to participate. It is, however, a guide, bringing together major elements of a holistic intervention response.

ASSESSMENT

Whilst assessment is not the main focus of attention in this chapter, it provides the essential cornerstone to all intervention with young people who have abused and their families. Assessment is an ongoing process which extends into the therapeutic process, so that hypotheses formed in the assessment are continually tested and revised, agreed goals and targets are reviewed and assessed needs are met. To this effect, G-MAP has developed a structured assessment model, which involves a minimum of three clinical interviews with the young person who has abused and at least one interview with carers (see O'Callaghan & Print, 1994).[32] We have formulated semi-structured questionnaires for young people and parents to complete separately. These aid the important task of information gathering about a young person's background and personal history, as well as family history and parental response to the abuse. Additionally, a pack of psychometric questionnaires is completed with the young person, covering broad aspects of personality, psychosexual and psychosocial presentation and offence specific areas. Completion of these questionnaires provides not only data against which we can balance clinical judgement, but, through re-completion at intervals, also allows for important evaluation of progress in attitudes and functioning.

Parents are also asked to complete questionnaires relating to family environment and parental stress. Parental involvement in assessment emphasises to all involved that the 'family' will be a crucial dynamic in both current and future work. We do not feel that it is appropriate to ask the victim to directly contribute information to the assessment. It is, however, important to have victim statements, where they exist, in order to set in context the account of young people who have abused, as their reports of the incidents are so often characterised with distortions, minimisation and justifications.

CONTRACTING

Following assessment, it is important to formulate agreements with young people, family members and other professional workers. These should clarify boundaries on contact between the young person who has abused and his victim(s), protection issues and responsibility. The process of ongoing work should be detailed and the limited nature of confidentiality in respect of the young person's work explained. Attention should also be given to how feedback will be offered between all family members and professionals involved. Importantly, there should be space to highlight individual goals and review points. These should not merely reflect the therapist's own agenda, but include any additional aims identified by the young person, for example giving up smoking, starting college, controlling anger, as these often reinforce a joint sense of purpose, are useful motivators and provide indicators of progress at reviews.

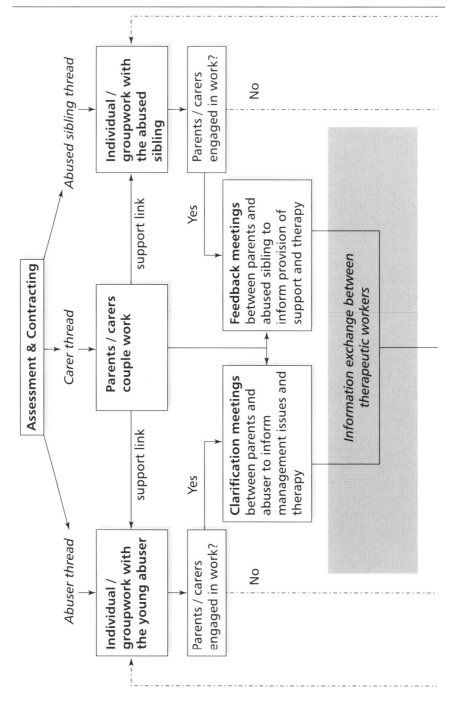

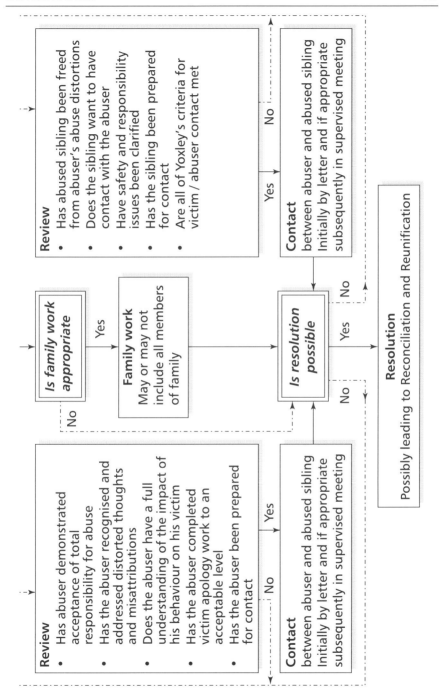

Review
- Has abuser demonstrated acceptance of total responsibility for abuse
- Has the abuser recognised and addressed distorted thoughts and misattributions
- Does the abuser have a full understanding of the impact of his behaviour on his victim
- Has the abuser completed victim apology work to an acceptable level
- Has the abuser been prepared for contact

Is family work appropriate

Yes

No

Family work
May or may not include all members of family

Review
- Has abused sibling been freed from abuser's abuse distortions
- Does the sibling want to have contact with the abuser
- Have safety and responsibility issues been clarified
- Has the sibling been prepared for contact
- Are all of Yoxley's criteria for victim / abuser contact met

Yes

No

Contact
between abuser and abused sibling
Initially by letter and if appropriate subsequently in supervised meeting

Is resolution possible

Yes

No

Contact
between abuser and abused sibling
Initially by letter and if appropriate subsequently in supervised meeting

Yes

No

Resolution
Possibly leading to Reconciliation and Reunification

HEALING THE VICTIM

Whilst our attention in this chapter is on young men who have abused siblings, it is important to identify a number of themes that extend across abuser and victim work.

It is to be stressed that the offer of work to a sibling victim should be separated from, and unconditional on, work with the young person who has abused and his family. Whilst this appears a shockingly obvious point, we have experienced situations where workers have left the victim, however unintentionally, with the view that she or he would only be offered work if the brother who had abused engaged in similar work. Alternatively, victims have been put under pressure to accept therapy, with the suggestion that if they did not accept the offer of help at this point in time, their abuser would also not be helped. Interlinking the intervention needs of young people who abuse and their victims implicitly replicates the abuse dynamics, muddies the waters of responsibility and provides ample scope for further victim guilt and abuser excuses.

We believe that the different workers involved in the healing of victims and adolescents who abuse have much to gain in communicating and not maintaining silence, which mirrors the dynamics of the abuse process itself. There is a need to respect confidentiality and therapeutic boundaries, for example, the therapist working with the young person who has abused should not directly pass on to him information provided by the victim, but may benefit from this information in planning interventions.

HEALING THE YOUNG PERSON WHO HAS ABUSED

As far as is known, there are no models of intervention designed specifically for adolescents who sexually abuse siblings. This is undoubtedly due to the lack of research and knowledge about this particular group of abusers and the consequent lack of specific theories or concepts relating to their behaviour. For most young people who sexually abuse siblings the cycle of offending developed by Ryan and Lane (1991)[33] is applied. This model highlights the self-reinforcing nature of the abusive behaviour and how it is accompanied by a distinct and traceable pattern of thoughts and feelings. The model also stresses the notion of control, rather than cure. A cognitive behavioural therapeutic framework, used to identify a young person's individual cycle of abuse and to develop strategies to prevent relapse, has become the central treatment methodology in work with both adult and adolescent sexual abusers in this country. G-MAP has developed from this framework a therapeutic programme, which aims to address the following issues with young people who have sexually abused others:

- Education regarding sexual aggression, sexual abusers, victimisation and human sexuality
- Taking responsibility for the thinking, feeling and behaviour that enables abusive behaviour
- Understanding an individual's own sexual assault cycle and how this can be inhibited, for example by improved anger management, social skills, giving up use of pornography, etc.
- Understanding and restructuring cognitive distortions
- Development of victim awareness and empathy
- Victim apology and restitution work
- Understanding and modification of deviant arousal patterns
- Assertiveness and anger management
- Interpersonal communication and social skills
- Self-esteem
- Relapse prevention skills
- Dealing with own victimisation.

For further information on methods and techniques in delivering thera-peutic programmes of work with adolescents who sexually abuse, the reader is referred to Smets & Cebula (1987);[34] Ryan & Lane (1991);[35] O'Callaghan & Print (1994):[36] Morrison & Print (1995).[37]

Whilst such models and texts are helpful in developing programmes of work with all young people who sexually abuse, they do not generally assist in considering some of the additional areas that often require attention in the work with those that have abused siblings. Such intervention neces-sitates increased attention to issues of wider family history, dynamics and relationships and work on family resolution, reconciliation or reunification.

G-MAP has developed the following approach to young men who have sexually abused siblings:

1. Involvement in a generic programme of therapeutic work for adolescents who sexually abuse as outlined above. This may be via groupwork or individual work, whichever is most appropriate.
2. Additional individual work provided by a mixed gender co-working pair which focuses on:

- *Personal/family history.* The young person's family experience is central to work with young people who have sexually abused siblings. Many of these young people hold distorted views of their family experience. Restructuring such views and reappraising personal history is central to his developing an understanding of his behaviour and in identifying work that is necessary with other family members. This work also allows the young person to identify significant life events and to consider how these may have impacted on himself and other family members.

- *Own victimisation* (if appropriate). Given that a relatively high proportion of sibling abusers have been victims of sexual abuse (O'Brien)[38] and that a majority of others are likely to have suffered from neglect, physical or emotional abuse, this work may require considerable attention. A primary goal is for the young person to gain a sense of perspective on his own abuse experience. This should not allow him to excuse his own behaviour or avoid responsibility, but should help him to express the painful feelings associated with his own abuse and better understand its impact upon his subsequent life choices.

- *Family relationships*. Family dynamics and relationships have particular importance in work with this group of young people. Many adolescents who abuse siblings have experienced seriously dysfunctional families where relationships may be abusive, boundaries blurred and power dynamics oppressive. Work with the young person aimed at helping him to recognise the consequences for himself and others of such experiences is an essential component of developing the young person's insight into his own behaviour and recognising the possible impact of his abusive behaviour on others. Care should be taken that the young person does not use the understanding gained from such work as an excuse for his own behaviour, for example in concluding, 'I couldn't help what I did.' Instead, it is important that the young person is encouraged and motivated to understand that he has choices about how he responds to negative experiences and that subsequent work is provided to help him identify and develop skills in positive coping strategies.

- *Preparation and support for family work* (where appropriate). Most young people who engage in family work at any level find it a difficult and stressful experience. They require considerable support in considering their agenda for such work, how they express themselves, how they manage aggressive or unassertive behaviours, and how they cope with feelings such as embarrassment, anger or fear. Often opportunities to rehearse family meetings and practise the skills they may require are important components of this work.

- *Preparation for contact with the abused sibling* (where appropriate). Whilst work on developing victim empathy is likely to be part of the general therapeutic programme, for those young men who have abused siblings additional work is often required, particularly in cases where contact with the abused sibling is a consideration. This work is likely to occur at a late stage in the therapeutic programme, once there has been agreement by all involved that contact will be beneficial to the abused sibling and that they, too, will receive preparatory work for contact. Work on preparation for contact is likely to include:

- Accepting full responsibility for the abuse—this must be demonstrable not only in terms of broad statements but also in the absence of comments which reflect distorted thoughts, self-pity, inappropriate attitudes or misattributions.
- Empathy for the abused sibling—that is a true recognition of the actual and possible future impact on the victim not only of the abuse itself but also of the accompanying betrayal of trust, abuse of power and denial of feelings. Empathy should include a genuine desire by the adolescent to assist in the healing of his sibling. In too many cases the young person views contact with his victim only in terms of meeting his own needs, for example, to reduce guilt or to progress the possibility of family re-unification.
- Written letters of apology, which are not sent, are a useful method to rehearse and check the young man's thoughts, understanding and intentions towards his victim.

Further criteria to guide practitioners in making decisions about contact between the young person who has abused and his sibling victim are offered below.

HEALING THE FAMILY

The use of the family in therapeutic intervention with young abusers has been perhaps the weakest part of practice in the field. The unfortunate tendency of 'treating' the individual offender in isolation has become equated with pushing the abuser to accept sole responsibility for his actions. Within this framework, family work has often been associated with a dilution of this process; that is, misattributing the problem as a 'family thing'. Furthermore, the complexity of family dynamics has sometimes meant that engaging families is more difficult than merely focusing upon an individual young person, particularly when there is seen to be no possibility of reconstituting the family after therapeutic intervention has been completed. Practitioners have sometimes felt that it is not worth putting efforts into engaging a resistant or ambivalent family.

Nonetheless, the sense of family is so ingrained in us and, whatever the context and nature of our own particular experience, it is the benchmark against which all other social interactions are measured. It is therefore an essential element of addressing any young person's abusive behaviour. This is regardless of the young person's previous family experience and his current position vis-à-vis the family. As Thomas (1991)[39] has said: 'all young people enter therapy with a family attached'.

It is, however, important to acknowledge the different needs of various family members when sibling abuse has occurred and to work to accommodate these needs within a dynamic, holistic framework of change and healing. One of the essential tasks of the therapist in sibling abuse work is therefore to bring into tandem the conflicting needs of abuser, victim and parents. This necessarily calls for a heavy emphasis upon concepts such as:

- Acknowledgement—establishing all the details of abusive behaviour and demonstrating the benefits of openness and honesty
- Responsibility—the need to re-designate responsibility; i.e. the abuser acknowledges to self and to others responsibility for all of the abuse perpetrated, thereby providing a basis for the victim to shed responsibility
- Accountability—resolving crises of blame, minimisation and guilt in order to promote accountable behaviour from all in the family.

ISSUES IN THERAPY WITH CARERS OF YOUNG PEOPLE WHO HAVE ABUSED SIBLINGS

Below are some of the most common issues which we have confronted in working therapeutically with those who are parents of abuser and victim.

Perceived failure of self as parent

Discovery of the abuse is often accompanied by a disabling sense of failure as a parent. This is particularly powerful in relation to sibling abuse as parents have to face not only the abuse of their own child and the feelings of anger and guilt that this brings, but also the feeling that they have been responsible for raising an abuser. Many parents feel that they have failed on both counts and that they must therefore be 'bad' or 'useless'. It is important to allow them to give voice to these feelings, encouraging them to re-appraise themselves as parents, without a blurring of blame or responsibility. Teaching and exploring the concept of responsibility with parents is often the key to allowing a better sense of perspective-taking on their part. Mobilising guilt into positive resolve for action or change (either individual or family) is an important goal here.

Parental guilt, shame and blame

Linked to the above, parents often express feelings of guilt in relation to having been caring for the victim and abuser at the time of the abuse. It is common for parents to struggle with the questions, 'Should I have known/ could I have known?' and 'Was it my fault?' A parent will often direct anger at self, partner, abuser or the victim. Being able to express and own the guilt and shame they are feeling is an important step in harnessing this energy into a force for support and change.

The need to seek to unite the family

The discovery of the abuse is often a crushing blow to parents, for whom their sense of certainty and normality is shattered. Faced with this, many parents deny all or some of the information they have been given and want to pull the whole family closer and 'make it all better again'. Others feel that they are seemingly not able to accommodate the conflicting needs of victim and abuser. Parents may be forced into making choices that are seemingly impossible, for example having to choose between victim and abuser. There is a need here to allow parents to grieve for the loss they are experiencing; either to their sense of family or to their own self-esteem.

The search for reassurance about the future

Many parents seek reassurance that the future will be without problem and seek solace in thoughts that the abuse was a 'one off', with no possibility of reoccurrence; 'Yes, I believe it happened, but I won't allow it to happen again.' Educating parents about the nature of sexual abuse and the circumstances that led their child to abuse can lead to a greater acceptance of issues of risk, relapse and the cyclical nature of abuse.

The search for 'why'

For many parents, the need to search for meaning in, and reasons for, the abuse is the prime unresolved issue. Having accepted that the abuse has taken place, they are nevertheless left uncertain about why their son has behaved in this way, and what this means about him: e.g. 'Does this mean he is a paedophile?', 'Does this mean he is gay?' etc. Working on these issues involves the use of core concepts, such as the cycle of abuse, in order to allow for development of insight and a framework for the family to understand the motivation behind the abuse and its meaning for the future.

CLARIFICATION MEETINGS

The purpose of clarification meetings is to allow young people or parents, whilst engaged in the 'individual work' thread of the model, to meet together in a structured way in order to ask questions and seek clarification from each other about any aspect of work to date. These are structured meetings, facilitated by the therapists. They provide opportunities to verify, clarify and explain information, concerns or questions. They also enable parents to gain a more developed overview of the work being undertaken with their son and allow them to give the young person feedback on their views on his progress. They have the benefit of modelling open communication about abuse issues and paving the way for later, more formal family work. Often major issues are identified in ongoing individual work, which cannot be left until formal review points. For example, the young person may be being blocked in his attempts to be honest for fear of his parents' response. Through the use of a clarification meeting, where he is able to ask his parents what their response would be, he may be able to overcome this barrier to progress.

CONTACT BETWEEN THE YOUNG PERSON WHO HAS ABUSED AND HIS VICTIM(S)

This is not a therapeutic structure which relies heavily upon victim and abuser contact, unlike that of 'Victim Sensitive Offender Therapy', proposed by Bera (1994).[40] Whilst we are aware that there may be benefit in some cases in bringing together victim and abuser therapeutically, we are concerned not to provide pressure, uncertainty or overload for the victim. It also is often difficult to check the victim's ability to understand why she or he is being brought together with the abuser, particularly when the victim is a very young child, or when under pressure from others to comply with such a request. At the same time, there will be situations when it will be inappropriate to prevent contact. Yoxley (1990)[41] sets out criteria for victim/abuser interventions, which we have adapted as a minimum guide for practitioners in cases of sibling abuse:

- Victim safety and benefit is primary
- (Contact) should always be voluntary, at the victim's discretion, and in the victim's best interest
- (Contact) should involve only abusers who accept full responsibility and have appropriate levels of victim empathy
- The offender and the victim should be carefully prepared and should be supervised at all times

- The offender should use responsible, victim-sensitive language
- The victim can be empowered and supported through early provision of information about the offender. This improves the victim's understanding of the offender's behaviour, for example, the victim should be told why her/his brother has left the home, not told he is on holiday.

RESOLUTION, RECONCILIATION AND REUNIFICATION

We have many examples of workers making statements to sibling abusers early in the process of therapeutic intervention that they are working towards unifying the family at the earliest opportunity. These statements are often well intentioned, but misguided and inappropriate.

Workers often have an investment in bringing families back together as soon as possible. The danger in this is when they operate from a 'rule of optimism', unaware of the degree and nature of risk posed by the young person and believing that, should he return home, everything will be for the best. Sometimes this is because young people who abuse are amongst the most difficult to place in substitute care. There is a general lack of appropriate residential and specialist foster care placements available, often leaving workers with the stark choice between returning the young abuser home or putting other children, already vulnerable and abused, at risk. We have also observed workers who have a strong desire to 'make it better', as the following case examples demonstrate:

> Having abused his stepbrother (see previous case study), Andrew was removed to a specialist children's home. His stepbrother remained with his original foster carers and requested contact with Andrew. His foster carers were supportive of this, seeing it as an opportunity to bring the two siblings together. Andrew, who was engaged in the early stages of a groupwork programme, refused to see his brother. This was despite quite protracted and intense pressure placed upon Andrew by his social worker. In turn, Andrew's foster carers saw his refusal to have contact with Christopher as evidence of his lack of commitment, feeling and his unwillingness to move on his abuse behaviour. They terminated all association with Andrew. Andrew, in later therapeutic work, identified that his refusal was based on the chronic pain and guilt he was carrying at the time of his brother's request, as well as his uncertainty about being able to manage a meeting with his brother.
>
> Kevin, aged 17, sexually abused his sister and was removed into care. His social worker told him this was a temporary measure, pending an assessment of his level of risk and need. In the assessment, Kevin highlighted a return to his family as his only motivation to participate in therapeutic intervention. Also in the assessment, Kevin's parents made it clear that they would not consider his return home, however they would support him in independent

living. Kevin's response was to withdraw and refuse to participate in any
work.

At the other end of this continuum, however, there are other occasions
when practitioners, following a rule of pessimism, exclude contact prematurely and write off any ability on the part of the young person to change
his behaviour, or for the carers to find alternative ways of managing family
interactions. This is demonstrated in the following case:

> Michael abused his sister and following the discovery of this was placed
> many miles away from home in a specialist residential project. His parents,
> who had adopted Michael when he was a young child, expressed a desire to
> work to have him return home, acknowledging realistically the difficulties
> ahead in this process. However, the Local Authority social worker, who
> attributed the young person's abuse as evidence of a wider abusive family
> system, immediately stated that Michael would 'never be returning home'.
> This effectively undermined the parents' resolve and commitment to Michael
> who, in turn, accepted this as evidence of his lack of self-worth and hopeless
> future.

The preceding case examples highlight the need to examine and differentiate between three important concepts: resolution, reconciliation and
reunification.

Resolution can be defined as working with the victim, the carers and the
young person who has abused to finish the unfinished business that so
often accompanies the discovery of abuse and subsequent professional
intervention. Resolution is a primary therapeutic goal for young people
and their families. For resolution to occur it is not necessary for all parties
to forgive, or to feel that an ongoing relationship of any kind is appropriate.
It may involve reconciliation, or sometimes reunification, although these
are not always necessary.

Reconciliation can be defined as the process of seeking balance, post-abuse,
in family relationships. For reconciliation, it is not necessary for the young
person to be re-united with the family, nor for the young person to be
forgiven by the victim or parents. Reconciliation may be one outcome of
therapeutic intervention, but not its primary goal, although family members
(parents and abusers) often hold this as their personal goal.

Reunification can be defined as bringing the young person back into the
family having adequately ensured the protection of actual or potential
victims. This may, in some cases, be the outcome of therapeutic intervention,
but is never an exclusive goal of therapy. It needs a great deal of careful
planning and attention.

Matthews, Raymaker and Speltz (1991)[42] studied the functioning of reunited families, particularly how family members perceived and experienced reunification in situations where incest occurred. Whilst sibling incest was excluded from the study, they describe a set of desirable preconditions for family reunification, which we have adapted and extended to relate specifically to situations of sibling abuse. Whilst the issues surrounding reunification will very much depend upon the particular circumstances of the abuse, the particular family dynamics and risk issues, we see the following points as comprising the very minimum basis upon which reunification should be considered:

Victim

- Able to acknowledge and discuss the sexual abuse
- Does not blame self for the abuse
- Willing for the sibling who abused to be united with the whole family
- Confident about own ability to report any further abuse
- Feels safe and protected in the home if the sibling who abused is to be returned.

Young man who sexually abused

- Accepts full responsibility for the sexual abuse
- Has been able to demonstrate empathy for the victim and awareness of the impact of his behaviour on other family members
- Shows remorse for the abuse
- Is willing to talk with the victim, and other family members, at their request about their abuse, making appropriate apologies, but does not overwhelm (flood) the victim or family members with unrequested and self-serving apologies
- Demonstrates understanding about his motivation for the abuse
- Is able to acknowledge ongoing risk factors and can communicate these to those inside and outside of the family, as appropriate, in order to seek help to prevent relapse.

Parents

- Are able to put victim's needs for protection first
- Have been able to confront the young person who abused and express feelings about the abuse

- Are able to discuss the impact of the abuse upon themselves as carers
- Hold the young person who has abused as responsible and do not blame the victim
- Can accept the differing needs of the victim and the brother who abused and yet can accommodate these within their schema of the family
- Can make any necessary changes in parenting style and skills, in order to manage risk and facilitate openness.

The family

- All family members have made an informed choice for reunification
- Therapeutic intervention has been offered according to the concentric circles model and this has been successful at all levels
- Potential risk situations are shared and the family has a holistic protection plan, involving external supports or checks, as appropriate, which are agreed and in operation
- Family dynamics are open, whilst boundaries sufficiently protected
- Evidence exists of healthy family interactions
- Physical issues in the home requiring attention have been addressed (e.g. location of bedrooms, etc.).

SUMMARY AND CONCLUSIONS

We have offered a holistic model of intervention in cases of sibling abuse. In our experience, this is a rewarding and demanding area of work, which demonstrates the need for clear, principled boundaries and models of therapy with explicit direction and goals. We conclude by offering a poem written by an adult man, who had abused his sister as an adolescent. This was completed within the context of work done with him on his abusive behaviour and, we feel, demonstrates the painful and difficult process of facing up to abusive behaviour:

I am your brother

I am the pain of the boot that kicks,
   steel toe-capped, hard hearted.
My breath is of anger,
   my step of secrecy.

I am the beast
  prowling the night.
My twisted logic confirms
  the excitement that poisons me once again.

I am the boy, raped at five, at sixes and sevens,
The runt of the class,
  the pitiful fool, playing at life.
I wept my soul away, my feelings
Leaked from my fingertips
  and everything I touched, turned to stone.
Until now.
I search for my truth.

I am your brother.

REFERENCES

1. Home Office (1995) *Criminal Statistics 1994*.
2. M. J. O'Brien (1991) 'Taking incest seriously', in Michael Quinn Patton (ed) Family Sexual Abuse: Frontline Research and Evaluation, 75–93 (Sage: Newbury Park, California).
3. J. Saradjian (1996) *Women Who Sexually Abuse Children: From Research To Clinical Practice* (John Wiley & Sons: Chichester).
4. D. O'Callaghan & B. Print (1994) 'Adolescent sexual abusers: research, assessment and treatment' in T. Morrison, M. Erooga, & R. Beckett (eds), *Sexual Offending Against Children*, 146–177 (Routledge: London).
5. D. Glasgow, L. Horne, R. Calam & A. Cox (1994) 'Evidence, incidence, gender and age in sexual abuse of children perpetrated by children: towards a developmental analysis of child sexual abuse', *Child Abuse Review*. **3**, 196–210.
6. H. Masson (1995) 'Children and adolescents who sexually abuse other children: responses to an emerging problem', *Journal of Social Welfare and Family Law*, **17**(3), 325–336.
7. Dolan, Holloway, Bailey & Kroll (1996) 'The psycho-social characteristics of juvenile sexual offenders referred to an adolescent forensic service in the UK', *Medical Science Law*, **36**(4) 343–352.
8. M. J. O'Brien (1991) *op. cit.*
9. K. C. Meiselman (1978) *Incest: a psychological study of causes and effects with treatment recommendations* (Jossey-Bass: San Francisco).
10. J. L. Herman (1981) *Father–Daughter Incest* (Harvard University Press: New York).
11. D. E. H. Russell (1986) *The Secret Trauma: Incest in the Lives of Girls and Women* (Basic Books: New York).

12. I. Weiner (1964) 'On Incest: A Survey' *Excerpta Criminologica*, **4**, 37.
13. D. Finkelhor (1980) 'Sex amongst siblings: a survey on prevalence, variety and effects', *Archives of Sexual Behaviors* **9**(3) 171–194.
14. D. O'Callaghan & B. Print (1994) *op. cit.*
15. M. J. O'Brien (1991) *op. cit.*
16. J. V. Becker, M. S. Kaplan, J. Cunningham-Rathner & R. Kavoussi (1986) 'Characteristics of adolescent incest sexual perpetrators: Preliminary findings', *Journal of Family Violence*, **1**(1) 85–94.
17. M. J. O'Brien (1991) *op. cit.*
18. G. Richardson, F. Graham, S. Bhate & T. Kelly (1995) 'A British sample of sexually abusive adolescents: abuse and abuser characteristics', *Criminal Behaviour and Mental Health*, **5**, 187–208.
19. D. Finkelhor (1980) *op. cit.*
20. M. Laviola (1989) 'Effects of older brother–younger sister incest: a review of four cases', *Journal of Family Violence*, **4**(3), 259–274
21. Kaplan, M., Becker, J. & Cunningham-Rathner, J. (1988) 'Characteristics of parents of adolescent incest perpetrators: Preliminary findings', *Journal of Family Violence*, **3**(3), 183–91.
22. H. Smith & E. Israel (1987) 'Sibling incest: a study of the dynamics of 25 cases', *Child Abuse and Neglect*, **11**, 101–108.
23. M. J. O'Brien (1991) *op. cit.*
24. H. Smith & E. Israel (1987) *op. cit.*
25. L. H. Pierce & R. L. Pierce (1987) 'Incestuous victimization by juvenile sex offenders', *Journal of Family Violence*, **2**(4), 351–364.
26. S. P. Bank & M. D. Kahn (1982) *The Sibling Bond* (Basic Books: New York).
27. M. J. O'Brien (1991) *op. cit.*
28. L. H. Pierce & R. L. Pierce (1987) *op. cit.*
29. M. J. O'Brien (1991) *op. cit.*
30. J. V. Becker, M. S. Kaplan, J. Cunningham-Rathner & R. Kavoussi (1986) *op. cit.*
31. Starhawk, (1992) 'A men's movement I can trust', in Hagan (ed.) *Women Respond to the Men's Movement: a Feminist Collection* (Pandora), 27–39.
32. D. O'Callaghan & B. Print (1994) *op. cit.*
33. G. Ryan & S. Lane (1991) *Juvenile Sex Offending; Causes, Consequences and Correction* (Lexington Books: Lexington, Massachusetts).
34. A. C. Smets & C. M. Cebula (1987) 'A group treatment program for adolescent sex offenders: five steps toward resolution', *Child Abuse and Neglect*, **11**, 247–254.
35. G. Ryan & S. Lane (1991) *op. cit.*
36. D. O'Callaghan & B. Print (1994) *op. cit.*
37. T. Morrison & B. Print (1995) *Adolescent Sexual Abusers: An Overview* (NOTA: Hull).
38. M. J. O'Brien (1991) *op. cit.*
39. J. Thomas (1991) 'The adolescent sex offender's family in treatment', in G. Ryan & S. Lane (eds), *Juvenile Sex Offending; Causes, Consequences and Correction* (Lexington Books: Lexington, Massachusetts).
40. W. Bera (1994) 'Victim-sensitive offender therapy: a systemic attributional per-

spective', in Gonsiorek, Bera & LeTourneau (eds), *Male Sexual Abuse: A Trilogy of Intervention Strategies* (Sage: Newbury Park, California).

41. J. Yoxley (ed), (1990) *The Use of Victim–Offender Communication in the Treatment of Sexual Abuse: Three Intervention Models* (Safer Society Press: Orwell, Vermont).

42. J. Matthews, J. Raymaker & K. Speltz (1991) 'Effects of reunification on sexually abusive families', in Michael Quinn Patton (ed), *Family Sexual Abuse: Frontline Research and Evaluation* (Sage: Newbury Park, California).

10

SECONDARY ABUSE

Jeff Hopkins

INTRODUCTION

The experiences described in the foregoing chapters elaborated the nature of the work to be done with children who have been sexually abused. There is a long tradition of psychoanalytic literature on direct work with children. This acknowledges the way that the workers' own unmet needs of childhood interplay with the needs of the child and confuse the helping process. The significance of the mutual influence of child and worker has long been appreciated. Although it is recognised that the work is both stressful and distressing, attention has rested, primarily, on the distress of the child.

Research on the effects of the work on staff is sparse. Earlier sketches have described the experience of staff working with children (Hopkins, 1984).[1] Two further small studies have described the experience of child protection workers (Hopkins, 1989),[2] and their managers (Hopkins, 1991),[3] and these provide the backcloth to this chapter. More extensive studies on stress amongst child protection workers draw attention to the pressure of workloads (Fryer *et al*, 1989)[4] and the stress of worker dissatisfaction (Fryer & Miyoshi, 1989).[5] In the rush to provide guidance and procedures to protect the child and to preserve the rights of parents, the needs of staff have been largely overlooked. Concerns expressed about the level of stress and its effect on practice have been made in a number of official reports, but these are seldom cited (e.g. the *Cleveland Report*, 1988 and the *Kimberley Carlile Report*, 1987).[6] This chapter is an attempt to restore the balance and to ensure that a high standard of child-centred practice is supported by a high level of commitment to the care of staff providing it.

The material in this study is drawn from the experience of helping a small group of staff, working directly with children who were sexually abused, across a short period of transition in their worklife. Their experiences were set against the experiences of members of a child placement team. The purpose of the chapter is to place their personal accounts into a wider context and to identify the stresses that are created as a result of the work, and as a result of the attitudes of those around them.

The framework of the discussion is an exploration of the interrelationship between the experiences of the worker and those of the child. The chapter begins with a classification of the pressures and stresses that are part of daily life at work. It moves on to address the themes of powerlessness, stigmatisation, betrayal and sexuality—commonly identified as features of the child's experience, and explores their relationship to the worker's experience. It concludes by describing how the workers respond and offers a number of observations on the care of staff.

This chapter does not address the experience of fosterparents or residential workers. Their experience is different, but not separate, from the experiences described here.

STRESS IN THE WORKPLACE

The concept of staff care is elaborated in *The Code of Practice for Staff Care* (1991).[7] This identifies a number of general features of working life that may impinge on work performance. These are: organisational change; the effects of violent and intimidating behaviour; the experience of a staff team in disarray; the experience of discrimination and harassment; the intrusion of personal problems into worklife; the impact of disciplinary procedures; and the particular stress and distress generated by the work itself.

Organisational change appears to be a permanent feature of worklife in social welfare agencies. This not only threatens the support structures built up by staff undertaking direct work with children, it also threatens their place in the agency and brings with it demands for attendance at meetings and time for planning. The workers cannot afford not to be involved in shaping the world in which they work. The reality is that whilst they are struggling with the emotional demands of the children, their own position at work may be unsafe.

Working in an investigative role can also expose workers to the threat of violent and intimidating behaviour from the adults involved. This is not a threat that all agencies take seriously. In one case it was the police who installed an alarm system into a worker's home after the management had ignored her concerns. It is not unusual for threats to be made against the worker's own children.

Working in child protection demands a high level of trust in immediate colleagues, including secretarial and administrative staff. However, the pre-vailing climate in the agencies has meant a greater emphasis on work management skills than on the ability to provide support to others. Workers are issued with practice manuals but few agencies prepare their staff for the emotional impact of dealing with child sexual abuse. Significant support systems are overlooked, notably the support provided by the other members of the team. The secretaries in one team could tell when the workers were upset. One worker walked differently, another said little. The secretaries responded with a cup of coffee and a supportive word. In turn the workers recognised how distressing some of the material was that had to be typed and stayed with the secretaries while some of it was being done.

Experience suggests that most of the staff, working with cases of sexual abuse, are women and the majority of senior managers are male. One group of workers were dismissed by their manager as being 'all females together'. Another was left smarting when a male legal officer, describing court pro-cedures, implied that as women they would be able to use 'their feminine wiles' to further their case in court. The women believed that they were stereotyped as wanting to do only the 'personal' work with little interest in power and status. They recognised power and status as essential to command attention, both within the agency, and in relation to other organis-ations. Paradoxically, because of the image of sensitivity in interpersonal relationships, more may be expected of women in direct work than of their male colleagues. For added measure, more than one woman worker found that parents sometimes gave more authority to male opinion than to their own. The disadvantage extends into practical issues. Members of the place-ment team were having to fight their employer, in order to get the same right for car allowances for part-time staff as for full-time staff. When women senior social workers took maternity leave and came back as part-timers, they were only allowed back as social workers. There was resent-ment at the time and energy taken up trying to get the kind of conditions from employers that were available to their male colleagues.

One of the major problems created by the focus on child-centred practice was the assumption that social workers were somehow immune to the ordinary concerns of life. The workers proved as vulnerable to bereavement, separation, debt, and other experiences as the rest of the population. However, they tended to neglect their own needs for the needs of the child, to their personal cost.

Public interest in the world of child protection meant that the risk of media exposure was a reality. The price of a mistake, or even an alleged mistake, came high, and not only for the child and family. The social effects of an investigation were very distressing for the workers, their colleagues and their families. Investigations tended to be prolonged and to dominate their life. All the workers recognised that in Child Protection they were either centre stage, or in the wings waiting to be called on. Nobody was more aware of the shortcomings in practice and resources than they were.

The workers shared the problems and difficulties of other employees in the personal social services. What was lacking was any serious attempt by the employers to recognise that there was both a personal and professional cost in neglecting the care needs of staff. It is against this general background of indifference to the wellbeing of staff, that the experiences of those who work with sexually abused children will be explored.

POWERLESSNESS

The sense of powerlessness, as experienced by the workers, came not only from the feelings expressed by the children, but from the inability to influence the outcome of their work in the interests of the child, and from the lack of resources to meet the high standard of service that the child needed.

They knew that their investigative work placed the child at risk. If the child shared the secret, the family might be split apart. If the child kept the secret, the abuse went on. Secrecy perpetuated the abuse. Breaking the secret was breaking the power of the abuser, but it left the child exposed.

> It can be overwhelming to hear what you are being told. This is followed by a sense of helplessness that you are not able to help them to make it better. It's very hard to cope, with the pain and the awful things that we carry away from our work with the child. There seems to be a powerful bond to children who share their feelings with you; and a felt responsibility to be available to them.

> The work is real; when someone is telling you that it is happening to them, it is very difficult to stay apart from them. I'm forever surprised by the strength of children to put up with the things that are done to them. If I'm OK I can give, but I know that there are times when I am vulnerable to their distress.

One worker described how she was afraid that her own feelings would crowd out her ability to stay with the child as she let go of the pain. She knew that behind the distress, children sometimes believed that they were responsible for what had happened. There could therefore be no walking away, only a commitment to stay alongside as the child was buffeted by the events that followed. High-quality support was essential to help the worker reassure the child in pain. So it was too where emotional demands threatened to engulf a worker. For instance, when only one worker had been allocated to the whole family and the work was untenable, because the interests of family members were incompatible. Worker and child both need reassuring and both need help, but this worker was not offered suitable supervision or therapy and she had to provide this for herself.

It became clear that one of the ways in which the workers' experiences mirrored those of the child was their powerlessness to control events after the disclosure. Once the worker had 'spoken', others took control. People who were not involved with the child were the ones that made the decisions about the child. Even the decision as to how the worker's report would be used rested with others within the agency. If the case moved on and went into the judicial arena for decision, the child's fate was determined by the quality of argument and the presentation skills of lawyers and their knowledge of the system.

> The relationship between the judge and the barristers appears as important in determining the outcome as all the work you put in with the child.

> It's their game. In the wardship court you present your findings and then they scurry about the corridors, trying to do deals that give something to both sides, and which sort out the immediate problem over access arrangements, rather than the long-term plan to prepare the child for a permanent placement. The bench then declares how helpful it is that agreement was reached between the parties.

The sense of powerlessness is conveyed in the day-to-day practical arrangements of the court. These are devised to accommodate the interests of the adults who run the system, and not to meet the needs of the child, or the worker who is acting as her witness.

Some workers were pushed into powerlessness. They were put in impossible situations. Faced, quite literally, with piles of work, unallocated or not dealt with, they could only respond by limiting the goals of their work to a series of actions which did something about the situation. There was no time to address the problems. They were tinkering at the edges, trying to make the child's life more bearable with visits to McDonalds and holidays. As long as there was no great crisis, they kept the case limping along. The experience of powerlessness was made worse by the promulgation of idealistic guidance and more training. The workers were unable to deliver what was already expected of them. Yet every new procedure or training course meant more was expected of them. They believed that they would be held to account for their failure to deliver, even though the resources including staff, facilities and time, were not there.

> Training is the only place where there is money going into development and this just raises the level of frustration.

> At a personal level you have to make it clear what you are doing or you are

powerless. Being a child care worker may give the illusion of power but, in practice, you are rendered powerless. You cannot change the situation without jeopardising the client, the agency or the system through which children are offered some help or protection.

The workers recognised that the public image of themselves was as a powerful disruptive influence. But, like the sexually abused child, much of their time was spent just trying to survive.

STIGMATISATION

Public attitudes towards social workers vary according to the political, economic and social climate. In the last few years child protection work became a particular focus of media interest, providing not only a source of human stories, but also evidence of the incompetence of professionals, and the abuse of children and families by the state welfare system.

Working in child protection at present means being associated with public controversy. Investigating the practices of child protection has become an industry for lawyers and journalists. As workers have identified ritual and organised abuse, so the boundaries of child protection stretch public credibility further. Investigative reporters have won prizes for their exposure of the injustices perpetrated by child protection workers. The workers were aware of the surfeit of inquiries into child protection, which left the collective impression of a service that was damaging to the public health. Ironically the purpose of each separate one was to restore public confidence in the child protection service. This was usually done by seeking out any evidence of malpractice or mismanagement by the staff involved, and making recommendations that would prevent the same mistakes occurring. To the workers whose practices had been subjected to investigation, there appeared to be a number of hidden agendas, which reflected more powerful interests than professional concern.

The workers were aware of only a few beleaguered colleagues who had chosen to protect themselves from criticism by rigid adherence to procedures manuals. They saw themselves amongst the group of those who would choose to speak out on behalf of the child and were prepared to engage indirectly in the public controversy. They felt that if they became only patchers of wounds they would lose their self-respect as professional child care workers. They were aware that they could be seen as troublemakers by their agencies, but they were very experienced and confident in their expertise. They had the choice to go along with the inadequacies or to fight them; in effect, the choice between burn-out or battle fatigue.

One group of managers felt very threatened by the high public profile of child protection and were concerned to protect the public image of the agency and their own position within it. They appeared to view evidence of staff burn-out, and of shortcomings in practice, as a matter of personal incompetence and not as a managerial problem. The workers were aware of colleagues who, feeling exposed, sought to cover up their errors and their failure to carry out procedures. It is possible to identify a cycle of attrition in which public hostility towards the child protection services leads to a climate of fear within the agency, which in turn leads to a concern by individuals to protect themselves, and then to a tragedy which fuels the public hostility. To be proactive as a worker meant breaking the cycle and risking the hostility.

The court setting provided experiences in which the maligning of the child protection workers' practices were actively condoned. The adversarial nature of the contest meant that the 'other side' would attempt to discredit the evidence presented, or to show that it was unreliable because it had been contaminated. The barristers therefore set out to show that the worker mismanaged the process of gathering evidence, or that they implanted the notion of sexual abuse in the mind of the child. This was normal courtroom practice. One worker found a particular irony in her situation. After having her professional and personal credibility hammered in public, and still reeling from the impact, she was left to pick up the distressed parent on whose behalf the attack had been mounted. Everyone else had gone. Their business was done for the day.

Child protection workers were also stigmatised by some of their colleagues in the workplace. These workers who believed that having pretentions to be expert was damaging to social work generally, because it placed a social barrier between the workers and the undervalued groups, who were the main users of their services. They therefore resisted the concept of specialist skills and specialist workers. Their attitude towards the child protection 'specialists' was patronising.

There was an inevitable wariness of child protection workers among the families of the children they work with. Child protection does imply a parental failure to protect the child, and does sometimes lead to taking children away from home. Many of the families saw the workers only as agents of control. Some of the foster parents appeared uncomfortable with the workers. They saw them as the people who wanted to know about 'the dirty things'. They may well have felt abused by the interest of the social worker in the detail of the child's behaviour and of their own attitudes towards it.

Workers and families have different agendas and their assessment of the needs of the child were sometimes very different. The workers knew of situations where this had led to the discounting and labelling of the one by the other. It was not always possible for the social worker to work this through with the foster parents. They did not always have the time or energy, and in some cases it would have been inappropriate for them to do so.

The workers were concerned that the lack of credibility given to child protection workers would mean that their accounts of the child's experience would not be believed, and the voice of the child no longer heard.

> My greatest fear is that the child goes on to become an abuser; and that I don't impact on the structure that might prevent it. That I don't have a system of supports. I am not given credence. My greatest fear, when working with boys, is that I won't be able to help them and they may go on to become abusers or rapists.

The stigma associated with child protection carried over from the workplace into their social life. They all felt uncomfortable, in describing themselves as social workers or child protection workers, when meeting new acquaintances or casual strangers.

BETRAYAL

Direct work with a child who has been sexually abused, meant working to a script in which the worker played a rescuer to the child's part of victim. If the interventions of others, or the changes generated by other agendas, undermined the trust that the child placed in the worker, then both child and worker felt betrayed.

The workers believed that uncovering the confusion and distress locked into the experience of sexual abuse, was both necessary and right for the child. They walked a precarious line each time they approached a case, and needed a strong commitment to their work in order to stay with the level of distress that was exposed. They were not only exposed to the pain of the child, but also exposed to the professional risk of making finely balanced judgements on the basis of tenuous evidence and their own experience. With so much invested in their practice they expected no less a commitment from others.

When managers demanded that they give priority, instead, to activities that met the agency need for funding, they felt they were being exploited. They believed that the more successful they were, or were likely to become, in generating money through consultancy, or by selling places on training courses, the greater the pressure there would be to go on doing it. From their point of view, it was the managers' responsibility to secure the necessary resources, and not theirs. The resentment was aggravated when all the additional income disappeared into the agency and the underpaid workers felt they were now subsidising the agency twice over. The group of child placement workers was told to 'recruit and sell' five families to other agencies, and to train and service other workers in intercountry adoptions. No additional time was to be allowed or extra resources made available. Their personal and professional priority was working with the children on their own case load. Whether they accepted or resisted the new demands, they were in for more aggravation.

The workers were also pushed by managers into direct work when a child wasn't ready for it, because they needed details which the child had not disclosed. They may have wanted confirmatory evidence of the abuse for their own information or to satisfy the court. Working with a tired and upset three-year-old was distressing itself, and continuing the work was seen by the workers as further abuse of both the child and themselves. It is not unknown for paediatricians to expect workers to bring the child back to the hospital for further examinations, not because they doubted their own diagnosis, but because they want to cover themselves, or even to show colleagues an 'interesting case'.

The failure to resource child-care practice effectively meant that managers looked to the existing staff to resolve the problem of expertise. In one situation the agency could not afford to bring in experts to do the direct work in a particularly difficult case, and asked the child placement worker with the most experience to do it.

> I was made to feel second best and expected to grab a bit of training on a course somewhere if I could find it. If you come over as competent or you've got previous experience in direct work, you get all the difficult cases.

Workers were identified by their managers as experts because they had read a book or had been on a three-day course. One made two comments at a case conference and was identified as an expert with non-communicative children. The manager's response to the reluctance of one worker to accept their designation of her as an expert, was to give the label to someone else and to regard her as a disappointment. In some agencies the pattern of bestowing expertise onto workers is extended by the custom of diverting staff into 'specialist' teams, without providing the level of professional support or training necessary.

It suited one particular manager to claim that his staff were experts in working with children. He labelled the workers as experts and promoted himself as a manager of experts. The workers accepted that this was the price they had to pay for the opportunity to spread information about good practice in child care, through him, to others in the agency. But it didn't happen because he was promoted quickly, and moved upwards and out of sight.

The relationship between the workers and management is bedevilled at times by a lack of trust. This arises, in part, from their different agendas, but it is often experienced as a lack of support and sometimes as a betrayal. The test came when managers were faced with the choice of maintaining their credibility with their staff or with more powerful forces.

> I was working with a foster child placed with assertive, middle-class foster parents. I was worried about an incident and reported it. The managers believed the foster parents and I felt branded a liar. I was put on trial. I was told to report back on the situation monthly. I felt weary, frozen and lonely. The offers of help and the support systems never came to fruition. I began to feel maybe it never happened.

In a number of cases, the feeling of betrayal started with promises made at the recruitment stage that were never fulfilled.

> At interview, the managers said how impressed they were by my experience and gave the impression that I was somebody that they saw as special. In reality they just wanted another body. The rest of the time they have piled stuff onto me without any regard for my own feelings. I feel that I was ensnared. The promise of supervision has never been kept. All I get is a caseload check. It's left up to us to get supervision for ourselves. Things that we know are wrong, or not good practice, are being approved by managers in some kind of misguided attempt to nurture us. Yet we do not confront this, because we know it will create difficulties and we just don't want any more hassle.

When the agency fails the child, by failing to deliver the positive experience of public care that the child needs, the workers can feel that their work has been disregarded and that they have been party to a second abuse of the child. Their knowledge of the lack of resources available to the child casts a long shadow over their worklife.

> I know that removing the child does not ensure that the child will be cared for. He or she may well be placed in an unsuitable placement and moved around. Kids are betrayed by the system. We are party to the abuse of children in care. The emotional abuse that comes from the poor quality of care. Not even 'good enough' parenting. In some cases the child is perpetually on the move between places and people. In other cases you get the child to share his or her feelings, to the point where they need therapeutic help, and it's not available or court proceedings hold it up. The service is determined by what is made available. It's like taking a 'Chance' card as you move round the board in Monopoly. As the child deteriorates so he or she becomes labelled

as a problem. Every move is a loss, and it gets harder for the social worker as well as the child.

The cynicism towards managers can also extend to colleagues. It can be difficult to accept the support that they offer.

> You realise how hard you are working when they try and support you, and you feel uncomfortable because they don't usually do this. You know that if you started talking seriously they will have to dash off. You do not feel secure enough to admit to others that you haven't done very well, without feeling it will be used against you. The tension therefore builds up.

Given that the script of those working directly with children is to care for others, this may lead them to play out the role with their own colleagues, and team leader.

> When you know they are having difficulty with their work you take on work in order to rescue them. In trying to protect others you sometimes lose your objectivity. I'll do it because I know that I can do it, and colleagues come to see you as the one who does it all.

Like the disclosing child, the worker may sometimes refrain from sharing all of their burden because they are aware that their manager may not be able to handle it.

Interwoven throughout the fabric of the relationships between children, workers, colleagues and managers, is the experience of dependency on powerful authority figures. This generates both the need to believe that they are unfailing and beneficent, and a fear of their power to make life unpleasant. This illustrates that the issue of care and control, at the heart of all child protection work, infuses both the worklife of the service providers and their practice. Workers treat managers as parents and yet fear their powers. Managers honour their workers yet exploit them as servants. The life of the worker mirrors the experiences of the child in the confusion of promises, trust, nurture, betrayal and appeasement.

SEXUALITY

Just as the experience of sexual abuse clouds the child's own sexual development, so working with children who have been sexually abused casts a shadow over workers' own sexual relationships.

All the women workers reported that the work had an initial, and profound, effect on their own sexual relations. This reaction has been reported also by some male workers. The women's perception of men in general was thrown by the discovery of what some of them had done to the children. This affected their own desire for sex with their partner. Given also the emotional drain of their work they inevitably went to bed in search of sleep rather than sex.

> My head is churning with all the stuff I've been dealing with during the day. Trying to make sense of it.

> Because of my experience, I work from the basis that almost anyone can be a perpetrator. Every situation a possible perpetration. This leaves me wondering . . . Is my partner capable? Is my child vulnerable?

> I believe that sex is a fun thing, a positive part of a healthy relationship. Working with abused children, sex is all about power, violence and cruelty. You continue to have sexual relationships but the framework has changed, but you can't share it without your partner believing that you don't trust him, that you are doubting him. I'm having sex but not giving the love I need to give.

There may be a number of different feelings for the worker to resolve:

> I am still aware of my own feelings and prejudices. I still find it difficult to understand female perpetrators. How could a woman . . .? I know I have to sort this out or I am giving her an extra burden on top of everything else.

It isn't only the work that can touch the core of the worker's own experiences. Training courses intended to prepare workers for direct work with children can sometimes stir their awareness of their own childhood. This leaves them having to come to terms, in their adulthood, with experiences that have remained unresolved for many years. Help is not sought and is seldom offered.

> Courses and training have made me aware of sexual experiences in my own childhood and young womanhood, which remained unresolved. I had to come to terms with them but didn't seek someone to help me work them through. I didn't acknowledge my own vulnerability.

The influence on intimate relationships can be insidious and undermine their spontaneity. The workers become oversensitised and caution their partners about their behaviour with children. When observing her partner's casual play, one worker felt that she had to ask whether he was aware how other people might interpret what he was doing. She was also aware that her own children were growing up and, as adolescence loomed, she was very conscious of their emerging sexuality. She began to question why she was noticing this and found herself being careful, rather than spontaneous, in her approach to the children. This left an edginess to her relations with her family which she resented but seemed unable to resolve.

There was little opportunity for the workers to deal with the effects on their own sexuality and on their intimate relationships. Few were willing to discuss this with their line-manager, and some women would have particular difficulty sharing it with a male manager. Although a highly personalised experience, it appears to be a general hazard of working with cases of child sexual abuse. The workers observed that the situation would be even worse for a colleague who did not recognise it as a side-effect of her work, and who assumed that the fault was hers that she was unable to relate to others in a 'normal' way. She would then be experiencing directly something of the situation of the sexually abused child.

COPING

The responses of the workers to the stress and distress generated out of their work experiences were varied. However, there did appear to be a general need for some form of gratification, usually an indulgence and sometimes one that was knowingly self-abusive.

> Smoking, eating, abusing myself. Having sex but not the kind I need. I also spend money inappropriately. Treat myself and my kids. I get out of control with the finances and this creates more pressure on our marriage.

> I waste time. Talk about things in a way that is not helpful. I perpetuate the uncaring way we work together, by talking about colleagues in a disparaging way.

The response of one worker was to split her life in two.

> The real me doesn't go to work, I have to shut off between being a mother myself and a someone who works with sexually abused children.

The workers acquired a very strong sense of commitment to seeing the child through, and to trying to prevent the abuse from recurring. They believed that no-one really wanted to know just how flimsy the mask of civilised behaviour could be. People could not handle the messages that some of the children were giving. The workers therefore looked to each other for support. Their work became a way of life, and there was a risk that their own identity would become subsumed within their work; that they became what they did.

> I go on because I have to. I expend myself until I have nothing left to give.

> I live to work. Where are the outside interests, the hobbies? All seem less important. I have no mental space to attend to my own home.

> I'm not tackling the real problems in my life. I don't want to go out and socialise. I've no energy, I feel on the edge of things. I've lost my social skills. Lost my sense of fun. I feel like an adolescent in my lack of confidence. I feel insecure out of the workplace.

Workers have different ways of coping, but whatever the way they choose they are obliged to draw on their inner strengths to sustain them. Their work exposes them to the test of experiences for which they were seldom prepared. They learn that anyone is capable of sexually abusing children. They learn that child sexual abuse can have as much to do with power, subjugation and the wilful destruction of innocence as with sexual gratification. They are forced to re-examine their own motivation to do social work, in the light of a painful awareness that the further they push the boundaries the more their work is marginalised, and attitudes towards them and the children they work with, become hostile and abusive. Where the experience of stress reaches into the core of self-identity it becomes traumatising. Nightmares, flashbacks and other symptoms of post-traumatic stress were not unusual.

DISCUSSION

The authors who prepared this book recognise that accounts of practice, in which the work is presented outside the context of the workplace, provide an essential but limited understanding of the parameters in which they work. They therefore thought it important to conclude with an account of the work experience of staff working directly with sexually abused children. The experiences described are based on the experience of a chance sample of workers known to the writer. These may not represent the experiences of other workers, but until the position is established more clearly they must suffice as the basis of discussion.

The work experiences of staff were set within the same framework as the one in which the experiences of sexually abused children were presented in Chapter 1. In this way it proved possible to show how the experiences of the practitioners mirrored, to some degree, the experiences of the children they worked with. Their accounts of the stress and distress within the work situation added a second dimension to the pain and distress arising from the process of helping itself. The workers felt exploited and abused by those with power over them. They were themselves at times guilty of both abusing others and self-abuse. They felt uncared for.

The concept of staff care remains neglected within the personal social services. The workers described how stress and distress amongst staff impeded the service that they provided, and both created and reflected problems within their agencies.

The fact that there is little discussion of the workplace experience of child protection workers, within the literature of child protection, and even within their own agencies, suggests that there is little acknowledgement of the personal cost of working in child protection. The fact that this disinterest encompasses a number of different agencies suggests that it may be a reflection on the present culture of the personal social services. This introduces a third dimension into the present discussion, alongside the stressful effects of the work itself and of the work situation; namely, the effects of the culture of the organisation on the faculty to practise effectively. If the agency ethos is dominated by the need to maintain the fabric of the organis-ation, or to work within economic priorities, it can be of no surprise if the workers who provide the front-line services feel themselves to be treated as functionaries, or perceived as unit costs. This group of staff may be among the most skilled and experienced of the workforce but felt dis-counted within the organisations set up to help sexually abused children. Their worklife offered only uncertainty about the security of their own position, neglect of their personal needs and indifference to their point of view. Their practice was performed against the continual struggle to main-tain their professional and personal integrity. This is not a case of special pleading but a recognition that there is a price to be paid for this, in terms of the quality of service to children who deserve better.

The conclusion of this chapter must be that a high level of service to sexually abused children must be supported by a high level commitment to meeting the personal and professional needs of the staff providing it. A staff care response to the three dimensions of stress should also be three dimensional. It must address not only the practice need, providing thera-peutic supervision to enable the workers to disentangle their own experiences from those of the child, it must also address the stress and distress generated within the workplace itself and, finally, explore the pos-sibility of changing the culture of the organisation from one dominated by administrative or managerial values into one that is user-friendly for workers and children alike.

It yet remains to establish how representative are the experiences described. In the meantime, it is left to the workers themselves to raise their concerns within their own workplace, and for the managers, themselves under pressure and experiencing stress, to recognise that getting the care of staff on the agenda may be as much in their own interests, as in the interest of the children in their care.

REFERENCES

1. Hopkins, J. (1984) 'Caseworker' *Social Work Today*, 9 April 1984, p. 18; 23 July 1984, p. 16; 24 August 1984, p. 18; 20 Dec 1984, p. 20.
2. Hopkins, J. (1989) 'No words . . . just tears, stress and distress amongst staff working in child abuse cases', *Child Abuse Review*, **3**(2), 3–8.
3. Hopkins, J. (1991) 'Managing stress in child protection', *Child Abuse Review*, **5**(2).
4. Fryer Jr., E. F., Poland, J. E., Bross, D. C. Krugman, R. D. (1988) 'The child protective service worker: A profile of needs, attitudes, and utilization of professional resources', *Child Abuse and Neglect*, **12**, 481–90.
5. Fryer Jr., E. F. & Miyoshi, T. J. (1989) 'The relationship of child protection worker attitudes to attrition from the field', *Child Abuse and Neglect*, **13**, 345–50.
6. See, for instance, the (1988) *Report of the Inquiry into Child Abuse in Cleveland 1987*, HMSO, p. 247 and (1987) *A Child in Mind, The Report of the Commission of Inquiry into the Circumstances Surrounding the Death of Kimberley Carlile*. London Borough of Greenwich, p. 200.
7. University of Keele Centre for Occupational Studies with the Local Government Training Board (1991) *The Code of Practice for Staff Care in the Health and Social Services*.

INDEX

Aftermath   3, 6, 10, 20
Anatomically correct dolls (AC dolls)   24, 121
Anger   31, 88–9, 110, 145
Art (therapy)   14, 16, 41
Assessment, risk assessment   10, 22–3, 78–85, 128, 143, 162–3
Auxiliaries   19

Behaviour categories – *see* Information Processing of Trauma
Betrayal   11–12, 13, 187–90
Bexley   56, 57
Borderline personality   98
Boundaries   8, 12, 143, 160–1, 166
British Association for Dramatherapists   37

Catharsis   14–15, 30, 104
Childline   59
Child Protection Registers   2
Children Act 1989   70, 82
Class   8, 9
Cleveland   1, 61, 68
Cleveland Report   60, 61, 73, 180
Cognitive interviewing   61–2
Cognitive restructuring   87
Confidential doctor service   59
Confidentiality   11, 34, 60, 166
Consequences of childhood sexual abuse   98, 126–8
Contracts   43, 146, 163–5

Coping strategies   20, 85, 127, 143, 192–3
Countertransference   105–7, 111–14, 115
Crown Prosecution Service   36, 48

DHSS   56
Defence mechanisms   10, 25, 97, 99, 100–1
Developmental play   39–40
Dissociation   10, 97, 127
Dolls   18–19, 24–30, 39, 48–9, 50, 103
Drama (therapy)   7, 14–16, 39, 41
Dysfunctional Response Cycle   146

Eclectic approach, eclecticism   20, 102
Experts, expertise   188

Family therapy   7, 20, 169–70

Gender   8, 9, 97, 101–2, 125, 153
G-MAP   153, 155, 163
Group issues   7, 8, 9, 13, 18, 89, 105–14, 136–7
Group support   56

Holistic framework   161–2, 176
Home Office   56, 57, 72

Individual work   18, 102, 146

Information processing of
   trauma   127, 143
Institutional abuse   67
Interactive approach   13–14
Integration   14, 15, 16

Joint interviewing   3, 56, 58
Kimberley Carlisle Report   180

Leading questions   64–5
Learning difficulties   28, 31, 40
Legal issues   56–7, 58–9, 65

Media   36, 182
Metaphor   40–1, 45
Mother-blaming attitudes   73–8
Music (therapy)   14
Myths and siblings   154

National Adolescent Perpetrator
   Network   120
National Children's Homes   120
NSPCC   1, 2, 3, 58, 144, 153
NSPCC   Child Sexual Abuse
   Consultancy   2, 6, 11, 143, 144

Object relations   37–9
Organised abuse   2

Perpetrators   2, 59, 119, 156, 157
Person shield   45
Pigot (Judge)   57
Play (therapy) and playing   14,
   16–17, 37, 39
Post-sexual abuse syndrome   98,
   99
Post-traumatic stress disorder
   6–7, 99
Powerlessness   8–10, 13, 99, 110,
   128, 183–5
Puppets   18–19, 24, 39
Protagonist   18, 19, 26

Psychodrama   7, 17–18, 26, 32,
   102–5

Race   8, 9, 47
Reassurance   14, 18, 33, 171
Re-enactment   15, 18–19, 33
Rehearsal   18, 19, 31, 33
Research   2, 6, 7, 76, 120, 125, 143,
   144–50, 154–8
Reunification issues   175
Risk assessment – *see* Assessment

Safe environment   36
Salford Mental Health Services
   153
Security   14–15
Sexualisation and sexuality
   12–13, 38–9, 110–11, 127–8, 132,
   147, 190–2
Stigmatisation   10–11, 13, 185–7
Stress   181–3
Supervision   114–15
Support networks   43
Survivors   8–9, 109
Symbolism   19, 103–4

'Tele'   102–3
Therapeutic groups – *see* Groups
Therapy issues   170
Training   2, 3, 6, 191
Transference   12, 105–7, 111–14,
   115
Trust   11–12, 69, 109
   in colleagues   181

Validation   15
Victim characteristics   155
Victim therapy and
   victimisation   31, 119, 126,
   153–4
Videotaping   11, 57–8, 59

Welsh Office   56